Dedicated to the memory of

Gilbert Nicholson

THE GREAT MIGRATION ADVENTURE

The story of the Marfleet family's migration to Canada

By Sarah Agnes Marfleet (née Lee)

Introduction

In 1903 a large contingent of immigrants from Britain, Scotland, and Ireland led by Reverend Isaac Barr arrived in Canada with much fanfare in the media, and support from the Canadian government. They were supposed to colonize the largely empty Northwest Territory, which would later become the provinces of Saskatchewan and Alberta.

Among the colonists were three Marfleet brothers, Harry, Fred, and Ted who came in advance of rest of their family headed by their father William and mother Elizabeth to settle the area chosen by the Reverend Barr.

Fred, my grandfather, later married Sarah Agnes Lee, who came from Ireland in 1913 as a lone immigrant to teach school in remote regions of Canada. The following is their story told by Fred and Sarah Agnes in a manuscript written in the early fifties.

I have researched the background for this story and included information not in her original from other family histories, historical archives, and the excellent historical narrative, 'Muddling Through' by Lynne Bowen. This story is not complete as many threads are, as yet unresolved. However, as it is, the story is a compelling insight into the lives of early settlers on the western prairies of Canada at the turn of the last century.

Brian Marfleet

Marwayne

Table of Contents

PROLOGUE

January, 1903. In a pub in Lancashire.

"Ast thee heered owt o' that theere bloomin Pahson as wants hall hus blokes t'go hout t'Canadar Bill?"

"Naw, wat's 'ee a wantin hus t'go t'Canadar for, Jim?"

"Well, hit would appeer as there's lots o'land hout theere an 'ee wants t'gie hevery man has will go hout a underd an'sixty hacres o'land! Is t'man daft?"

"A dunno. It's hall in t'papers habout 'im."

"Well! Bah gum! That's a rum un! A 'underd and sixty hacres 'o land!! 'Oo his 'ee?"

"Ee's a pahson somewheres in Lunnon."

"A ruddy pahson! Well I'll be blowed! What's 'is name?"

"Ah forget 'is name. The lads wir hall a talkin' habout 'im last neet in t'Arts 'Ead."

"An' ees givin haway a 'underd an sixty hacres o' land!"

"Well not hexactly givin' haway. 'Ee wants hevery one t'pay a couple o' quid for hit."

"A couple o' quid! Aw that's an 'oss o' another colour! Ha!ha!ha!"

"But Bill, a underd and sixty hacres o' land for a couple o' quid! That sounds darned good t'me."

"Theer's ha catch hin hit somewhere, I bet. W'er ad t'lads has was a talkin' 'eered habout hit?"

"Sum o' them ad read habout hit hin t' papers."

"Ah never seen nowt habout hit in t'papers."

"Naither 'ave hi but 'ee wants hany one has wants t'know more habout hit t'write t'im."

"Weere'd ye write to?"

"I dunno rightly, but 'Erbert 'Arper seemed t'ave a lot o' hinformation habat hit."

"Erbert 'Arper! 'im as keeps t'fried fish stall in t' Market Place?" Weer'd 'ee get hall 'is hinformation from?"

"Ee wor a readin t'hus hall aht o' t'paper, **an 'ee 'ad soom papers, - pampters 'ee calls 'em,** 'an they was hall real hinterestin'."

"Wat wor hinteresting in 'em?"

"They say has t'grass grows knee 'igh an t'cattle and t'hosses stand hup t'their knees heatin t'hay."

"W'y dun 'ee go hout there and farm hit 'isself?"

"Aw, Hi dunno. You coom along t' t'Arts 'Ead with me t'neet an ask 'im. Then ye'll 'ear fer yersen hall habout hit."

"Hany one helse spoutin las neet in t'Arts 'Ead?"

"Just 'Arry 'Opkins. 'ee got a-gate habout t'hinjuns scalpin men an'women an' lads an' lasses. 'ee sez, sez 'ee, "Read them Buffalo Bill yarns hif yer don't believe me."

"Aw 'ees a hass! 'Ees ploom daft! 'Ees nobbut a neddy. What 'ee wants is a good clip on t'lug."

"You coom t'neet an' ear 'Erbert 'Arper."

"Ah reet. Hi'll coom."

Later in 'The Hart's Head'

Herbert Harper: "An now this 'eere pamplet his Hall habout t'seasons. Now let me see wat hit says. Hit says 'eere:"

"The winters hare cold, but hits a dry cold. One does not feel hit has we feel cold hout hin this moist climate. There will be 'ardships and 'ard werk. Omesteadin' his no lazy man's job, an' Canadar his no country for t'weak and t'hidle …"

Bill, interrupting, "'Au t' 'ell wi hit. That's wat hi says. An t' 'ell wi t' blinkin owd Pahson – that's wat hi says. W'y go away t' 'at cold country and werk 'ard? Wat hi says is, wen hus blokes go haway to hanother country, lets go t'himprove ours'ens. Wat hi says his, t' devil ye knows his better than t'devil ye dunno."

(Laughter)

A voice: "Wat's 'ee wantin hus t'do hif we goes hout theere?"

Harper: "Farm. Ye get a underd an' sixty hacres o' good lan giv t'ye."

Voices: "Dah ye know hany thin' habout farmin'?"

"Naw! Never seen one has hi knows of."

"What ud hus miners know habout farmin?"

Some miners, but not many, joined the Barr Colonist Scheme, and many of those who joined, prospered in Canada.

In a bank in the Midlands:

"Did you go to the meeting in the Drapers Hall last night Bill?"

"Yes, but only stayed a short time. Jack Cook sat next to me, and he began talking about this Barr Colonization scheme for Canada. I hadn't taken much interest in it before, but Jack had some pamphlets with him and 'bah jove', Canada sounds a bit of 'All Right' to me. We left half-way through the meeting, and went into the "Horse and Groom", and as we sat there talking, others soon joined us and we had a real rousing discussion on this scheme of Barr's - a meeting of our own, as it were."

"The Pater was talking about that Barr business at tea this evening, but I did not pay much attention; thought it was just another hair-brained scheme to got money out of innocent people. One hears of' so many such things in these days of unemployment."

iv

"Well, it sounds to me as if a chap could have a pretty easy and independent life out in Canada."

"Oh!"

"Yes. You see, you get one hundred and sixty acres of good land given to you free."

"The devil you do. One hundred and sixty acres! Bah Jove, that sounds fantastic!"

"It does, doesn't it? And you should read some of the pamphlets! I tell you that's the climate to broad strong healthy men. The sports, too, are wonderful. There's wild game - deer, elk, moose - all in your own park, a real happy hunting ground for a sportsman to come along. There are also grouse, two or three different kinds; also wild geese and ducks on the lakes in one's own park. I tell you it really sounds most marvellous."

"Yes. Quite Acadian, don't you know! A veritable Land of Cockaigne! You don't suppose there's a catch in it anywhere, do you?"

"Oh no, I don't see how there can be. Jack Cook had a copy of Barr's prospectus with him, and everything is all so well planned and thought out. Things just can't go wrong."

"You seem quite enthused about it all."

"I am - we all were, in the 'Groom' last evening. Quite a few of us have decided to go out and give it a try."

"It gets quite chilly out there, I understand."

"That's another thing. It <u>is</u> very cold, the thermometer, drops to 35 degrees below zero in the winter, but it is a dry cold - one does not feel it."

"One doesn't feel it! Why, the damned thing is giving me chills right now. Why that's away colder than anything we ever get here. It seldom drops down to 10 degrees here."

"Yes, I know, but it's the altitude. It is 2,000 feet above sea level out in the North West Territories. One just does not feel the cold, nor the heat as much as we do here. You should read the pamphlet about it."

There was quite a large number of Bank Clerks and Bank Managers, etcetera among the Colonists, who came out with the Barr arrivals.

In a store:

"Were you at that Baa meeting at the "Flying Swan" yesterday evening, Frank?"

"Oh, just part of it. Art Fleming had told me about it, but it was almost over when I got there. The Missis was out to a tea fight or something, so I did not get there for the beginning of it. Who is this man?"

"He is an Anglican Curate in Hendon, or somewhere in the North of London, I understand. He was born in Canada, and knows the country well. He has travelled all over the North-West Territories in his missionary work among the Indians."

"What do you say the name is?"

"Baa."

"How do you spell it?"

"B-A-A-H-AH."

"Oh, Baa."

"Yes, Baa."

"Is he touring the country?"

"No. He advertised in the papers, and has had pamphlets distributed."

"Oh, he does not go speech making! How did he happen to be speaking here?"

"He was visiting friends here and just dropped in at the 'Swan' one evening. Art Fleming got talking to him, so Art asked him to come again yesterday evening, and he would have a lot more of the boys there to hear about Canada."

"He's a bit of a boozer, from all accounts."

"Yes he got pretty well soaked before the evening was over, but he's a clever old cuss. He knows what he's talking about!"

"He certainly can give vivid descriptions! The way he described the country and the seasons, he surely held his audience."

"Yes, you could have heard a pin drop."

"What I can't understand is this business of giving the land away. He said each male adult would get one hundred and sixty acres of good land free. That's a most astounding offer! There must be something wrong with it. It must be bog or fenland or something."

"What good would that do him, to take a lot of people out and put then where they'd starve?"

"Well if each one paid him two pounds, he could skedaddle. There's a lot of that kind of thing going on these days, you know. Do you know of any who want to go out?"

"They all seemed very enthusiastic about it yesterday evening."

"Would you like to go?"

"I certainly would. I tell you, the free independent life of a gentleman that he described has this counter-jumping beaten all to pieces."

"Yes I get fed up with it too. Sometimes I feel as if I would do damned well anything to get away from it."

"Yes, and if we miss out on this chance, Lord knows when another will come - if ever. The offer can't last long. Lots of people will jump at it. A hundred and sixty acres of land all one's own! It's like getting a lifetime's wages in a lump sum. I sometimes wonder if I'll wake up."

"And see your fairy godmother flying out through the window, eh?"

"Oh, you can laugh, but you know, 'Strike whilst the iron's hot'…"

"Yes, and that other old adage about, 'Fools rush in..''

"Oh, go to hell - I'm going to give it a try anyway."

"Here! Here! You'll write and tell me when you get there I hope. By the way, what about schools out in that wilderness? Don't children have to go to school to learn, or do they acquire their education in the lump sum too?"

"There you go again - always the doubting Thomas. Baa' says that when the settlement materializes, the Government will build a good school, right away, in the centre of the district. He says that is what is always done and those children that live at a distance ride to school, either horseback or in a buggy, that is a kind of cart or trap, I take it."

"Bah Jove – horseback! Do you know all my life I've wanted to own a horse of some kind?"

"Me too! I used to be crazy about those cunning little donkeys on the sands at Skegness."

"Would a man be able to buy a horse out there?"

"Why Baa' says all the land-owners have lots of horses. Just imagine your own paddock and your large fields of corn all in your own park. When you go to town you drive your own horse and dogcart."

And so, all over the British Isles people were discussing this wonderful free gift of land.

* * * * * * * * * * * * * * * *

B arr first launched his idea through the medium of advertising, in the latter part of 1902. England was in the throes of a hangover rife with unemployment and restlessness. The Boer war had ended and soldiers had returned from South Africa - those who would ever return - clad in uniforms of khakis, a new color with a new name learned from the Boers. Wages were low and men who had married during the comparatively prosperous years of the war, now found themselves out of work with no likelihood of obtaining adequate employment in the near future. Their memories were full of the past few years of adventure, and of the exciting, maturing experiences of warfare; they found life in their native land unsatisfying and drab. Some of these returned men went back to their pre-war jobs, only to find them tedious and uninteresting. Many others could find no jobs and these roamed the streets of the cities, often hungry, and always seething with discontent, incipient rebellion swelling in their hearts. Violence against the economic and social conditions of the day often broke out, and the pallid gestures of charitable organizations in providing soup kitchens for them, only incensed them to further and more violent demonstrations. What to do with them and how to handle them became the problem of the day.

Right out of the blue, news came of a migration scheme, sponsored by a Mr. Barr, a clergyman of the Anglican Church, which offered a free gift of one hundred and sixty acres of land, in Canada, to any adult male who would immigrate to that country. One hundred and sixty acres of land! It sounded stupendous! It was the answer! It was a dream, come true!

News of this startling offer spread like wild fire throughout the whole of the British Isles. No pibroch of Donald Dhu ever called forth readier or more eager responses. They poured in by the hundreds. Men of recognized mental stability, who, if they had ever thought much about Canada before, had thought of it only as a land of snows and of scalping Indians with perhaps a few polar bears and a seal or two, thrown into the very white monotony, now found themselves caught up in this maelstrom of migration fervour. Visions of parks, studded with lakes, of fields of corn (grain), of herds of cattle and bands of horses, filled their minds. Many of them, who knew nothing about farming, saw themselves as large landowners, 't'squire', out riding horseback overseeing their farming operations or strutting around their demesnes, with their gun under their arm and dogs at heel. The very, very gentlemen!

Among those caught up in the fever of anticipation over the prospect of emigrating to Canada was the Marfleet family of which I, Fred Marfleet, along with my brothers and sisters are the subjects of the following history.

Part 1   Baa's Lambs

CHAPTER 1

It's a dry cold, you don't feel it

One evening in early February, 1903, Gilbert Nicholson came bounding into the drawing room of his home in Kent, England where my sister, Fan, was sitting crocheting.

"Come here, Fan, I want you to hear what Ritchie is telling us." He said to her, excitedly.

Ritchie was a traveller, who called, periodically, at the "Nicholson Chymist" shop on the Pantiles, Tunbridge Wells, Kent, to solicit orders for his wares in such commodities as "Discreet Stationery", and the pallid, surreptitious cosmetics (if, indeed, that word had, as yet, reached inclusion in the dictionary) of those days, and other such luxuries – then not much in demand.

Gilbert was not the 'bounding' kind, nor was he easily given to excitement, so as she rose to accompany him, in eager surprise, into the shop.

Fan exclaimed, "Why Gilbert, whatever's got into you?"

As they entered together, Ritchie was saying, "Yes one hundred and sixty acres free for the taking!"

"What's all this?" Fan asked, interested at once.

Part 1   Baa's Lambs

"Ritchie here is telling us about a marvellous migration scheme that's afoot in London," explained the elder Mr. Nicholson, and Mr. Ritchie, turning to Fan said.

"Yes, Miss Marfleet, not only in London, but all over the country. I'm surprised that you have not heard of it down here. In London, indeed, all over the country, one hears it being discussed wherever one goes."

"But what's it all about?" Fan asked him.

"Well a man named Barr, an Anglican Clergyman by the way is proposing to take a party of men, and their families, out to Canada to settle there. Each male, who is eighteen years of age or more, will be given one hundred and sixty acres of land free." He went on to speak at some length about Barr's scheme, the salient, "Anglican Clergyman", and "one hundred and sixty acres of land free" recurring with almost the same emphatic repetition of Poe's Raven 'Never More'.

"But surely there's a catch in it somewhere." Fan said as he finished.

"There doesn't seem to be; the offer seems to be quite genuine." he told her.

"Have you spoken to this Mr. Barr?" Gilbert asked.

"No, I've never met him, just read his pamphlets."

"And you say every man over eighteen is eligible for this free land?" Fan asked ponderingly.

"Absolutely! There are no strings attached, as far as I can see, or read. There will be certain expenses, of course. Everyone has to pay his own way out to the colony …"

"And where do you say it is?" Gilbert asked.

"Oh, away somewhere in the North West Territories, the pamphlet says, near where the Vermilion River enters the Saskatchewan River. I don't know enough about the geography of Canada to know where that is, but I looked it up in an old atlas map, and it seems to me it must be near the Rocky Mountains." Ritchie told them.

"By Jove, that would be a wonderful opportunity for an adventurous young man." Gilbert said, wistfully.

"That's one thing the pamphlets stress." Ritchie told them. "In one it says 'there will be hardships and hard work a plenty. There will be isolation and, sometimes, even want. Only the rugged and the strong need apply. Canada is no place for the weak or the idle."

"I wonder if the boys would be interested." Fan mused. "They are all strong and hard workers, when there's something to work for."

"We should write and tell them," said Gilbert. "I'm sure Ted would jump at an opportunity like that."

"And Dad, too" said Fan. "If there's any chance of getting a farm of his own, he'll be right after it, no matter where it is."

3

"Where do you say this man Barr hangs out?" Gilbert asked.

"I haven't got his address with me, but I can send it to you when I get back home. I'm certainly surprised you haven't heard of it before." Ritchie said as he took his leave.

That night Fan and Gilbert sat talking until the early morning hours about this Barr scheme. They both thought it would be a good venture for every one of her brothers to go out and settle in a new country. If indeed, each of them could get this wonderful free gift of land.

"But it sounds so fantastic" said Fan. "Why the whole of Canada would soon be taken up by new settlers."

"Oh, Canada is a very big, country." Gilbert told her. "I think it would take many, many years before it would all be taken up."

"But think, Gilbert, there are five boys in our family and ..."

"Five!" said Gilbert. "Who's the five?"

"Well there's Harry, and Bill, and Fred, and Ted and maybe Bert would go too. I wonder if he would."

"I'd forgotten about Bert. Yes, he'd probably want to go also."

"Well that's five and Dad would make six. Six times one hundred and sixty acres is a tremendous am..." She spoke wistfully.

4

"Seven", said Gilbert. "If they all go, we'll --you and I, Fan – will go too, and I will also try for this grant of land."

"Oh, that would be wonderful!" said Fan and she looked at Gilbert with pride and solicitude. Gilbert was a very frail, undersized fellow, who wore very thick lenses, which intensified his apparent frailness. He was deeply in love with Fan.

"What did Ritchie call it when he was speaking of this grant of land, a - a -"

"Homestead" supplied Gilbert. "Seven homesteads would mean 1120 acres."

"Yes, that's it, homestead. Oh Gilbert, it would be like being back on our own farm again." There were nostalgic tears in Fan's eyes for our old home on the farm that she still remembered, loved and yearned for.

A few days later Gilbert got a letter from Ritchie, enclosing some of Barr's pamphlets.

'These are all the pamphlets I have at the moment,' he wrote. 'I hope to meet you all in the arms of the 'Lady of the snows' someday. For me the die is cast. I haven't been making my salt at my job for over a year now, so I shall probably not be seeing you again. Wish me good luck. Ritchie P.S. Enclosed herewith is Barr's address. R.'

Fan and Gilbert read those pamphlets, over and over again. They seemed so honest and straightforward. There were no 'end of the rainbow' or other extravagant promises, contained

in them, "And of course there wouldn't be" said Fan. "An
Anglican Minister would say of the country only what is honest
and true." Such was the confidence in the scheme inspired in
everyone by the fact that its promoter was an Anglican
clergyman; but Fan, like many others, was to learn that even the
clergy have their frailties, not the weakest of which - in Barr's
case - was an itching palm.

"I think it would be a good idea for us --you and me,
Fan -- to run up to London and have a chat with the Rev. Barr,
before we begin to think too seriously about this migration
scheme," Gilbert suggested, and Fan agreed.

So Gilbert wrote to Barr and made an appointment
with him, and some days later Fan and he met Mr. Barr at his
home in North London. They both found him very
approachable and liked the way he spoke.

"So --so -- not fatherly exactly, but paternally -" Fan
said later.

"What's the difference?" laughed Gilbert.

"Well, there is a difference," argued Fan, who was
always a talker, and who prided herself on her 'Nicety of words'
as she phrased it. "Anyway," she continued, "I liked him, and
so did all those others that were there. He inspired one so with
confidence and-- and-- fortitude, now that's the word, Gilbert,
that's -"

"I'm not arguing." Gilbert laughed again.

"No. but you smile as if I didn't -"

6

"Tut-tut, my dear," said Gilbert. "I was just smiling at your enthusiasm."

"Well, you seemed to be enthused yourself, and so were all those others. I couldn't help but laugh at the big strong woman that asked about the hospital. She almost got out of breath telling him about her ailments. She began, 'ever since my last baby was born I just get so out of breath I can hardly ...', and Mr. Barr interrupted her. "Yes, lady, I understand just how important it is that we should have a hospital. For this purpose, also for the purpose of establishing our own co-operative store where we shall be able to get our necessities, or most of them, at little better than cost, I am asking for a substantial contribution from each intending homesteader, so that we can begin on these two vital projects, even before we set sail for the colony.'"

"Who were these others you speak of?" asked the elder Mr. Nicholson.

"People, who, like ourselves, had come to find out more about the country and what life would be like out there," Gilbert told him.

"Did you find out much more than you knew already?"

"Much more," said both Fan and Gilbert. "He says he has felt colder right here in London, when our East winds are blowing, than he ever felt in Canada."

"How does he explain that, or does he give explanation?" asked Mr. Nicholson.

"He says it's the altitude." Gilbert told him. "The altitude of the North West Territories is over two thousand feet, and though the temperature falls to away below zero, sometimes as low as fifty below, one doesn't feel it because the cold is so dry."

"Hm-m-m" Mr. Nicholson mused. "That's a mighty obliging kind of cold. Fifty below zero and one doesn't feel it. I have read of people getting frozen to death out in Canada."

But by this time, both Fan and Gilbert were so enthused about Barr and his migration scheme that, if all the frozen bodies that have ever been found in Canada had passed in procession in front of them, each warning them, with its frozen eyes and frozen voice, of the severity of the climate; Fan would have simply smiled and said, "But, my dear, it's a dry cold. You should never have felt it." Such was the faith and trust everyone seemed to have in all Barr's statements.

The phrase, "It's a dry cold; you don't feel it," was to become later, among the colonists, a saw of ridicule and disbelief in any disputatious statement; and when the word "Amen" was added, it became the final statement of utter incredulity.

Fan's enthusiasm gathered momentum almost with every breath she drew, "If only we could all get out and have a big farm like the one we had in Wainfleet! If only we had the money to get out there! If only -"

"Do you think the boys would all want to go?" Gilbert asked.

"Oh, I'm sure they would. I believe every one of them would like to own a farm."

"Why not write and ask them to make sure?"

"Well, I don't know. I might just get them all worked up and then find there's no possible chance of their going?" she said dejectedly.

"I've always held the theory that if anyone wants a thing badly enough he'll attain it." Gilbert said sagely.

"I believe you are right," agreed Fan. "I shall write to them all on Sunday, and ask them."

However, before Sunday arrived, she got bad news from home. Mother had had a stroke and Dad wanted to know if Fan could come home for a week or two. Molly did not feel she could look after mother alone, as she required nursing night and day. Anne, my oldest sister now Mrs. Harry Alcock, was already in Canada with her husband and family at the time. So Fan went home, and Barr's colonization scheme was, for the time being, thrust into the background of her immediate concern. When she returned at the end of two weeks, she was so depressed by Mother's illness and by the hopelessness of our family ever being able to take advantage of this wonderful offer that the subject remained un-broached, between her and Gilbert, for several days. Seeing how spiritless and sad she seemed and hoping to revive her interest in the Barr scheme Gilbert asked her, "Did you write to the boys?"

"No, Gilbert" she said. "I had a talk with Dad and he would love to go, but he says we just can't even think of it. He seems to think it would take a lot more money than we ever

9

thought it would, so I suppose we must forget all about it." she ended tearfully.

"So you didn't write?" he asked again.

"No, what's the use?" still weeping.

"Lots of use," he told her. "Now buck up, Fan" He consoled her as she continued to weep.

"I've been thinking a whole lot about this homestead idea while you have been at home, and I've decided that I would like to go out and take a homestead there. Dad seems to think it might make me stronger and better in health, but I wouldn't want to go alone, Fan. I would want you to come with me." He said.

"You and me, go alone!" Fan exclaimed. "Oh, I couldn't, Gilbert, I couldn't leave mother now."

"No, no. Hush now, Fan, I don't want you to leave your mother. I plan to have the whole family go out to Canada, and---"

"But we can't Gilbert. It's out of the question. We could never raise the money. Why Dad says it ..."

"Listen, Fan, I have a few thousand pounds in the bank that Granny Nicholson left me when she died last year. I shall draw that out of the bank, and I'm sure it will be enough to get the whole family to Canada."

"But, Gilbert, you couldn't, you must not – I won't even thin -"

Part 1   Baa's Lambs

"Yes I will, Fan. I have decided to do this. I know I couldn't ever make a better investment." He said, determinedly.

"But you don't know, Gilbert. We may never be able to repay you."

"Don't worry about the money, Fan, even if you never pay it back I shall be amply repaid in other ways, so we shall forget all about that part of it." He said.

"Oh Gilbert, you darling, to do all this for me -" She began weeping.

And so fate, in the form of Gilbert Nicholson, ordained that the Marfleet family come to Canada.

I was in the British Navy at the time. My ship, H.M.S. Mars, had called at Gibraltar for a stop after cruising along the shores of North Africa to the Suez, where we had coaled,(always a dirty job in the Navy), and back again, calling at the various stops of the Middle East and the Southern European Ports. To my great surprise, a very bulky letter awaited me there. It was from Fan and Gilbert. So enthused were they by what they had heard from Mr. Barr about Canada and the possibilities that seemed to be waiting there for families such as ours, that they had finally decided to emigrate and move the whole family out to this new land of hope and glory.

I have spoken glibly, of Fan and Gilbert. In those days, the two names were rarely disassociated. Even now, I often think of Gilbert, and never without a deep feeling of remorse of how devoted to our family he was. Also, looking back I can now realize the sterling qualities of his nature; qualities of which I was completely incognizant at the time.

11

His sincere desire to help others, we took for granted.
The energy and effort he put into the plans he made for the
benefit of our family evoked little, if any, gratitude or
recognition from any of us nor did he expect any, I believe. He
was an ardent patriot. England to him was first and foremost,
and for this reason, or at least strongly motivated by this reason,
he too envisioned a large, thriving British Settlement at the
juncture of the two rivers. He had read enough about
colonization and the experience of colonists everywhere to
assess fully, the value of a plentiful supply of good, fresh water
to a settlement. I have heard him say often, after we came to
Canada, "It is a great pity that Barr's plans miscarried."

The Nicholson's were druggists - chymists more
voguish in those days. They owned a high class and prosperous
drug store on the Pantiles in Tunbridge Wells. In 1903, the
Senior Mr. Nicolson and his two sons operated the business.
Mrs. Nicholson died a few years prior to this time, and my sister
Fan was then housekeeping for them. Fan was, at that time, a
tall good-looking girl, very smart in her clothes and a good
tennis player. Gilbert, who was as I have said, delicately
constituted and of very frail physique, was attracted by health
and vigour in anyone, and more particularly so in Fan. They
became engaged to be married, just about the time that they
decided our whole family should move to Canada.

I have often wondered just what attraction Gilbert had
for Fan. Maybe his physical weakness appealed to the strong
mother instinct in her nature; or it may have been his innate
goodness and kindness, for no one could know him and not
sense the virtue that was in him.

He was, indeed, one of Nature's Gentlemen.

Part 1   Baa's Lambs

After almost fifty years, I still have the same feeling of affection for him, the same admiration for his integrity and resourcefulness and the same feeling of pity for his frail physique and his intense consciousness of it. His sight was very poor, though he was only twenty-eight years old. I have seen him look up, peering at me and say, "How lucky you are Fred, to be so tall". I was just over six feet then.

He would ask me to describe some distant object, or tell him something he wished to know about it, or he would move his hand up and down my arm and say, "If I were only as strong as you!"

As I write this, he is still living at the home on the Pantiles in Tunbridge Wells, now an old man, totally blind.

CHAPTER 2

"For I am a sailor in the Queen's Navee"

Gilbert and Sullivan

The Marfleets came from Wainfleet St. Mary in Lincolnshire. My father had been a tenant farmer, renting a farm near Skegness, which had been rented by generations of the family for over 300 years. This may seem odd, but renting in England at that time was on both a permanent and a secure basis. The farm Dad rented belonged then to St. Bartholomew's Hospital in London, bequeathed to it by a former owner.

Each field on the farm was numbered, and a scientific rotation of crops to which the tenant unfailingly adhered, together with a systematically applied fertilizer ensured that the soil could not ever be impoverished. It was the duty of the bailiff to oversee the operation of the farm and to help the tenant with advice and suggestion. Thus, both property owner and renter were assured of the utmost in returns.

The tenant farmers of those days belonged to the upper middle class - a tenant gentry forming a class of society almost exclusively their own. They sent their children to the better schools, owned their own carriage horses; some of them, even as my father did, owned their own hunters.

There is an oil painting of my father 'in the pink', that is the scarlet and white worn by huntsmen, somewhere in existence. Some member of the family has this portrait, but I,

14

being now the youngest living of Dad's children, am not likely
ever to possess it.

When I was about eight years old, my father lost his
farm partly through his own fault, but more still I maintain, by
reason of the bad times through which agricultural England was
then passing about sixty years ago - a "Depression" it would be
called these days. The family had to leave our lovely old farm
home, which as I have said had been the home of the Marfleets
for many generations. We went into Cambridgeshire and lived
in a little hovel of a house in a place called Cockowlets. I
wonder if this place is still called by the same odd name. My
father got work there as a labourer and it was there that we all
got our first bitter taste of poverty, and bitter and galling that
taste was. How my mother worked, she who had hitherto had
servants to do most of the work, now did the washing, mending,
etcetera, with too little of everything and always trying to "make
do".

I still remember every detail of the night we moved.
We made a "midnight flit" - I guess to evade the Sheriff - the
"bum bailiffs" as they were popularly (or un-popularly) called.
Dad packed all our bedding, some pieces of furniture, including
the piano, cooking utensils, the brass bed warmer and all us
children into a large wagon. He and mother then shook hands
with two uncles, my mother's brothers, who were there to lend a
hand, and we started out. Mother was weeping quietly, Dad was
very silent, and we children sensed something of the calamity
that had befallen the family. When Dad spoke to the horse to
guide him, he did so in a subdued voice, which added to our
fear. How we clopped and, rattled along - breaking the stillness
and peacefulness of the night and giving us the feeling that we
would be caught, for surely, it seemed, we were running away!

15

After we had bumped along for some time, Dad began to sing, still in a low soft tone:

> Oh some men, you are aware
> Build castles in the air,
> But very soon they vanish and decay,
> While others strong and sound
> Build castles on the ground.
> Oh, it's easy if you only know the way.

This assured us greatly and we began to feel better.

We now wanted more singing. It made us feel so good. We asked him to sing "Cockles and Mussels", a favourite with him and us, and we all joined in - first lustily then drowsily, and soon we were asleep.

My eldest sister, Anne, went to live with Mother's other's sister, Aunt Rose. She went to a good school, where she received an excellent education. Her music came in handy in later years when she gave music lessons at Onoway, thus adding to the family income. She was also Secretary of the Onoway Hospital for many years.

My oldest brother, Bert, got work on a barge that plied on a nearby canal. Mother and I very often, in fact every Saturday, walked the three miles to the barge to collect Bert's wages, to help the family needs, - poor Bert.

This still left eight children to feed - the youngest, Katie, was only two years old. She was pretty as a picture and so loveable. She died in a few years, probably a victim of malnutrition.

How hungry I used to be in those days, and how good everything we got in the way of food tasted! After I was married, I told my wife one day of a rice pudding with beef gravy mother used to give us. She had been a teacher prior to our marriage and had never done much cooking. She puckered her brow and asked,

"Rice pudding made with milk and sugar?"

I vowed that was it. She made a rice pudding and served it to me with beef gravy.

"Aren't you having any?" I enquired.

"No! I don't believe I would like it." Decidedly

I tried to eat it, but it did not taste the same as it had in those far off days of hunger. The main ingredient, namely my boyish appetite I guess, was missing. Some time later, I told her of Mother's roly-poly pudding and of Mother's dumplings with beef stew. Both of these she tried, with the same disappointing results. Then one day I began to tell her about a dish mother used to make with boiled wheat. This was the supreme climax! She turned on me with a "Fight to the finish'" look in her eye and said,

"Look here! I'm glad your mother's dead."

I was hurt and shocked, but I was also cured. I never mentioned my mother's cooking to her again.

When I was seventeen, our family was very poor indeed. Fan and Floss, two sisters, were both out working, but Dad could get no regular employment. There were more

17

labourers, than available work. We had made several more
'midnight flits', each one landing us in deeper and more dire
poverty. Brother Bert had gone broke in a butcher's shop in
London and I, who had been helping him in his business, found
myself without a job and seemingly no hope of getting another.
One evening I was without money and tired out with having
walked all day, from early morning, in a fruitless search for
work of any kind. Bert had left London and I had no place to
sleep that night - my landlady had told me, very sorrowfully, I
could not have my room any longer, as I had not paid my rent
for two weeks. I did not blame her. I had had nothing to eat
since a very sparse breakfast the morning before, and all the
tapeworms of all my overfed, gouty ancestors, seemed to be
gnawing the very vitals out of my body. I had walked up and
down, up and down, up and down in front of one of "Harris'
Sausage and Mash" Shops, breathing-in the tantalizing aroma
that came from the open door, and getting hungrier and hungrier
with every sniff. I hardly dared look at the window where the
sausages were cooking; luscious, and temptingly brown. This
had always been a favourite meal with me, when I had money.
One got a good helping of sausage cooked to a turn, fluffy
mashed potatoes and a good thick slice of bread and butter and a
large cup of coffee for sixpence - twelve halfpennies! I went
through my pockets – just one ha-penny. I flung it toward the
window, and turned away feeling gaunt and weak. To add to my
misery my feet were killing me in the old worn-out boots I was
wearing. I felt I just could not go on any longer!

'Hell,' I thought aloud, 'what am I to do?'

"Like a good meal, lad?" Out of the blue, a voice
asked. Surely, it came from Heaven!

Part 1   Baa's Lambs

I wheeled around expecting to see blessed Michael the Archangel or some other celestial apparition. There was only a big, burly recruiting officer standing in front of the recruiting station next door to "Harris Sausage and Mash." I turned away hope dying in my heart.

It came again, "Like a good meal lad?"

I now turned and looked at the officer. He had a kindly smile on his face, but a "this is my meat" look in his eye. I approached him hesitantly, hardly daring to hope it had been he indeed, who had spoken those heavenly words. He repeated the question for the third time and he had me, right there.

He took me inside the recruiting station, and after measuring me, told me I just fulfilled all the requirements for the Royal Marine Artillery. He showed me pictures of the South sea barracks, described the life of an R.M.A. man, making it sound very alluring indeed. Life in the barracks, according to him, was one round of pleasure. The good food he made a special feature of, also boat rowing and sea swimming. He showed me pictures to prove all this. Then the pretty girls on the South sea esplanade, he dilated upon, almost drooling over their charms. He then went on about life at sea, the foreign ports I would visit and the popularity of the Marines in these ports, and all in all, the life of a gentleman, that would henceforth be mine if I joined up.

To a youth of my age, and in my circumstances, all this was very appealing, so when he said,

"All right boy, just sign here. Put your name and home address." I hastened to do so.

"And now go down to the kitchen and have all you want to eat!"

How I went! Mercury on winged heels never moved faster.

I was given sleeping accommodation for that night and next morning was marched, with three other new recruits, to the railway station and put on the train for Portsmouth.

It seemed real fun to all four of us!

Upon, arrival at Portsmouth, we were met by a sergeant, who spotted us the moment we got off the train. He told us to follow him, which we did gleefully. Outside the station, he mounted a bicycle and told us to keep up with him.

As we walked along, one of the lads said, "I am going in here to buy some fags." but the moment he dropped out of step with us, the sergeant let out a yell like the war whoop of a wild Indian.

"Here, you! Where are you going? Didn't I tell you to follow me? You are in the Marines right now, boy."

So we were!

That was the first severe military command we had heard. We were to hear many more in the days and weeks to come. We soon grew to expect them.

I laugh now when I think of our first uniforms. They fitted where they touched, but we wore them proudly and thought we looked quite cocky in them.

Part 1   Baa's Lambs

It was 1897. We were in the Queen's 'Navee'!

After some months of intensive training, we did indeed look quite snappy. I soon chummed up with Bowdy, and we became real pals. I believe he was older than I was. He seemed so much older in the ways of the world. He was the smartest man in our company. I always tried my best to beat him at the guard's parade, but never once succeeded. He and I used to talk a lot about girls and our experiences with them, pretending - at least it was pretence on my part - that our sex relations with them had been both manifold and varied.

I well remember one evening meeting a couple of girls on the esplanade. They seemed to be out, as we were, for a little sex adventure. Bowdy soon went off with one of them, leaving the other with me. We went on the sands and I suggested we sit down. She giggled and said "Oh, it's fah too damp."

I proceeded to spread my handkerchief - a six inch square thing – for her to sit on, so we both sat down and cuddled and kissed and had almost got going, when Bowdy and his girl returned. They had lost no time.

They sat down beside us and we all four began fooling around, rolling over each other and really being rough and daring, until Bowdy said,

"We have just time to see you girls home and rush back to barracks before midnight." We were on twelve o'clock leave.

Sometime after kissing them good-night, I missed my gloves but made no mention of the fact. Next day Bowdy gave them to me.

21

"Where did you get them?" I asked in surprise.

"I found them in that girl's drawers." He answered quite nonchalantly.

One evening we went to a music hall, and after the performance, I was rhapsodizing over the beauty of one of the actresses, and Bowdy said grimly.

"She is no tender chicken. You should see some of these painted hussies, when they are taking in the milk in the morning. I've seen them in Brixton, where my people live, and they look like old hags, wrinkled and mouldy."

Somehow, I felt more adult after chumming with Bowdy.

After we passed out of training, I really did enjoy life in the barracks. It was truly the life of a gentleman.

It was around this time that I first met Gilbert Nicolson. I was on a furlough and went to Tunbridge Wells to visit my sister, Fan, for a week. During the next six months, I met them both frequently, and always had a good time with them.

Then one dour, dreary day orders were posted. We were told to hold ourselves in readiness for embarkation, and a few days later I was drafted to H.M.S. Mars and was marched on board with the draft. The thought of leaving England and life in the barracks, and all my friends and relatives, so filled my heart with misery that life became empty and hollow. Bowdy, I missed most of all - he was drafted to the "Renown".

We were shown the mess deck in what seemed to be the bowels of the ship and the beds, which were hammocks suspended with hundreds of others by hooks from the rafters of the deck. I thought of the comfort and convenience of the beds in the barracks, and of our leaves when Bowdy and I would go "square pushing" and all I was leaving behind. I felt I just could not take life at sea, so watching my opportunity, I climbed the hatchway determined to run away there and then.

A big, buck Marine Sergeant stood on deck, no doubt on the look-out for would-be deserters such as me.

"What do you want?" He asked.

"How long before we start?" I evaded.

He pointed to the now receding coastline of the Isle of Wight and said, "We are underway right now, boy. We are ten miles out to sea."

I made up my mind right then to make the best of it. I cannot remember any more nostalgic pinning's for the life of the barracks and the girls of the esplanade.

It was always a kind of home-coming to get back to Gibraltar – "Gib", as it was affectionately known. It always meant leave for most of us. Then we high-tailed it up to "Jack up the Ramps", a public house that provided both drinks and merriment.

Girls?

Yes! In birdcages and every other kind of cages, to prevent unwarranted intrusion, I guess. Only men in naval uniform were seen on the "Ramps" when the fleet was in. The soldiers then became "Cheap guys". They only had sixpence, whereas naval men could sport "two bob" - two shillings. Also, there was great rivalry between the Blue Marines and the able seamen. I could recount many an amusing episode arising out of this rivalry but remember particularly one occasion when a "big buck Marine" as the seamen nicknamed us, and a "flannel-foot" as we, in turn, nicknamed them, met at the same cage. Both were three sheets in the wind and could hardly stand up and both wanted the same girl. They began to fight and somehow in the scuffle they got their backs to each other. Each thought the other was looking over his shoulder and tried to hit his opponent in the face. It was funny! The bystanders convulsed with laughter. Finally, the combatants realized the situation, and joined heartily in the laughter. Then two girls dashed madly out from the cages and each grabbing an arm of one of the erstwhile pugilists marched him off to his reward, I guess.

Five years passed - six months in barracks, six months at sea. The Boer War was fought and won although, despite the vigilance of the British Navy, Kruger escaped to Holland.

But Rule Britannia!

Still, we cruised the Mediterranean. Coaling at Suez and coming back to 'Gib' until, as I say, on this memorable occasion I picked up the letter that was awaiting me.

I read it, re-read it, and read it again.

How very enthusiastic Fan seemed to be! Gilbert, too, was very serious and earnest in his letter. Fan and he had

24

weighed the pros and cons, of moving our whole family out to
Canada, as soon as arrangements could be made to do so. Bill
was in the Metropolitan Police Force in London at the time so
they would have to procure both his and my discharge. It was a
case of buying me out of the Navy, and they did not anticipate
much trouble about doing this. England was then at peace, and
no country dared to disturb that peace.

That is how secure the English Channel and our
British Navy used to make us feel, in those far off days of
England's glory.

They went on to tell me just what Canada had to offer.
Mr. Barr had said each adult male in the family could get a
quarter section of land or one hundred and sixty acres, which we
understood better. There were six of us, including Gilbert. That
would mean six times one hundred and sixty acres of good
fertile soil. It sounded stupendous! Harry and Ted, they said,
were already making plans to go and that they were all talking,
thinking, dreaming Canada every moment of the day and night.

I read the letter to some of my mates on "The Mars'".
It was the first any of them had heard of Barr's scheme and they
all thought it sounded fabulous. One hundred and sixty acres of
land free for the taking! Six of us would be going out to get six
times one hundred and sixty acres!

"Six noughts, nought" computed little Chapman, a
cockney. "Six sixes, thirty-six; six one six and three is nine.
Nine hundred and sixty acres of land! Why blimey, Fred, you'll
'ave a hestite! A blinkin' hestite!"

I saw it.

I saw thick stone walls surrounding it with high
wrought iron gates opening onto a long driveway with beautiful
shady trees on either side. Oh, I saw it all, and how good it
looked. I began to wonder how soon I would be free. I would
never polish another damned button as long as I lived - but how
soon? It should not take too long! How soon?

A few days later, I got another letter from Fan.
Gilbert had begun to negotiate the purchase of my discharge and
they - Fan and he - had written for three reservations on the ship
that was to carry the Colonists to Canada. They thought if
Harry, Ted and I went out with the first shipload, we could write
back and let them know just what the chances were of work for
the others.

Then if conditions were satisfactory, Mother, the girls
- Fan, Rose and Mollie – with Dad, Gilbert and Bill could come
later. So sure, they were that my discharge would come through
in time!

But, as Burns wrote the best laid schemes of mice and
men 'gang aft agley'. When the ship, the Lake Manitoba,
chartered by Barr to carry the colonists across the Atlantic
sailed, Harry and Ted were among the passengers, but my
discharge was still pending.

After receiving Fan's letter saying that Gilbert and she
were buying me out of the marines, I was in a fever of
expectation and excitement, waiting each day to hear that I was
free. One day at the mess, the officer called my numbers 9015,
and told me to report right away, to the captain's cabin. I went,
in a dither of excitement, thinking that my discharge had at last
come through. When I entered the cabin, the captain smiled a

friendly smile and said, "I understand you are intending to leave the navy?"

I saluted and said, "Yes, Sir."

"What are you going to do?"

"I'm going to Canada, Sir." I told him, and went on to tell him that my family was going and that we boys and Dad were going to get homesteads: all this in reply to his questions, of course.

"Do you know anything about Canada?" He asked me then.

"Very little, Sir, I'm afraid."

"Well now, I'm surprised that an intelligent young man like you should elect to quit a secure job in the navy to go to a country like Canada." He then painted a tough, cold picture of the prairies ending up with his regrets that I should want my discharge as I had been slated for promotion. "You are the type of man we want in the marines, I assure you there is a good future in the service for you. Don't you think you had better reconsider?"

But, adventure beckoned. I told him. "No, I have definitely decided to go."

He said again, "I'm sorry to see you go."

My shipmates were just as excited about my getting my discharge as I was. "God, you are a lucky dog." They would tell me. "Why the hell can't I have rich relations that would buy me out?"

It made me feel very lucky at the time.

My discharge came through about a month after my visit to the captain's cabin.

I went home, at once, to see my parents. They were living, then in a small village, named Woollen's Brook, in Cambridgeshire. It was the first time I had seen mother since she had had her stroke, and I could scarcely repress the tears that gushed to my eyes when I saw how crippled she was, she who had always been so active and nimble. The memory came to me of how, when my older brothers and sisters were learning to dance, she would pick up her skirts and show them the steps. Although, she was then dropping into the heaviness of advancing years, how light and gay she was on her feet; and oddly that is the most vivid memory I retain of her still through all these years.

After being at home for a week, I went to visit Fan and Gilbert. In those days, I always looked forward to a visit to Tunbridge Wells. The Nicolson's were nice people and always gave me a gracious and hearty welcome. The first evening at tea, I told them about my visit to the captain's cabin. Repeating what he had said about Canada. "He almost made me shiver with the cold of it." I laughed.

"But", said Fan, the earnest light of faith in Barr's statements shining in her eyes, "didn't you tell him it's a dry cold and that you don't feel it?"

28

Part 1   Baa's Lambs

Mr. Nicolson laughed, "That's your and Barr's secret information about Canada, I think, Fan. I've read a lot about the country and I've never before heard of this 'dry cold that one can't feel'. It seems absurd to me." he said.

Fan gave him the look that one could imagine a rabid fanatic bestowing upon a declaiming apostate. Then she asked me, "What else did he say?"

"He tried to dissuade me from taking my discharge. He told me that I had been slated for promotion and that there was a bright future for me in the marines, and asked me if I wouldn't reconsider my decision." Before either Fan or Gilbert could remark on this, Mr. Nicolson said,

"Yes, I'm sorry, too, to see you quit the marines, Fred. I think you've made a mistake in not listening to the captain."

Had I? I've often wondered, but 'The moving Finger writes'.

CHAPTER 3

Baa's Lambs

The S.S. Lake Manitoba on which Harry and Ted had passage had been built to carry between eight and nine hundred passengers, but which was crammed full with almost two thousand human beings packed together like herrings in a barrel. Many of them were single men, bachelors, most of whom would retain that status to the 'bitter end'. There were families with children, and families without children, and some with children in the making - one baby was born somewhere on the trek from Saskatoon to the final goal. And some minority of single women, whose hearts, like those of the bachelors, throbbed to the promise of high adventure, in a new and bountiful land.

Mr. Barr, it seemed, was an Anglican Minister, who had spent many years in Canada and had travelled widely in his missionary work among the Indians in the North West outposts. On one of his missions, he had been struck by the possibilities of forming a British settlement at or near the point where Vermilion River joins the North Saskatchewan, far away in the North West Territories, as the area was then known.

He envisioned a prosperous farming community from which would, in time, emerge a thriving city, and from which the vast and fertile territory stretching from Saskatoon, Saskatchewan away into the North West Territories would be brought within the fold of the Anglican Church, and the Christianizing influence of its culture and religion.

Part 1   Baa's Lambs

I still believe that, had his plans materialized, the large
city he envisioned would, indeed, now stand on the site he had
chosen. The area later came to be called Lea Park.

Here, one of the busiest ferries on the North
Saskatchewan River plies back and forth daily during the
summer months from its North to its South Bank. When the
river is frozen over in the winter, the road which crosses on its
frozen surface is a heavily trafficked highway, serving settlers
north of the river and the populace of Onion Lake, Cold Lake
and other small villages.

Barr told, in his pamphlets, about the richness of the
soil in the territory, the rolling prairies covered with wild grass
or hay – prairie wool he said it was called – which grew so
bountifully and lushly, and which would feed and shelter
thousands of head of stock, cattle and horses, the year round.
He spoke of heavy yield of grain on the new fertile soil, and the
wealth of natural forestry – bush he said it was called – which
would supply both fuel and building material for years and years
to come. He spoke of the healthy climate 2,000 feet above sea
level, and of the asset the plentiful supply of good water would
be in a mixed farming district.

Then he spoke of the seasons.

The long cold winter that some years came early in
Autumn – Fall he called it – and lasted till well into April, but
other years did not set in until around Christmas and lasted till
towards the end of March, dissolving over night, almost, into
verdant Spring.

He tried to describe the cold, how intense it could be,
how it gripped with icy tentacles and held, how when the wind

31

blew in a sub-zero temperature neither man nor beast could
withstand its piercing blast that seemed to cut through the
heaviest and warmest clothing. Even thickly lined and heavy fur
proving often to be quite inadequate against its penetrating
clutches. So vividly did he describe it, that his readers
shuddered and huddled closer to the fire as they read, and felt
they really knew just how cold the prairies could be. Not one of
them really knew it.

Then he spoke of Spring: how it came overnight
always with a rush, how as if at a wave of a magic wand the
long and dried-out grass of the prairie would put on a cloak of
greenish hue, and begin waving in the soft mellow breeze. Then
soon the mauve and purple of the wild crocus would everywhere
greet the eye, and man would here realize the glory of the
awakening new life as only those who have endured the rigors
of a northern winter can realize it. How, about the middle of
April the dull, cold silence of the winter days would one
morning be suddenly broken by the rollicking song of the
meadow lark as he flew from tree top to tree top, lustily and
cheerfully singing and evocative of the best impulses of man.

Then Summer with its long, long days of sunshine,
when crops grew and ripened so quickly. The wide open spaces;
where one breathed free and untrammeled, where the music of
the soul felt unrepressed and unrestrained. The beauty of the
sun rise, and even more beautiful sunsets could be enjoyed
without obstruction of buildings or haze of smoke. Waving,
golden wheat of autumn and harvesting time with the myriads of
wild duck, honking geese and v-shaped flights of wild turkeys
filling the sky. The plentiful supplies of wild bird life – prairie
chicken, rabbits, duck, geese – all of which were good eating
and easily obtainable. His readers avidly drank in his words and
began to long, with an aching longing, to leave the sordid,

32

Part 1   Baa's Lambs

crowded and inhibited life of over-populated England, and get to
this country where freedom and plenty beckoned. Pen-pushers,
artisans, counter-jumpers, bank clerks, bricklayers and farmers –
thousands of them – wanted to join in this great new pioneering
adventure.

The SS Lake Manitoba sailed from Liverpool,
Mar 31st, 1903 with 1,960 souls on board a vessel
whose registered rating of passengers was between eight and
nine hundred. They were packed together like sardines in a tin.
Many others who had taken earlier departures would join the
trains heading west to the homesteads. In one report a total of
2,684 persons eventually joined the Barr inspired immigration
movement.

After a day or two at sea the overcrowding, the fetid
air of the cabins, the lack of privacy, the inadequate sanitation,
the evil smelling drinking water, sour food, and other such
discomforts began murmurings, soon to become grumblings and
loud-voice discontent. Barr, "Baa" as he was called by most of
the English and which he loathed, was the chief target of all the
abuse. For, was it not he who had made all those wonderful
promises? Had he not given his word that everything would, at
least, be comfortable? Why then was there not sufficient good
food?

Everywhere there were disgruntled groups, speech
making and spreading the dissatisfaction. One would be orator
voicing the grievances said, "What I says is, we are being led
like lambs to the slaughter." Another would be wit called out
derisively.

"Aye, Baa's Lambs."

Part 1   Baa's Lambs

And so the nickname "Baa's lambs" originated for the Barr Colonists, who came out two thousand or more strong and settled in and around Lloydminster in 1903.

About the middle of April the SS Lake Manitoba docked at the port of St. Johns, New Brunswick. It soon became very apparent that "Baa" was on the make. He had bought up a large quantity of bread which he was offering to the colonists at ten cents a loaf. It was soon discovered, however, that the same identical loaf was selling in the town for five cents. After this discovery not one loaf of "Baa's" bread was bought by the colonists.

Eventually on April 17th, 1903, there arrived at Saskatoon, then a little hamlet on the prairie wilderness, some twenty-three hundred Barr Colonists, all already somewhat disillusioned and disenchanted, but still with eclectic visions of landownership, in the varying degrees of demesnes, park or even a moderate estate, looming large, "Ever a little further. It may be beyond that far blue horizon still capped with snow."

The papers en route, announcing the arrival of this large number of Colonists, were loud in their praises of the type of settler to arrive. Not only were they superior, both physically and intellectually to any other influx of immigrants Canada had ever known, but also financially. It is estimated that these people brought with them from the Old Country, at least half a million pounds sterling. There were doctors, lawyers, druggists, clergymen, merchants, aristocrats, artisans, labourers, and some farmers among the arrivals, all in excellent health and eager to become good citizens.

Here again further evidence of Barr's greed and selfishness soon became apparent. It was revealed that he had

34

made arrangements with the implement dealers and others to pay him a substantial commission on all purchases made by the colonists. For example, he had bought a large quantity of oats at twenty-five cents per bushel and sold them to the colonists at one dollar and fifty cents per bushel.

The discomforts, hardships and disappointments which they suffered, both on the SS Lake Manitoba and later on the trek across the continent, more particularly after leaving Saskatoon, where they left the railway line, caused so much antagonism against Barr that he found it expedient to disappear. These other such unethical practices on his part ultimately aroused so much ill feeling among them that he had to make a hasty get away to escape their intended violence.

Then the reverend Mr. Lloyd, who had joined the Colonists in England as Chaplain took over the leadership. He led them through many more trials and tribulations resulting from Barr's inadequate preparations for the journey overland to their promised land.

He was both courageous and resourceful. But, though animated by the best motives, I believe, he made some poor friends by trying to keep all but true British out of the Colony. He was generally popular. He later became Bishop Lloyd, and the town of Lloydminster was named after him.

I maintain that I, who was just prevented by a technicality from being with them on the SS Lake Manitoba and who came a few weeks later, have every right to be associated with that most exalted and honoured society of Baa Lambs.

Here we shall leave the rest of these colonists for the time being, to follow the fortunes - good and

Part 1   Baa's Lambs

ill, of one family - the Marfleet family as told in the following
chapters by Fred Marfleet, son of Will and Elizabeth.

Harry and Ted had left the colonists at Saskatoon.
There they had been told that there were good chances of getting
work in Prince Albert, then a sizeable town of about two
thousand population, about two hundred miles north on a branch
line from Regina. So to Prince Albert they went, hoping to earn
enough money to continue their journey west to the Barr
Colony. As had been arranged, they sent home a cable, "Come,
Lots of Work." I was now all ready to go and sailed from
Bristol on the first available boat -- a cattle boat. There were
only a dozen passengers on it and the trip was enjoyable. We
landed at Three Rivers, Quebec, where the cattle were unloaded
and replaced by a return cargo of lumber. We passengers went
on by train to Montreal, where we spent the day sightseeing.
Next morning we boarded the train on the next lap of our
journey west.

What a train! What a journey!

We sat on bare board seats all day, and at night slept
on bunks with mattresses so sparse as to be almost negligible.
How my bones ached each morning after a night spent on those
uncomfortable bunks with their meagre coverings. Each night
there was a change of conductors, usually around midnight, and
we were then awakened to show our tickets. Half asleep and
with bleary eyes, we would rummage through our pockets for
the damned things. We all hated this nuisance. Some of the
conductors, waited very patiently and with genial banter; while
others seemingly were out to cause us all the trouble and
inconvenience they possibly could. One in particular used to yell
and hurl epithets at us. We all hated him. I felt I would like to
choke him.

36

Part 1   Baa's Lambs

Day after day on the same noisy, chugging train, sitting on the same hard seats! They became harder each day, I vow, and always the same discomfort at night. One evening there was a little diversion - someone called out, "There's a mosquito".

I sat up all attention looking for something as large as a bumblebee, at least, but it was killed before I saw it. I had to wait for that pleasure until a few days later. Meals were snatched at refreshment stands at the small stations where we stopped. We always welcomed these stops, as they gave us a chance to get a breath of fresh air and stretch our legs.

One morning a woman was making "flap jacks". We all ordered some. She came with them and a jug of syrup and enquired, "Sirp boys?"

We all wanted "Sirp".

She said, as she poured it over the cakes "Well, 'tain't no fav'rite with me. It gives me the indigestion". The cakes were cold and tough as leather. We all had "the indigestion" after eating them! The train sang as it chugged along through rough rugged scenery, 'hot and dirty', 'hot and dirty'. It was indeed hot and dirty!

I thought of coaling the ship at Suez - always, a hot, dirty job, but we had always had fun. All pitched in from the captain down to the lowest rating, and the fantastic dress in which many of them appeared! Swallow-tail coats and top hats, ladies' evening dresses, ladies' bathing suits, ladies' night gowns, one once appeared in a lady's blouse and old fashioned lady's drawers which reached down to the ankles around which were lace ruffles. These opened at the back each time he stooped, and then we all pelted him with coal. The more bizarre and ludicrous the attire - the more fun, and when the job was completed the mad rush to be the first to wash - one small tub of fresh water for approximately a dozen men. Then the cool, refreshing swim in the sea! How gloriously healthy and well that had always made us feel.

However, avaunt such memories!

Was there not a "hestite" waiting for me, out in that grand beckoning west?

'The winters, would be cold - a dry cold you don't feel It, The summers would be hot - a dry heat you don't feel it ...'

So the literature had said. I would not permit memories of the past to blur the vision of the life of freedom and plenty that awaited me.

At Winnipeg, all my shipmates had come to the end of their journey. I had some time to wait there, so we all spent the time together viewing the town, then in 1903, just a Main Street with a few distorted looking streets branching off. There were few buildings of any consequence, which I can remember.

The people in the town seemed to be mostly French!

Here my fellow passengers tried very hard to dissuade me from going any farther West. They said, "It is an unexplored, uncivilized country, where Indians, still wild outlaws, buffalo and many wild and fierce animals roam at will. It is a no man's land, whose climate no white man can endure."

But, "Excelsior"! I would not be diverted.

38

Part 1   Baa's Lambs

I would put my banner with the device "Hestite" on those high wrought iron gates and my posterity would rise up and call me blessed.

My ticket was paid through to Prince Albert, Saskatchewan, North West Territories, so I boarded the train for Regina. At that time a branch line ran from Regina, on the main Trans-continental line, North through Saskatoon to Prince Albert, approximately two hundred miles.

If I had hoped for better travelling on this lap of the journey, I was to be disappointed. The view from the window as the train sped west had changed to a flat, uninteresting plain with, even in those days, large fields of wheat with the crop already showing well above ground.

'Ah!' I thought, 'The wheat! The bountiful grass knee-deep! The forests! Surely Barr had spoken truly.'

The next morning, after reaching Regina, I entrained for Prince Albert. I had sent a telegram from Winnipeg asking Harry to meet me.

It was still daylight when the train pulled into the station at Prince Albert. On alighting, I looked around for one or both of the boys but only two men, who, from their copper colour faces, I assumed were Indians, were waiting on the platform. Their clothing was odd - black shirts and bib overalls (the first bib overalls I had ever seen), but absolutely no paint or feathers.

As I looked around for the boys, these two strangers approached me, grinning, and then one of them spoke my name! Sure enough, it was Harry and Ted come to meet me!

Part 1   Baa's Lambs

Harry asked, "Have you been sick?" I looked so white to him.

"Where can I get a nice hot bath and a good meal?" I asked.

They both laughed and Ted said, "I am afraid you will have to wait until Saturday night for the bath, and the cook's in bed, so there will be no meal till morning. Breakfast is at six. We start work at seven."

I had turned down the chance of a snack at a little station about two hours ago thinking of the beef-steaks I would have with the boys when I reached Prince Albert!

"Where's your grips?" asked Harry, and when they explained that 'grips' were suitcases, we picked mine up and started off.

How rough and uncouth they both seemed!

Harry had always been inclined to be bluff, but Ted had always been gentle and refined. How dirty their clothing was! They did not seem to bother about my need for a meal and a bath. It had seemed to amuse them. I felt hurt and rebuffed.

We followed a road, which led up a hill, for about a mile and as I walked along, I filled my lungs with the cool fresh air. How exhilarating it was after the hot stuffy train. I breathed deeply, wondering, at its cool refreshment. In a little while, it seemed to become quite nippy.

"This is the dry heat," I thought. "You can't feel it".

Part 1   Baa's Lambs

"What's the temperature this evening?" I asked.

Harry sniffed the air in the way I have seen so many men do when trying to gauge the temperature and said, "It must be damned near freezing."

In June!

'Oh, he's just showing off.' I thought.

At the top of the hill I saw in the now fading daylight a number of small huts, one of which we entered. A small, smelly, coal oil lamp dimly lighted it. There were three most uninviting looking bunks in the room spread with hay and covered with two dark blankets.

Not even the scant mattress of the train.

Harry and Ted undressed at once and got into the blankets! Harry said to me, "Blow out the lamp, before you turn in, Fred". I surveyed the blankets and straw with mistrust and distaste. They were dark gray in color, but no unpleasant odour from them - they smelled new. This gave me some little assurance. But, remembering how clean our beds at home had always been; this thought gave me a feeling of resentment against Harry and Ted for not seeming to mind the crude, coarseness, of the beds. I thought of the hammocks on board ship and the beds in the barracks - always spotlessly clean, and a depth of misery and despair, such as I had never known before, assailed my soul that night.

Harry and Ted were already sound asleep, so I blew out the light and lay down on the blankets without even removing my shoes.

41

Next morning the alarm went off at 5:45. Harry and
Ted both leaped out of bed, Harry gave me a shirt, and bib
overalls saying, "You had better wear these, Fred. You can pay
me for them when you get some money." I donned the shirt
and-overalls and burst out laughing. How ridiculous I looked in
them.

Harry said, "You'd better hurry up." and hurried out
of the shack.

Ted waited for me saying, "Come let us go, Fred, or
we'll be late". I detected sympathy in his voice and he was
younger than I was! I felt ravenously hungry so I went along.

We entered a long shed, where a table made of bare
rough boards laid on trestles was spread with a most sumptuous
breakfast. There were stewed prunes, steaming hot porridge,
bacon and eggs, sausages, brown and white bread, hot biscuits,
honey, marmalade, lots of butter and a most enticing smell of
coffee. Harry was already sitting half-way up on one of the long
benches that served as seats on each side of the table. The
benches were almost full of men and all were laughing and
joking and seemed entirely care-free and happy.

Everything tasted good and well cooked and I ate
heartily and was surprised at the amount of food Ted tucked
away. He looked stronger and healthier than I had ever before
seen him look.

After breakfast, he introduced me to a Mr. Itner with,
"Itner, this is my brother Fred. He's going to work with us."

Mr. Itner said, "Good! Good!" shook hands and spat.

Part 1   Baa's Lambs

The form of the introduction seemed odd, but in keeping with all I had seen so far. The thought came unbidden, 'It's dry - you don't feel It.'

I liked Mr. Itner's, friendliness and handshake and began to feel more at home in my rough surroundings.

Mr. Itner, or just Itner, as he insisted we all call him, was an American from Nebraska, where he had had some experience in making bricks. Hearing that Western Canada was being opened up, he had come to find out what were the possibilities of establishing a brickyard in one of the mushroom towns that the propagandists of those days spoke of, and had drifted into Prince Albert and decided the clay there was suitable for his purpose.

He had driven all the way from Nebraska with a team and wagon and had brought with him a brick-making machine.

It had taken him a year in Prince Albert to get ready to start. One day, as he was leaning against the corner of the hotel, picking his teeth and spitting -- I have never seen anyone that could spit like Itner; it was pure artistry the precision with which he could hit his target -- looking for man likely to be his kind, along came Harry and Ted and other Barr Colonists just newly arrived.

"Want work boys?" Itner asked and spat.

They assured him that was what they were looking for.

"Well now," he said, spitting, "I'm looking for boys to work for me. I want to start a brickyard here. I am sure it will do well," pausing and spitting, "but - I have no money," spitting

43

and a long pause, "will you boys risk working for me at $1.00 a day and good food and sleeping and I'll pay you in the Fall." Spitting again and cocking his head on one side, and as Harry said, afterwards, mesmerizing them into accepting his offer.

The boys thought it was a pretty good proposition; the good food appealed strongly to them after Barr's "off-colour grub"-, so they agreed to take his offer. He then told them to go up to the brickyard and there await his coming.

He then went to the trade's people and told them his circumstances, and asked them to 'stake him' for the summer months. Two took the risk and soon the brick-yard was in operation.

Now anyone who has worked in a brick-yard will know something of the nature of the work required. My job was to hew clay out of a bank and wheel barrows full of it up an inclined plank to the pit where it was mixed with water ready to be moulded into bricks."

Never shall I forget those first few days until I caught on to the knack of handling the barrow. It took every ounce of strength in my body and just about wrenched my shoulders apart. Perspiration poured from every pore and the mosquitoes - - millions - billions - trillions of them chewed me up! Such heat I had never known 'Dry heat,' I thought. 'You don't feel it!'

The only thing that made me stay with it was the thought, 'Ted stayed with it and he is much slighter and less robust than I'. The seconds, minutes, hours of each day dragged mercilessly on from seven in the morning until six in the evening. I was done; only the thought of the bath that Ted had said we should get on Saturday night kept me going. When we

44

Part 1   Baa's Lambs

dropped tools at six o'clock on Saturday evening, Itner said,
"Come on boys," and away he went on the run with every man,
including myself, trying to keep up with him, until we reached a
slough where he first, then all the rest of us jumped in and swam
around.

This was the bath! However, no bath in the world
could have been more refreshing. Not only did we have a bath
we washed our clothes at the same time. Then after swimming
around till all the ache and tiredness had gone out of our bodies
and our limbs were well limbered up, we ran back to camp, hung
our wet clothing on the surrounding trees to dry, put on dry
clean overalls and shirts and then to supper - a good wholesome
meal that always smelled delicious and inviting. The food at
Itner's camp was always good and appetizing.

I soon caught on how to use the barrow with little or
no effort, and then couldn't believe or even understand why I
had found it so difficult those first awful days.

Itner used to go into town each day to order supplies
and, as the volume of work increased, to look out for new men.
I remember one man, an Englishman, he sent out to the yard.
He looked us over as we wheeled our barrowful up the plank
and asked, "Good food?"

We assured him it was good.

"How much beeah are you allowed?" was his next
question.

We all laughed and told him "None".

45

Part 1   Baa's Lambs

"None," he exclaimed incredulously. Then, as he saw we meant it, he said, "Well, bah gum, that's a rum un!" Then over his shoulder, as he walked away, "I wouldn't do that there ruddy job for $5.00 a day with no beeah. That's hass's work."

Another came, also an Englishman, who spoke with an Oxford accent. He was about my own age and very slightly built. We were all surprised that he undertook the job. He enquired in his aristocratic voice, "By-the-way, what pay do you get for making these jolly little mud pies?"

When we told him $1.00 a day, he jestingly asked, "What do you do with the bally thing? Buy fags?"

Then looking at our black shirts and bib overalls, he remarked, "Jove, what cunning togs you all wear. Must I?"

Another Englishman, as rough as they come, answered sneeringly, "No, you wear yer ruddy swaller tiles and bring yer 'untin crop halong to fight these here skeeters, or one of 'em will eat yer hup."

Next morning he turned up, not in his swaller-tiles, but in black shirt and bib overalls. We watched him struggle, the sweat pouring off his face and every muscle of his body taut and straining to balance the wheel barrow on the plank and push it along. Hordes of swarming mosquitoes added to his discomfort. After about two hours, he fell flat on his back in a seemingly unconscious collapse, his eyes rolling around and his breath coming in gasps. We all stood feeling helpless until the Englishman, who had spoken to him so uncivilly the day before, said, "Give 'im a drink of whiskey," and produced a mickey. We gave the unconscious one a cupful, which he emptied at one gulp and asked, "Is there any more?"

Part 1   Baa's Lambs

The donor of the whiskey now looked down on him spurning and contemptuously, as if he would like to crush him as he would a worm, and then turning away, he said, scornfully, "Gee I 'ates them bloody dooks."

'Dook' for the man, as he lay there, was funny, but how odd and unpredictable are human beings. Why should this Englishman try to revive the dook?

He stayed with us for two weeks, during which he learned to balance the wheel-barrow and handle it easily. We were all surprised he stayed with us as long as he did.

Could that man run and swim! I have never seen anyone so strong and graceful in the water.

He always spoke of his parents as the 'Mater' and the 'Pater'. We learned he was a remittance man. A remittance man, in case I should explain is a man whose presence with his family in England is undesirable and so his parents usually sent him out to Canada or some other colony and paid him a remittance regularly for keeping out of England. He said bluntly, "They shipped me out to this bloody country to get rid of me."

He had been to Sandhurst Military College and had all the hallmarks of an aristocrat. During World War I, we saw in the Daily Mirror, an Old Country Pictorial, where a man of the same name had won the V.C. (Victoria Cross)

The summer passed quickly with hard work, good food and sound sleep, we were as happy as larks. We all looked and felt better than ever before. Our only recreation was on

Part 1   Baa's Lambs

Saturday night, when after supper we would get twenty-five
cents from Itner with which we would buy apples and a ten cent
plug of tobacco. Apples were a luxury for us then and we used
the brown paper of the wrapping bag for cigarette papers.

During this time I heard many stories from Ted and
Harry about the harrowing trip aboard the S.S. Lake Manitoba.
Crowded conditions, lack of sanitation, bad water, and food
rationing with exorbitant prices were just some of the hardships
suffered by the unfortunate passengers. Then at the harbour in
St. Johns all the arriving colonists were kept on board for three
days while Canadian customs processed the paperwork. When
finally they were allowed to disembark all the possessions
people had brought were stacked on the wharf in a huge pile of
disorganized belongings which everyone had to pick through to
find their own. Needless to say, many did not find everything
they owned and cherished, and many claimed items which
belonged to someone else. I was soon counting my good fortune
to have crossed in relative ease on the cattle boat.

When the frost came in September, the brickyard
closed down for the winter. We had made over one million
bricks, all of which had been sold. Itner was pleased and we all
felt quite wealthy with our accumulated earnings. We decided
to go west to the 'Hestites' for the winter. The wrought iron
gates which during those first hellish days in the brick-yard had
dissolved in the sweat of my brow now loomed-up again, high
and handsome and 'Blinkin' in the setting sun.

48

It's a Dry Cold

CHAPTER 4

Barr decamps

When Itner heard we were thinking of going to our homestead, he made us a very good proposition. If only (the saddest phrase in the English language), we had not been too green to realize it was good. He said, "You will go back on your homesteads, and spend all you have earned here, and next spring you'll have no money to make a start. Now if you'll come and work for me this winter, getting logs out of the bush, I'll give you $1.00 a day and your grub and sleeping bunks. I'll need lots of logs for firing the kilns next summer. Then go on your homesteads in the spring and you'll have some money to start."

As we showed reluctance, he said, "I'll tell you what. I'll give you three boys that piece of land on the hill there."

This was a piece of land about the size of a city block, then about one-half a mile from the centre of the town. He had potatoes growing on it. Only a few years later the town had expanded to quite a distance beyond this same block, and Prince Albert had become a city.

Still we showed our reluctance to accept his offer.

He coaxed. "You'd have enough money to go on your homesteads and start breaking."

"Breaking?" we asked in bewilderment.

49

"My God!" He said aside and spat, then, "Yes, breaking up the prairie sod so you can seed grain on it".

"Oh yes," We said, understandingly, "ploughing."

"Hmm, yes, ploughing", He repeated after us, and looking at us pityingly. Then he spat again and said, "Now look here, you boys don't know much about this country. Why do you want to go away back there, where there's no settlers and where it may be years before a railway comes through. Why don't you get homesteads near the town here, and let them other distant fields go to blazes?"

He even went to the trouble of locating homesteads for us, on the confines of the town and later absorbed by the city. We could also have easily obtained land, which now forms part of the business section of the city of Saskatoon. But no! Barr had planned on a city where the Vermilion River joins the Saskatchewan. We must go there.

We surely had our moments, but we just could not see them. Green Englishmen!

We went back to the Hestite!

At Saskatoon many, who like Harry and Ted, now found their money all used up, and who had to seek employment dropped out of the ranks of the Colonists. The others began the trek to the mouth of the Vermilion, by all and every means obtainable. They bought up democrats, buggies, wagons, buckboards, horses, mules, oxen, all and everything that offered a means of transportation to their homesteads. The people already settled in and around the hamlet, hearing of the great incoming tide of settlers, flocked in with everything they could get to sell – their object: to fleece the newcomers, which they did unmercifully. This added fuel to the fires of hate and resentment against Barr already smoldering in the hearts of everyone.

The going was hard over the rough and hitherto untrodden prairie, through sloughs and creeks, where horses and oxen sank to their bellies and it required the combined efforts of all hands to get them free. The mosquitoes and bull-dog flies were cruelly pestering, progress was slow and tedious. Both children and adults were suffering from shortages of food and water, and the weather after leaving Saskatoon turned unseasonably cold. All this created hardships and consequent disaffection. Each night many of them quailed with fear of the ordeals the morrow might bring forth.

It was a motley collection of people and effects, all thoroughly incensed at Barr. The provisions he had made were totally inadequate. Looking back in later years and in the light of further pioneering experiences, most of them recognized that all this suffering, or most of it, was just what they should have expected. What Barr, in fact, had tried to prepare them to expect. It was just a challenge to the initiative, patience, and forbearance of would-be homesteaders.

There should have been no thirst or hunger had they used the bounties that nature freely and lavishly offered. There was plenty of good water everywhere, but not in a faucet; the prairies were rife with partridge, prairie chicken, rabbit, and wild duck, all good eating, - particularly when cooked on an outdoor fire. There was an abundance of dry wood for fires, but no fresh meat from a butcher shop.

Part 2   It's a Dry Cold

In later years when a number of them met at a picnic,
or dance, or other gathering, and began reminiscing one would
hear such stories as these.

"Do you remember when we all went to help Blythe
pull his horse out of a quagmire?" Brown said. "That's a nice
'orse you 'ave there." Blythe said, "'orse! W'y t'bloke as sold
it, said it were a mare." Brown said, "Well, you ruddy hass!
W'y didn't you lift hits tile an' look?"

"I think one of the funniest things I saw was that Alec
-- oh, you remember who I mean, the one that started the
nickname "Baa Lambs" on the ship. You remember who I
mean, Alec-- Alec--, well anyway he was trying to hitch up a
team of bulls. He had the written instructions tacked onto his
new wagon, and his wife was reading them to him. "Let's see--
but this damned hame won't reach the collar. Are you sure you
haven't missed a line?" he asked her.

"Yes, I'm sure. Come and read it yourself."

"Yes, it says 'hook the hames to the collar'. But how
in hell -". Just then a native came over laughing, "Say, pal", he
said. "them collars ain't right. You've got them upside down."

"Was he the one that said to his bulls, 'gee there,
Hercules, gee. Oh, I beg your pardon, boy, haw' …?"

"No that was Bob Addison. Remember Butler, he
tried to unharness a team from a wagon and undid every buckle
in the harness. We found him looking ruefully at all the pieces
spread all over the ground trying to figure out how to get it back
together."

"Yeah, it was Ashton I think who tried to hitch a team to a plough by backing them into the handles."

"How did the name, "Baa Lambs" originate?"

"Oh that was on the ship. You know how we English used to call Barr, 'Baa', and how Barr hated it. One day someone was making a speech, you remember how we all loved to make a speech - -?"

"Yes, a lot of us became better speech makers than farmers, I'm afraid. Weren't some of those speeches killing?"

"Yes, but the pity is they didn't kill Barr."

"Well, go on with your story about the nickname."

"Oh, yes. Well a cockney was declaiming, 'W'at I says is we are all being led like lambs to the slaughter ----,' and Alec called out, 'Ah, Baa Lambs' and the nickname has stuck, and a darned good name, too."

"Do you remember Bob Fletcher?"

"Yes, always drunk, wasn't he?"

"He sure was a boozer. Did you ever hear about the night he got into Huntley's tent by mistake?"

"No. What happened?"

"About a dozen of us got into a little poker game at Saskatoon that lasted all night. Fletcher left early and staggered into the wrong tent. He crawled into bed with Huntley's wife.

53

She didn't wake up until after he had been there for a while.
Apparently she woke up and felt for Huntley's curls and you
remember how bald Fletcher was."

"Ah, yes, as bald as a bladder of lard."

"She ran into Mrs. Malone's tent scared to death and
they both went back and kicked Fletcher's ass out of the tent.
Huntley was out at a poker game and didn't get home till almost
daylight. They never dared tell Huntley or he would have
murdered Fletcher."

"How did you get to hear it?"

"Well you know Mrs. Malone? It was just too good to
keep."

"Did Huntley ever hear about it?"

"Oh, I don't know. I'm not even sure it was Fletcher.
Anyway they're both dead now."

"Really? How did Fletcher die?"

"Well, he was always writing home to his father, the
Pater, you know for money to buy more and more stock. He
stuffed the Pater with stories of the wonderful purebred horses
and purebred herd of whitefaces he had acquired. After his
mother, the Mater, died his father wrote to say he was coming
out to see Bob's farm and stock. Bob didn't have a hoof on his
place. So he borrowed all the horses and cattle his neighbors
would lend him. One of the borrowed horses kicked him in the
gut. He died in just a few days."

54

"He surely was a character. I wish I had half the money he spent on utter foolishness. What was that he was trying to invent?"

"Oh, heaven knows. Could have been a cure for baldness."

"Or drunkenness."

"Were you there the night we were going to tar and feather Barr?"

"Yes, we were surely mad. That was when we discovered he had only paid twenty-five cents a bushel for the oats that he was charging us a dollar fifty for. I wonder who tipped him off."

"Oh someone that was afraid we would murder him."

"But you know all that suffering from hunger and thirst on the trek was unnecessary. There was plenty of good pure water lying all over the prairies, from the melted snow. We just had to strain it through our teeth."

"Yes, just! It was good water all right but full of bits of grass and insects."

"And the bush just teemed with prairie chicken and partridge and rabbits, and we all had guns. Why the dickens we didn't shoot them I'll never know."

"No. Too green, I guess."

Part 2   It's a Dry Cold

We all enjoyed getting together at a dance or meeting, more especially in later years when only a few of us original colonists were left. It is hard to believe we were all so green. It was just about where the town of Bressaylor is now situated that feelings against Barr rose to a boiling point. A number of the men, led by Clutterbuck I heard, decided at a private meeting that they would get hold of him and tar and feather him. With this worthy motive in mind, they went to his tent, only to find that he had pulled out and disappeared, decamped as it were.

Ed Griffiths, who was always at the rear of the trek, was on this evening well east of the vanguard. He was surprised to meet Barr and some other man, a stranger to him, in a buggy going 'hell bent for leather' toward Saskatoon. Ed was always quite proud of the fact that he was the "last baa" to see "Baa", and to "kiss him goodbye, as ye might say" – a favorite expression of his.

Poor Barr! He had only anticipated about nine hundred responses to his appeal for colonists. The overwhelming two thousand plus was just beyond his reach. He was unable to cope with the adventure on this large scale, and neither did he receive the support he should have from his co-operators for the scheme. Certainly, Lea Park, at the junction of the Vermilion and North Saskatchewan rivers, had more potential as a site for a city than Lloydminster could ever attain. Good water has always been, and still is, a problem there.

"And then when we came to where the fire had gone through! Never shall I forget the misery of that scene. Everyone was too heartbroken to speak, almost. Look where we would - just charred black desolation. Some of the men cried like babies! Quite a few turned right round and went back. I wonder if they went home."

56

Part 2   It's a Dry Cold

"Well, I know I for one, was all ready to turn right round. Mr. Lloyd surely showed great courage and good sense."

Soon after leaving Battleford, which was at that time a good-sized town with a strong detachment of the Mounted Police stationed there, the settlers came to a country charred and blackened by fire. They stood aghast. Even the strongest and most sanguine hearts among them quailed at this desolate scene. There was nothing to see but miles and miles of black desolation in every direction. So disillusioned were they that they could not proceed further.

Had it not been for Mr. Lloyd's encouragement and persuasion, the group would have dissolved. He told them that in only a few weeks the prairies, now burnt and barren, would again be a green fertile carpet. He said he had seen it happen before. They believed him and went forward for several more days. They again came to lush green prairie land. By this time they were so weary, worn and disheartened that they decided to call a halt at the place where Lloydminster now stands, on the 4th meridian.

When the provinces of Alberta and Saskatchewan were established, the 4th meridian was the designated dividing line, splitting the town of Lloydminster in two, one side in Alberta, the other in Saskatchewan.

"Yes, whatever success attended that venture was entirely due to him. We should have kicked Barr out at St. Johns when he tried to put across that bread deal."

"That was the first real evidence we had that he was on the make."

57

Part 2   It's a Dry Cold

"He was a rotter from the very start."

"Oh well, it's all under the bridges now."

Yes, it was under the bridges, but those people surely
did suffer. When Barr decamped, the Reverend Lloyd assumed
the leadership, at their request, and led the colonists forward
through the remaining hazards of the journey to the final goal,
where they founded a small town, and named it Lloydminster
after their now beloved leader. Here they pitched their tents for
the last time and it was here that we boys joined them at the end
of September, on our way to our 'Hestite'.

There was plenty of work to be done. Everyone
seemed to be trying feverishly to get some kind of habitation
built for the winter. Other settlers also had come in to be on the
ground floor in setting up businesses so there were quite a few
buildings in course of construction. We had brought with us a
team of horses, Nellie and Frank, and a wagon - all of which we
had bought in Prince Albert for $100.00. These were always in
demand. We got $2.00 per day digging cellars and hauling
supplies. We stopped and worked till nearly the end of October.

One day Bill Paling, who had already set up in a livery
barn business, came to me and said, "If you and your brothers
will put up twenty tons of hay for me, I will give you a mower
and rake."

"New?" I asked.

"Not quite, but new enough. Come and take a look at
them."

It's a Dry Cold

They seemed quite new to me so I told the boys and we agreed to take Paling's offer.

We had filed on homesteads before leaving England, and had paid our entry fee of $10.00 each, but all records and monies had been lost with Barr's disappearance, so we now entered on three others, about thirty miles northwest of Lloydminster, and exactly ten miles south of the mouth of the Vermilion River, Barr's original goal. Then we drove out to these homesteads, loading the mower on the wagon and dragging the rake behind. We took with us some provisions, a stove and a tent and began making hay.

It was now nearing the first week of November and there had been many heavy frosts. Frost destroys much of the nutritional value of the hay - as we were to find out during the following winter. We put up thirty tons for ourselves besides the twenty for Paling, which we delivered in good faith, hauling a load each time we went for mail. The grass was, indeed, knee deep and heavy as Barr's pamphlets had promised; the fifty tons we then put up could not be missed -- the growth was so abundantly plentiful.

After the haymaking was completed, we began to build a shack for ourselves for the winter. We built it of poplar logs, which we cut out of the surrounding bush, and chinked them with clay, as we had learned to do when working in Lloydminster. We roofed it with sods dug from the prairie, and surveyed the completed edifice with a feeling, in our hearts, of security against the coming winter whatever its severity! We had brought with us a gun, powder, and shot with which to make shells. So now, we made a quantity of these and hoped to have lots of sport, as the whole prairie seemed to be rife with game, prairie chicken, partridge and rabbits. These with the sowbelly

we had brought with us from Lloydminster, were our chief, and
I might say only meat all that winter, and indeed for many
winters afterward.

       J ust before Christmas, Harry and I took a load of hay
into Lloydminster to deliver to Paling. We found
the residents of Lloydminster almost devoid of provisions,
mainly groceries and tobacco. The hamlet was now quite a
sizable town of about 1,000 inhabitants with many small
business operations. Miller Brothers General store and Hall and
Scott Hardware were the two chief merchandisers. Almost as
soon as we arrived in Lloydminster, the Miller brothers
approached us. They were begging anyone with a team to go to
Saskatoon. "Where the hell have you lads been all this time?"
they asked. "We have been enquiring everywhere about you."

       "Did you ask Paling?" we asked them. "He could
have told you. What did you want us for?"

       "We want you to go to Saskatoon for a load of
groceries for us."

       We had told Ted we would be home the next day.
Saskatoon was two hundred miles away, so we hesitated.

       "To Saskatoon! Oh I'm, afraid --"

       "Look here! We are right out of grub, and not a bit of
baccy in the town. It is really serious with us. You can't refuse.
We'll pay you well."

       Not wishing to pass up an opportunity to earn a few
dollars, we agreed to go.

Part 2   It's a Dry Cold

The Reverend Lloyd was now firmly established in Lloydminster, and had won the esteem and affection of the residents, who, to show their appreciation of what he had done for them, had presented him with a team of purebred Clydesdale mares. These he offered to lend us on condition that we pick up some oats for him at Bressaylor on our return journey.

We started out for Saskatoon, Harry driving Nellie and Frank, and I driving the Clydesdales. The round trip took three weeks. Both wagons were heavily laden on our return trip. As we neared the settlement, one of the mares showed signs of great weariness. I was afraid she would play out, so I stopped at a house, just nearing nightfall, and asked if I might stay there for the night. It was the home of Laura Sisley - Saint Laura, as she afterwards became known. She was a spinster lady of about forty, I would guess. She had brought a number of youths from the East end slums of London, with the Barr Colonists, and had built that house to provide a home for them. She lived with them, paying all expenses, until they were all established on their homesteads, and then, her large inheritance all being spent, she worked among the colonists - cooking, housekeeping, nursing, or whatever other work she could earn a living at - for the remainder of her life. One of the boys "My boys", as she called them, froze to death that first winter, when he tried to walk "Home" from Lloydminster for Christmas. It was said that he was taking his first pay home to his benefactor. Laura mourned him as a mother would have mourned a well beloved son. She gave me supper that night, and wouldn't accept any payment for the food and shelter I had had.

Next day I caught up with Harry at Lloydminster. The weather had turned colder with heavy snow, so next morning we got up early to make a good start and went to get breakfast at Miss Fletcher's cafe. There were two sisters I believe, that

61

operated it. As we drew near we saw one of the women outside
scraping up the snow, which was, yet only about two or three
inches deep, from between the dog scat scattered everywhere
around. We did not much relish the porridge or the coffee on
the menu.

Melted snow was the only water obtainable in
Lloydminster that winter.

When we reached home that night, much to our
surprise, Ted told us he had caught six red foxes in our absence.
They were beauties! We sold the pelts later to Miller Bros. for
three dollars each. He also had hauled a huge pile of willow
fence posts out of the bush.

Ted was always a worker!

The weather continued to get colder and the snow
deeper. We had brought a good stock of provisions with us
from Lloydminster - mainly sowbelly and groceries, for our first
winter in the new land.

CHAPTER 5

'The wind doth blow and we shall have snow'

I believe it was about December twenty-eighth we had our first real spell of below zero weather and with a wind. We thought we had built our shack practically windproof, but now the wind seemed to rip through it as if it were a sieve. Looking back now, it seemed as if we were all three kept busy from the time we got up in the morning, not too early, till bedtime. One would be sawing logs up for firewood with a bucksaw - - outside -- until he just could not stand the penetrating wind any longer, and then carrying in an armful and piling it near the stove. Another was busy feeding the stove, which seemed to consume fuel at a rate a blast furnace in a smelting works would envy; while the third was getting booted and wrapped to go out to "take his turn on the buck". Ted was cook and during that extremely cold spell, there was little variety in the menu; beans, sowbelly, bannock, prunes -- prunes, sowbelly, bannock and beans, ad aeternum, ad nauseam.

We had made three beds; later we built bunks Canadian fashion, they take up less space, and, as we could not keep the fire going at night, we slept in all our clothes and piled on all the coverings we could amass.

Before leaving England, Fan had given each of us a dressing gown, which she made out of pure woolen, grey blankets. She had lined the hoods, a necessary appendage to a dressing gown of those days, with tartan silk. These were very warm and cozy and we each slept in them with the hood drawn snugly over the head and round the face and I even found it necessary to put my fur lined cap over the hood to keep my head

63

warm. I shall always blame that for my baldness. I had had a good crop of hair all my life, quite a quiff when I was in the Navy, and had never noticed any sign of it thinning till the following spring. Since then, it has gone like snow off a ditch on a summer's day.

The extreme cold lasted with temperature flirting between zero and forty below for six weeks. One of the longest and coldest spells I have ever known in all these years. It was so bitterly cold that pretty well every morning our frozen breath had formed a fairly thick sheet of ice on our blankets. One morning, when we got up, the cold was devilish - one of our coldest mornings - Harry looked awful, and as he got out of bed with his teeth chattering, he said, "It's a dry cold, you don't feel it". Ted, who was already booted to go out said, "Shit!"

Ted! Always the gentleman of our family.

The wrought iron gates had no place in our thoughts or hopes those days. We all three regretted, often and often, that we had not listened to Itner.

When there was no wind, we could keep tolerably warm in our shack, but could not venture any distance away as walking was impossible owing to the heavy snow into which one sank knee deep.

One day, we heard someone prowling around outside. We opened the door and found a stranger standing there. He was Billy Shaw, who afterwards became a brother-in-law. He said, "I heard you three boys were over here, so I just thought I would drop around and see how you are making out".

64

Part 2   It's a Dry Cold

We asked him in out of the cold; he seemed very friendly. He had walked over on his snowshoes and was very warmly clothed and comfortable looking. These were the first snowshoes we had ever seen and were just what we needed. We asked, "Where did you get them?" We did not know what to call them.

"Oh. I've had them years." he replied. "I bought them in Toronto."

We wanted to ask him how much they cost, but our snobbish reserve would not allow us to ask pointblank, so we parried, "I suppose they would cost more out west here than in the East?"

He said dryly, "I don't know where you would get snowshoes out west, but I can find out where you could get them down East."

"Snowshoes!" we thought.

"They are quite expensive." one of us suggested.

"Well, these cost me seventeen dollars."

Seventeen dollars! Aghast, positively prohibitive, but we could not let him know we thought so.

Poor but proud!

We examined them very closely, and as soon as he had gone, we all three set to making some out of willow twigs and saplings. We accomplished a shoe that was quite heavy and unwieldy, but as we had no money with which to purchase the manufactured article, they proved to be quite serviceable and enabled us to get around shooting prairie chicken and snaring rabbits.

How good that first prairie chicken tasted after our enforced confinement to the shack for so long, and when the weather warmed up a little in the second week in February, how luxurious those clean clothes felt after our first washday in five weeks or more!

Billy was very amused at the "door" we had contrived for our shack. Constructed of two upright poles, about three feet apart, with slats between them on both sides, the space between the uprights packed tightly with hay. When we entered the shack, we pulled the door in after us, so that no one outside could find an entrance. It did not fit tightly, but was helpful as a door.

One day we heard bells outside, and opening the door, we were surprised to see an Indian family drive up in a homemade cutter. It was a very cold day, but as we had nothing to offer them in the way of food, we did not think of asking them in to get warm. The brave was dressed in a suit made from what we have since come to know as Hudson's Bay white blankets and in which he looked cozy and warm. The squaw and two children seemed well wrapped up and comfortable, and they all smiled all the time, their little black eyes and white teeth gleaming brightly from their dark faces. The brave told me he was going to Stinking Lake, later called St. Ives lake, and later again, Stinking Lake, to spear muskrat. We boys had been there catching them in traps, but when he showed us the spear he had with him, I thought I would go along and watch him. I accordingly followed his cutter on my snowshoes.

66

His spear was made from a tooth of a hay rake straightened, pointed, and bound securely to a long, light spruce pole, with rawhide. This spear he put right through the nest, and with his years of experience he could tell exactly the position of the rat. He was certainly clever, because he never seemed to miss. In a very short space of time, he had speared about twenty-five. He seemed to realize I did not know much about it, and was trying to show me his method. He was astonishingly clever at pantomime, when he could not explain in English. We boys had spent a whole day trapping and did not have twenty-five. They seemed a very friendly Indian family.

A day or two later, Jack Fleming walked over with the two boys, all three on homemade snow-shoes. He said they had all had bad colds and that the two girls were home, too sick to come out. He wondered if one of us would go over to Billy Shaw's, and borrow a sack of flour for him. He had heard that Billy had brought thirteen sacks in with him in the fall.

We had met Jack when we first came out to put up hay for Paling. He had driven up one day with a pony and mule, in a wagon with the four children, two boys and two girls. He told us then that he was homesteading about two miles south of us and learning enough about us to realize we did not know much about winters in the Canadian West, he drove off promising to look us up during the winter. He had been as good as his word. I have never known a better neighbor or a more generous friend, than Jack Fleming and his family. If we boys were out of tobacco or anything, he would give us half of what he had, regardless of how precarious were his chances of getting a new supply,

He told us now that they had nothing to eat at home; they were right out of grub. I told him I would go to Billy's, at once, and he said the two boys would come with me and we could haul it home on their small homemade sled. Both the boys looked very pale and weak, especially the younger one. We set out at once. The going over the uneven snow was very heavy; we were all soon sweating and about half way there, the younger one played out. I took off my coat and spread it on the ground in a little clump of willows, which sheltered him from the light wind that was blowing. I tucked the coat well in around him, and the older boy, Lawrence, and I set out. We went as quickly as we could, got the sack of flour on the sled with as little delay as possible, and came back to find the younger boy rested and in good spirits and ready to undertake the walk home.

When we reached our shack, I cut what sow belly we had in two, also our tobacco, took half our tea and sugar, and a couple of prairie chickens and a rabbit, some homemade shells, and we set out. When we reached Jack's shack, I was very tired. I had hauled that hundredweight of flour over four miles of uneven crusty snow. Jack insisted that I wait and eat with them. He whipped up some bannock, feather light and snow white and fried sowbelly and prairie chicken. He made some syrup by boiling sugar and water together. In this, we soaked our bannock. We all had a real good meal.

After snaring rabbits for a few weeks, we invariably found that a coyote or fox had been ahead of us and stolen the rabbit. So to thwart the predator, we devised the scheme of bending over a high twig and fastening the snare securely to the end and then burying the twig fairly deeply in the snow in the path of the rabbit. Then, when the rabbit's foot caught in the snare, his struggles loosened the snow, and the twig sprang back into place, carrying both snare and rabbit high up out of reach of the would be robber.

68

All honor to the rabbit.

His importance in the colonization and settlement of this western country cannot be overestimated. Why the beaver should supersede him as emblematic of Canada, I shall never understand. The rabbit has supplied many thousands of settlers with meat during their first year or two of pioneering. That year they were there in thousands. Every bush and grove teemed with them. The Providence of God manifested.

The prosperity, health and fecundity of most wild animals rotate in cycles, those of the rabbit in a five-year cycle, I understand. That year, 1903, must have been at the very crest of a cycle. Their flesh was always fresh and healthy looking, next year we noticed small white watery globules on the insides of the skins of some of them, and the year after, their flesh looked very unhealthy indeed. When spring came that first year, we had a mound of skins at least six feet high and certainly six feet in circumference at the base in front of our door, and you should have seen the one in front of Jack Fleming's shack! The Indian squaws cure the skins and make them into very warm and comfortable robes, but we just burned ours, as we did not even have the comfort of a squaw.

After making our snowshoes and learning how to spear muskrats, two of us would go to Stinking Lake twice or three times a week. We had made spears after the model of the Indian's but not being as adept as he was at spearing, we were lucky if we got thirty or thirty-five for a whole day's work. These we would carry home in sacks on our backs, a distance of four miles. They were quite heavy, but we were young and strong. In the spring, we had between two and three hundred pelts; these we sold to Miller Bros. in Lloydminster at ten cents per pelt.

69

Our team, which we had fed all winter on frozen hay, with melted snow to drink, was now as thin as scarecrows. They were pitiful to look at. Each morning we almost expected to go into the barn and find one or both dead. We had enquired wherever we could about oats for them, but there were none to be had.

On March 19 that year, we heard the first crow.

Caw! Caw!

It sounded lovely. Never have I heard a more welcome sound. It made my spirits soar. I felt glad to be alive.

The weather had moderated towards the third week in February. March had come in wild and blustering with winds that were penetrating, but not so bitterly cold as in January and early February. After that first crow had made its presence heard, spring was here. Water seemed to come at once and be everywhere. The creek, about two hundred yards away from the barn, soon overflowed and we feared the barn would be washed away. We watched with alarm, the waters that had now almost reached flood proportions, rise higher and higher, and then, without warning, a Chinook blew down from the northwest and dried up the floods in a few days. We brought the horses out and the warm sunshine and exercise and the odd vegetation they seemed to find to nibble at, seemed to put new life in them.

Harry had left a sweetheart, Alice Warren, behind in England and during the winter, even in the coldest weather, he wrote to her each week and expected to receive letters each time we got the mail. Ted and I would tease him unmercifully about his ardor that not even forty-nine degrees below could tone down. He took it all good-naturedly.

Part 2   It's a Dry Cold

At that time, the mail came from Saskatoon to North Battleford by carrier with team and sled in the winter, team and wagon in the summer, and thence by another carrier to Lloydminster. We had to get ours from Lloydminster, so after the floods abated, we thought we would try to get in to get mail and some provisions, also oats for the horses. We might even get some work. During these winter months, Fan and Gilbert had sent us twenty-five dollars each month, and this little remittance might be awaiting us, so we started out with the team!

How those poor things made it, I shall never know. We three walked with them all the way, helping them through the miry spots and over the rough parts of the trail. It took us all day, about ten hours, to get to Lloydminster. Upon arrival, we were sorely disappointed to find no oats - not a kernel to be had, and next day no work! There was mail from home, however. They were all getting ready to come out to Canada towards the end of April and asked if we could meet them in Edmonton. They were enclosing twenty-five dollars, and hoped it would see us through till their arrival.

We had brought our muskrat pelts with us and got twenty-five dollars and forty cents for them, so we got a good store of provisions, including some cheese. Not much, but as Ted said, we could do as we had always been told to do as youngsters, "Eat our bread and smell our cheese." We also got some new footwear, and having made one last unsuccessful try to get oats, we started out for home. All this left us very little net cash to last till the end of the month.

We now got out more logs for building a house in the summer, also for fuel, also some willow pickets for fence posts. We always went with Jack Fleming and his family to get these logs and fence posts. He knew so much more about logging

71

than we did. We always took along some grub and made our lunch in the bush. Merle, his eldest girl, was even then a smart little cook, and used to make bannock and fry sowbelly and rabbit and dish up a real tasty meal, our dishes being our fingers, which Jack said, "Were made before forks."

On the first day of April, we saw a butterfly and then knew spring was, indeed, here. We now began making plans for going to Edmonton, to meet the family. It would be nice to see them all again and we all three eagerly looked forward to the reunion, although ever since that extremely cold weather in January and early February, Harry had always spoken against bringing Mother and Dad out to this country.

We hated to look at the team; they were still just like skeletons. Marfleets love horses, and it wrung our hearts each time we fed them the frozen hay, knowing full well how they must loathe it. We planned to give ourselves lots of time, and now that the snow was going and bare patches of prairie were beginning to show, we thought they might nibble a little grass on the way. Also, surely we would be able to buy oats from some farmer on the way to Edmonton. We started out on the twentieth of April.

The day before we started, two young men arrived with their turkey, which is to say their belongings, on their backs. They were the Websdale boys, who had filed on homesteads west of where the present town of Dewberry is situated. They are still farming their original homesteads there, together with other land they have acquired through the years. They had heard we were driving to Edmonton and they had walked to our place, a distance of eighteen or twenty miles, to ride with us. We explained the condition of our horses but bade them welcome, to put their turkeys in the wagon box and walk with us. We would be glad of their company.

We all five set out with the team the next morning, following a faint trail that had a nasty habit of fading out of sight and appearing again like the cat's grin in, 'Alice in Wonderland'. We had not proceeded far when we came to a swollen creek, rushing wildly much beyond its usual confines. We knew the horses could never pull the wagon through, but we must cross, so we all five took off our shoes and socks, those of us who now had socks, and waded through, pulling the wagon with the team tied behind, after us.

Brrr -- the water was icy cold!

No one had thought of bringing a towel, but Harry had a ragged old shirt in his turkey and this we all used to dry our feet and legs; the water in the deepest part had reached well above our knees. Ted, the last man to use the drier, did not get much of a dry. However, the warm sunshine helped a lot.

We had to repeat this ordeal at least twenty times before we reached Edmonton and by that time, did not even think of a drier. Our greatest challenge came at Vegreville. There the waters of the Vermilion River were swollen and rushing very rapidly and wildly and with great turbulence. We all five stood defeated. No one could see a way to overcome this obstacle. We were now more than half way to Edmonton and it had taken us six days to get so far; now must we turn back? We were beaten!

Then a man with a good, heavy, well fed team and wagon drove up. He turned out to be the enterprising kind and was hauling wayfarers such as us through, "for six dollars, per party, per trip."

St. Christopher!

We all five put together all the cash we could muster amongst us, amounting to $5.74, plus three, three cent stamps, proffered by Harry and withdrawn and proffered again. The stranger smiled grimly at this contribution but nevertheless, he waited till Harry made up his mind to part with the stamps before accepting the $5.83.

He hauled us across. We thanked him very gratefully.

After receiving our money, he became a little less grim, asked us who we were, and what we were doing on the trails. When we told him, he seemed very friendly.

Then Harry asked him if he had any oats.

The friendliness vanished at once and his steely eyes glinted as he asked, "Have you any money to buy oats?"

Almost with downcast eyes, we answered, "No", and pulled away from him, but not before Harry had spied sheaves in a field about a quarter of a mile away, and no doubt on St. Christopher's farm - now "Old St. Kit', as one of the boys said in venomous disrespect of our erstwhile savior.

It was now four-thirty or five p.m., and we decided to call a halt for the night. We proceeded till we were well hidden by the bush, which was everywhere. We shot some partridge, made a fire and fried sowbelly and partridge. We also made some bannock. We had no tea, so we drank the water from the

74

melted snow. This had been our fare all the way and how
deliciously good it tasted!

It was still not quite dark when we were ready to roll
into our blankets, so we waited and then went back to St. Kit's
farm and stole some sheaves. We all five went and brought
back two each. If this were sin, then may we be forgiven! I am
sure each one of us got as much enjoyment out of watching
Nellie and Frank eat those succulent sheaves, as they did in the
actual eating of them. We felt much happier now that we had
some nourishing food for the team.

From Vegreville on, the going was not so beset with
hazards, and as we neared Edmonton, we saw more farms, some
quite prosperous looking. They would be in the Clover Bar
District. These I compared with the "hestite" of my vision, and
found them all wanting in pretension. Mine would be much
more lordly and stately! However, it was nice to see these signs
of civilization. We had not seen one farm on our way between
leaving our shack and reaching Vegreville, excepting at Birch
Lake, where we saw some cattle in a distant field and guessed
there must be a farm near. However, it was too far to take our
starving team on the off chance of getting some oats for them.

We reached Edmonton on April 30 and pitched our
tent on the flats, near where the Low Level Bridge stands - then
the Fair grounds.

Part 2   It's a Dry Cold

CHAPTER 6

The good scow 'Marfleet'

The Websdale boys got work carpentering the day after we reached Edmonton and left us. The next time we saw them they were both married and settled on farms and doing well; that must have been twenty years later. Those were the days of horse and buggy travel when fifteen or twenty miles was a long, long journey.

My sister, Annie, and her husband, Harry Alcock, and their family of three children, were at this time living in Edmonton. They had come out to Toronto about six years prior, and had later moved west. Harry was now working here, trying to make enough money to get established on his homestead, about thirty miles away, near a lake bearing (to us) the romantic name of Lac Ste Anne.

We found their house the day following our arrival. When we knocked on the door, Annie, whom I could not remember ever having seen before, opened it.

"Does Mrs. Alcock live here?" I asked.

She laughed, "No, but Mrs. Alsop lives here," and then as I stood at a nonplus she explained, "We've chucked that disgusting name."

"Disgusting?"

"Yes! I wasn't going through life with that label stuck onto me."

76

Part 2   It's a Dry Cold

We all laughed.

"Well, what am I thinking about? Come in. You have all grown so much that I can scarcely recognize any of you!" Annie exclaimed.

"We wouldn't have recognized you either". We told her.

"My, you have changed so much. It's hard to believe you are the little brothers I left at home six years ago. You are all big men!"

"Not as big as Harry," My brother Harry said. Harry Alsop at that time was a very handsome man of fine physique and lordly bearing. A man whose appearance was always outstanding and drew admiration everywhere he went. I shall refer to him as Harry A from now on to distinguish him from my brother Harry Marfleet.

"Well, no. Of course, he has always to be the biggest toad in the hole," Anne said, laughing. Then she said, "There's a telegram here for you. I was wondering if you would get here before they did. Harry opened it as we didn't know just when either they or you would arrive. I hope you don't mind."

"Not at all," we told her. "We knew you'd be wondering where we were."

The telegram was just to advise us that the family was on their way from Winnipeg, and to be sure to have someone meet them at the Strathcona station, the terminus of the Calgary to Edmonton railway.

77

When Harry Alsop came home later and we got talking I said, "You changed your name, Harry, you couldn't take it.

"Goddammit no!" He replied laughingly. "I'm not what that name would imply," and then looking at Annie slyly, "though we do have a baby every two years, eh Annie."

"Oh you." she said, her face suffused with blushes, while we all laughed heartily.

Years later when Harry applied for the Canadian Old Age pension, one of the questions on the application was 'Why did you change your name?' He answered, "The reason is obvious". Harry was always out for fun.

Harry (Alcock) Alsop was born on a farm in Sherwood Forest situated in Nottinghamshire County in the year 1865. During his young adulthood, he farmed, worked in construction and was a member of the Liverpool Police Force. All of this provided him with experience, which he would find useful in his pioneering days.

On February 16th, 1892, Harry was married to Annie E Marfleet, and in 1893, they sailed for Canada with their baby son on the SS Parisian landing in Montreal, and from there traveling to Winnipeg by rail to settle near Brandon, Manitoba. Unfortunately, the land was marshy and mosquitoes forced them to leave the land they had purchased and eventually return to England in 1894, where they farmed and raised livestock.

It wasn't long before they became restless to return to Canada as the prairies were being opened up, so in April 1902, Harry sailed from Liverpool on the S.S. Tunisian to file on a homestead in the territory that would eventually become Alberta. Annie and the children followed later when he was settled.

Harry arrived at Strathcona, the end of the steel at that time, and took a ferry across the river to Edmonton. Edmonton, at that time, had a population of approximately 3,000 with one bridge over the river. He went to the Land Office and secured a block plan for the territory west of Edmonton. He purchased supplies which he carried on his back and began walking Northwest to St. Albert. His supplies consisted of tea, sugar, butter, bacon, bread, in a pack with frying pan, cup and kettle, a waterproof sheet and a blanket. A man and his son had been to Edmonton, where they sold some pigs for $.05 a lb. live weight, and were returning home when they came upon Harry and gave him a ride for about sixteen miles to their home. There the farmer fed and sheltered Harry overnight before allowing him to carry on with his journey.

The third night out it was snowing and Harry knocked on the door of a cabin where he received a friendly welcome from George Noyes, a son of an old-timer. It was now May 1st so the snow soon melted and was gone by noon. Harry proceeded on his journey across the Sturgeon River at a point that later became known as Noyes crossing. Soon after he crossed a creek and climbed a hill with tall trees on each side of the trail, he looked out over a fertile agricultural land where he and his family would live for the next twenty-five years.

He stayed initially at the homestead of Mr Beaupre, who was a great friend giving him lodging and advice, and on June 9th 1902, Harry filed on N.W. Section 36, township 54, Range 2, and west of the 5th Meridian. Here he built a new home for the family.

It's a Dry Cold

On October 31st, 1902, Mrs. Annie Alsop, together with their four children, Noel, Dorothy, Harold, and Sidney arrived by train in Edmonton. Annie went to the livery stable and hired a driver with a horse and buggy to transport them to the homestead. They arrived at Noyes Crossing where Mr. Noyes insisted on taking them across by wagon as the buggy was too frail to ford the river. The water was so high, the flour, sugar, and other perishables were placed on the wagon seat to keep dry.

They were thrilled at the sight of their new home and the children loved the snow. They bought a cow and managed frugally through the first and worst winter. Fortunately, groceries were cheap: good flour $2.00 per hundred weight, rolled oats $1.50 for 40 lbs., sugar $6.00 per 100 lbs, bacon 12¢ per pound, dried fruit 10¢ to 12¢ per lb. by the box of 25 lbs., however, both potatoes and milk were scarce. After that winter and from then on fruits and vegetables from Annie's garden, a pig or two butchered in the fall, eggs stored in water glass and crocks of butter and dozens of pork pies stored in the cooler made the winters cheerier.

On May 15th, 1903 a meeting of local homesteaders was held to establish a school in the District. From then on both Harry and Annie were active on the school board, as well as the church and the mission hospital later.

Harry moved his family to Edmonton during the winter in the first few years where he would find employment. The children and Annie soon decided they preferred to remain on the farm. However, on September 1st, 1905 the family was in Edmonton where they had the pleasure of witnessing the inauguration ceremonies for "the birth of the Province of

Alberta". There was a new member of the family in a carriage by then as a daughter Mable was born the previous winter.

That evening in 1904 we were recounting some of the experiences we had on the trip from the homestead to Edmonton. Annie said.

"How is mother going to make that trip back with you? It will kill her."

"We're hoping the prairie will be mostly dry by the time we're ready to go back." Harry said. "We'll have to carry her over some of the sloughs and creeks, or pull her in the wagon."

"It will be a very rough trip, I'm afraid. I wouldn't like to undertake it." Harry A said.

"Maybe she had better stay here with us until you get some kind of road to that godforsaken place." Annie said.

One evening before the family arrived, Harry A said to us, "Why don't you boys build a scow and float all your family down the Saskatchewan River to your homesteads? It would be much better than dragging them over the prairie."

"A scow?" we enquired.

"Yes" He said. "You've seen them on the Thames, haven't you? You know those big flat-bottomed boats that float with the stream? You could take your team and wagon and all your effects on it with you. There are people building one down at Walter's Mill right now."

81

Part 2   It's a Dry Cold

We remembered them, so at Harry A's suggestion we went down to the river flats next day, and each day thereafter until the family arrived and watched some men building one. We learned all we could about the construction, the quantity of material required and the approximate cost of one, but we had no money to make a start until the family arrived.

Each evening thereafter until the arrival of the family, one of us boys crossed the river to the South Side, either by the Low Level Bridge, the only bridge at that time to span the Saskatchewan River throughout its entire length, or by the ferry. Then we proceeded to the Strathcona Station to meet them. The ferry crossed from Walter's Mill, somewhere near the present site of the High Level Bridge. There is still a remnant of Walter's Mill near this bridge, and it is hoped that someday it will be made into a historical site.

At last one evening, as the train pulled into the Strathcona Station., I saw the three girls eagerly scanning the faces of the people on the platform, so I rushed onto the train and went joyously towards them, all smiles. They all looked indignantly at me and as I approached Mother, she looked quite scared and turned her head away. I remembered then how Harry and Ted had looked to me, when they met me at Prince Albert a year before so I asked, "Don't you know me, Mother?"

Then they looked at me intently, all their faces lit up with pleasure and they began to laugh and cry in turns. Fan rushed to me, threw her arms round my neck, and kissed me joyously. "Why, it's Fred!" Mother still kept looking at me a little dubiously, and no wonder; sun dried and burnt brown, I was topped with one of Harry Alsop's own haircuts. Harry was no fastidious barber, necessity rather than art guiding his hand,

82

quite a change from the military smart lad that had parted from them just after my discharge a little less than one year earlier.

They, in turn, looked good enough to eat, especially my sisters with their rosy English complexions; and Dad, Gilbert, and Bill surely looked comical in their Christie stiff hats.

Fan threw her arms around me and kissed me again and I hugged her to me. She then pushed me away from her and looked at me again. "Golly, I don't know whether I should kiss you, you look such a stranger," she said.

"Too late now" I told her, and then I turned to Rose and Molly, "Aren't you going to kiss the stranger?"

Rose just smiled her shy smile, and held out her hand to me, which was characteristic of her. I don't believe, in all her life, she ever kissed any man but her husband, and as I once heard Molly say, "I doubt if she ever kissed him of her own accord." Molly came to me and gave me a big resounding smack, and said, "That will do for both of us," meaning Rose and herself.

"Where are Harry and Ted?" asked Fan.

"They're talking to Dad and Gilbert," I told her.

"That's not them!" They all said incredulously, and then they sat down and laughed and laughed.

Harry had his hat off and his haircut was a masterpiece of the bowl variety, besides his being just as brown as any Indian I have ever seen.

83

"What are you all wearing?" one of them asked next.

"These?" I asked, putting my hands inside the bib of my overalls and pushing it out in front of me, "Oh, these are my bib overalls."

"Golly," said Molly, "Whatever made you wear those things? You don't have to wear them, do you?"

Harry and Ted then came up and the girls, even Fan, just held out their hands to them, giggling at them all the time. Harry stooped and kissed Mother.

"Oh, Harry, how you have changed." She said and began to weep, but when Ted stooped to kiss her she brightened up and said, "Now, Ted you really do look handsome". The girls agreed that Ted looked handsome, "and how you have grown". They exclaimed. Ted was very slightly built, and was six foot one inch in height. When they had decided that Ted looked handsome, they looked again at Harry and me and said, "You, too, really have improved in looks. It's just that you all looked so funny in those clothes". And they kept looking at us and giggling at our 'atrocious' haircuts.

"And those black shirts" said Mother. "I just can't like them."

"Oh, you'll get to like them," said Harry. "None of us liked them at first."

"Oh," laughed Fan, "I thought you were going to say that she would be wearing them herself before long." and we all laughed again, and there we were all were so happy that we wanted to laugh at everything.

84

It's a Dry Cold

Then Gilbert, who with Bill had been looking after the luggage, came up and said, "We had better be moving. We are holding things up here." and Bill, convulsed with laughter, asked Harry, "Who's your barber, boy?"

Harry made a ruffling motion over his head with his hand and said, innocently "Harry Alsop started it and Annie finished it". This started us all into peals of laughter again.

Then we three began to jibe at the Christie stiff hats that Dad, Bill and Gilbert wore, and this evoked more laughter and jests.

We got Mother off the train and to the Alsop home with little difficulty. Still unable to walk as a result of the stroke she suffered about two years prior, she of course, had to be carried everywhere.

That was a great family reunion; Dad, Mother and all my brothers and sisters except my eldest brother, Bert, were there, but Gilbert was with us, and accepted as one of the family. I often think of it and my heart fills with affection for every one of them. Mother, Dad, Bill, Molly, Ted, Annie and her husband, Harry A. have all passed away; there now just remain my sisters Fan and Rose, and my brother Harry at Vermilion.

The Alsop's had a large house, and what with the accommodation they could offer us, and our tent, we all slept comfortably till we were ready to start on the big adventure of going to the 'Hestite'.

Harry A was anxious that, before we started on the scow, we should all see his homestead and the log house he had built on it, so one day we piled some provisions and bedding

into the wagon box and all the men and Fan went out to see it.
The roads through the bush were almost impassable owing to the
spring thaw. In many places, we had to construct the corduroy
by cutting down trees, trimming off the branches and then laying
the poles, as closely together as we could get them, across the
swamps to make a passable road for horses and wagon. That
was, without exception, the roughest ride I've ever had. The
insides were almost jolted out of us, and we were all chewed up
with mosquitoes and bull dog flies, and deafened by the
whooping and yelling of Harry A as he urged his team through
the mud holes and quagmires, which were everywhere. We
were thrown from side to side, usually all ending in a heap in the
bottom of the wagon box, as the team lurched and strained at the
wagon, which sank to the hubs sometimes on one side,
sometimes on the other. We were bruised and banged all over,
but we pretended it was good pioneering fun. That was the first
time any one of us, except Harry A, had heard frogs sing. I do
not think they sing in the Old Country, at least none of us had
ever heard them sing there.

I think now of Gilbert Nicolson and his ever-evident
care and concern for Fan, who really was much better able to
endure the hardship and roughness of the trip than he was.

That was ever Gilbert's way, always self-effacing and
concerned for the welfare of others. How he tried to fend off the
flies and mosquitoes from Fan, and how, in their millions, they
punished us on the way through the quagmires and bush. Fan,
on the other hand, could not let Gilbert out of her sight. She
seemed to feel she had always to be at his side to protect and
help him.

Harry A called at Turnbull's, a neighbouring farmer,
for the key to his house which he had left there. They were all

in bed - it was about 10:30 p.m., and in answer to our knock the old man came down holding a coal-oil lamp high above his head, and in the most abbreviated night-shirt I have ever seen. When he saw Fan, he quickly turned his back on us and called over his shoulders, "Is there ladies in your party?"

Having got the key, we proceeded to Harry A's house where Fan soon cooked us a good meal, which we all enjoyed thoroughly. We then spread the bedding and blankets we had brought with us and slept so soundly that not even the mosquitoes, which harried us throughout the night, could wake us.

Next afternoon we were all out in the yard and Harry A was showing us his proposed layout of his barnyard, when a very spanking team and snappy buggy drove into the yard and a prosperous looking, but undersized man alighted and came towards us quite jauntily. Harry A was so engrossed in explaining his plans that he didn't notice the stranger, till someone asked, "Who is this, Harry?"

He looked around quickly and his face clouded over as he said, "I think I know the bugger," and went to meet him. When he came within earshot, Harry A asked rather truculently, towering above the stranger, "What do you want?"

The jauntiness dissolved instantly and the stranger answered quite meekly, "I am the Sheriff. I have come to collect this grocery bill for $100.00 for Mr. Jenkins."

Harry A said, "Oh, you have, have you? Then get the hell out of here. I shall pay that $100.00 when I'm damned good and ready to pay it. Now get and don't you come back – I'll send for you when I want you."

Harry A stood with arm outstretched, pointing to the gate, like a statue of some conquering hero of mythology, while the Sheriff almost ran to the buggy - looking back furtively over his shoulder as if he feared Harry A. would be after him. Then Harry A turned to us fuming, "The damned bum bailiff! I'll show the impertinent bugger."

Dad, who knew something - a whole lot in fact - of the awe in which the bum bailiffs were regarded in England, stood flabbergasted.

"That's the way you treat them out here?" he questioned.

"Yes" Harry A fumed "and wait till I get back to Edmonton. Old Jenkins will rue the day he ever sick'd his bloody bums onto me."

"Sicked?" seeked, I suppose sounded funny then.

When we returned to Edmonton, we set about building the scow. Harry, Ted and I had learned how to handle a hammer and saw, constructing brick drying sheds at the brickyard and we all felt that we now knew enough about the construction and proportions of a scow to warrant us at least making a start. All four of us boys, with Dad and Gilbert, worked on it. We built ours twenty-four feet square at the bottom with sides three feet high all around. Scows were built upside down. First the ribs or skeleton was constructed of two-by-six planks bevelled at the outer edges for the purpose of caulking. The front end sloped out from the bottom at an angle of about 45 degrees, I believe. Why this sloping front, I do not know, but all scows we saw were made that way and we followed the ordained pattern. It entailed quite a bit of work to bevel the edges in that heavy lumber to fit the triangular sides of the slope which as I say, was - like the goose's tail - more for beauty than use.

Having completed the construction, we now began the caulking. This consisted of inserting tow or pitch between the edges and joins of the planks with a caulking tool that we had purchased at the hardware store for that purpose. After the tow had been closely and very carefully packed in, we poured boiling tallow over it to seal it against water seepage. Dad, who had had some experience in caulking in England, was most particular about this and it paid well, for later when we tore the scow apart upon reaching the mouth of the Vermilion, there was not a sign of water seepage in the six-inch space between the bottom and floor of the scow.

The girls, my sisters, used to come down to the flats each day and help where they could, chiefly by cooking our meals over a picnic fire. In fact, those days in Edmonton and the trip down the river, including the rest of the summer and fall, were just one long happy adventure.

When the scow was completed, we were confronted by the problem of turning it over into the Saskatchewan River. Some performed this feat with the aid of a block and pulley, but we did not possess one and were too conservative to try to borrow one.

One evening, just before six p.m., when we were ready to turn it over, I said to the girls, "I dare any one of you to go over to the mill just before the whistle blows and ask some of the men, as they come out, to give us a hand."

Part 2   It's a Dry Cold

Molly the youngest, she was about sixteen then, took me up on it, "Of course we'll go," she said, "come on Fan and Rose." So off they went all three.

We watched them, wondering if they really would have the courage to approach strange men to ask a favour, but they did, and the men, as I had hoped, were only too willing to comply. About a dozen of them, all young and strong, came back with the girls and in short order, the scow was over in the river without either bumps or jars. Sometimes, with rough handling, the caulking gets shaken loose in turning the scow over. Happily, ours didn't. Now we laid a floor, leaving a space six inches deep between the floor and the bottom of the scow. The purpose of this space was to hold any water that might seep through the outer walls. We also made two sweeps of pine poles, about six inches in diameter and quite twenty feet long and each bladed at one end like an oar. These we placed in rowlocks, which we had built into the middle point of the topmost plank of the front and back ends of the scow. With these sweeps, we steered our course.

At the back end, we erected a canopy by raising the sides about two feet and placing an awning of heavy canvass over it. This was to provide shelter and shade too. Here the women slept while we men slept in a tent on the shore. Also, at a sufficient distance from the front, to admit of handling the sweep, we erected a platform with steps leading to it from the floor and over which we built a shade of tarpaulin. Here, Mother and some of the girls used to sit and converse or sew. Mother's hands were never idle, always busy with mending or embroidery, at which she was quite expert, and she was always ready with her cheerful and contagious laugh. We named this platform "Mother's crow's nest".

90

We were now ready to embark. It had taken us just eight days to complete our scow. Two Indians whom we had noticed covertly watching our progress, now approached us and introduced themselves as river pilots. They warned us of the treachery of the North Saskatchewan River. How it might be unsafe for us boys, inexperienced as we were, to venture forth without the aid of pilots. They said they knew the river from its source to its mouth, mentioned various parties whom they had guided through, warned us of some of the perils we would encounter, enquired our destination which, when we told them, they said they knew well. They said that there were many uncharted and dangerous waterfalls before we would reach the mouth of the Vermilion River, and ended up by casually stating that their fee would be $4.00 per day and their food.

We discussed their offer for some time and ultimately decided that we would make the venture alone, so we prepared to load up. My people had brought out from England some furniture including a piano, a relic of our former flesh-pot days, three beds, a set of mahogany highboys, Mother's rocking chair, a beautiful pink and gold breakfast set of dishes, together with many other dishes and knick-knacks, and a dozen pure-bred buff Orpington pullets and a rooster. We loaded all the furniture on the wagon box, placed Mother's rocking chair conveniently for her with two seats near her for two of the girls, then we put the crate of chickens right on top of the furniture and we all piled in.

Our team, by this time, had picked up and was in really good shape. Harry Alsop almost cried when he first saw them and for the duration of our stay at his home, he had made Nellie and Frank his special care. He loved animals I always think, as much as he did human beings. He could not bear to see a dumb animal suffer. When we said good-bye to the Alsop family, he clapped Nellie on the flank with his open hand and

91

his joy at the improvement in the appearance of both horses was most touching.

Edmonton then consisted mainly of one street, now Jasper Avenue, with odd scattered houses and many shacks here and there. There was no definite plan to the town. I remember quite well the Alberta Hotel, which is still on the same site. We always turned round the corner of this hotel each day on our way to the Alsop home from the 'flats' where we built the scow.

The completion of the Canadian Northern Railway from Winnipeg to Edmonton with the last spike driven on November 24th, 1905, and the original Canadian Pacific to Strathcona were the main reason for the growth of that area. Everyone co-operated to build and improve their farms; - a neighbour used his horses to break land for Harry, while Harry was putting a cement basement in the neighbour's new house.

As we drove along Jasper Avenue, we created quite a sensation. We were all in high spirits! We all felt and looked better for the time we had spent outdoors, and as we passed along with our quips and sally's of wit and continuous laughter, in response to which the hens cackled loudly and the rooster lent his lusty crow, we were indeed a worthy attraction.

As we proceeded, people wishing to purchase some of our chickens stopped us several times, but in spite of the very attractive prices, they offered, dad would not sell. Arriving at the scow, we loaded everything on it, including the team and wagon. The women folk slept on the scow that night while we men slept in the tent on shore. A few days before, we had purchased a small, quite water worthy, rowing-boat. Harry and

Ted, our pilots, started out next morning in this, about a half hour before we pushed off with the scow.

Then, on the morning of June 7th, 1904, we pulled out into mid-stream. Mother and one of the girls sat up in the look-out, while the rest of us on the sweeps steered our course! The Ferryman at Walters Mills, I have forgotten his name, had given us some very helpful advice about how we should proceed. One very useful piece of advice was that we notify the lumber mills downstream to let in their booms so we could pass in safety. This, our 'pilots' did, so we had no mishap on that score. As the scow passed under the Low Level Bridge, we were all surprised to see the crowd of people that had gathered to give us a hearty and encouraging send-off.

As we pushed away from the bank, Bill caught his foot on a root or submerged log and pitched head first into the drink, much to the amusement of the crowd watching from the bridge. We fished him out and floated away into the river. Most of the people watching, we had never seen before and, in all probability, would never see again. This gave us all a very gallant feeling and we felt quite elated by the hearty "Good-byes" and shouts of "good-luck" that reached us - some of them even throwing old shoes and rubbers after us, most of which missed the scow and fell to the bottom of the Saskatchewan River. Perhaps they were trying to show their sympathy for our foolhardiness in starting out unpiloted, for while we were building our scow we had seen several other parties start off, but all with river pilots to guide them. This made us think, "Are we, indeed, being so wise?"

Our first near catastrophe happened late in the afternoon of our first day out. It was a beautiful June day of brilliant sunshine and brilliant blue skies, dotted here and there with flocks of fleecy, white clouds idling around, apparently on no set course, while we below drifted lazily downstream, along with the current at about three miles an hour. The trees on the heavily wooded slopes of the high banks on each side of the river showed scarcely a stir, so little wind was there to create even a tremor among the leaves. It was a scene of incomparable beauty and restfulness. Suddenly our pilots ahead began to wave their oars frantically in the air and point to the South shore. We had been noticing, for a moment or two, a faint ripple on the otherwise almost placid surface of the stream, but now this ripple had become quite a swirl, and right in the middle of our course. "Pull to the south" rang out from dad, and everyone rushed to the sweeps. We could now see that the ripple was not as innocent as it first had appeared. There was a large boulder there, the sharp pointed top of which just appeared above the surface. We all pulled desperately, and as luck would have it, just the back corner of the scow was all that came in contact with the rock. No damage was done!

After we had safely gotten past this obstacle, we looked back up the stream and could see the boulder in all its voluminous danger quite distinctly. Needless to say, we mistrusted every minor disturbance that appeared to break the serenity of the surface water after that episode. Our nerves were quite disturbed for some time after, as we all realized that had it been the front corner of the scow hitting the rock, it might have meant disaster for some, perhaps many or all of us.

After this near mishap, the pilots in the boat would look back up stream and signal with upraised oar, thus directing us to steer north or south as the location of the rock or boulder might warrant.

94

Part 2   It's a Dry Cold

Always towards sundown, the pilots would be on the
look-out for a good snubbing tree on shore. Having spotted one,
they would signal to us to pull in and we would tie up for the
night with a good strong rope. Fan, usually, then got supper
while some of the rest of us busied about pitching the tent and
others, even on the first evening, caught fish. We ate like
fighting cocks! Dad, at that time, was a big strong man – six
foot two inches in height - and Ted, Harry, Bill and I were all six
feet and all strongly built. Poor Gilbert was short and slight and
a poor eater. Though he, also, seemed to improve in health on
this trip and afterwards on the homestead. Although he was frail
in physique, he was certainly not lacking in stamina or morale.

We had a cook stove with us, and Fan, who loved and
still loves to cook, would each day cook the evening meal. How
we ate! Each day we collected a dozen eggs, and these, with the
fish cooked with slices of sowbelly, homemade bread and
stewed prunes or dried apples, made a meal fit for a king.

Some of us ate on shore - some on the scow. That first
evening at supper, the men and Fan were on shore, sitting
around eating supper and discussing our journey so far, when
quite close to us we heard a low, clucking chatter. Looking
around, we saw two wood partridges regarding us most
inquisitively and chattering between themselves as if
exchanging their views on what and who we were. I reached for
the twenty-two rifle, which I had just been examining a moment
before and shot one of them. The other ran off into the
undergrowth, but emerged again in a few minutes, with its head
on one side and looking inquisitively at us, I potted her too.

I remember to this day the feeling of compunction I
had for shooting those two birds which nagged me for some
time afterwards. It has always been a mystery to me how bush

partridges survive. They seem so innocent and uninhibited by fear and so trusting. Quite different from all other small denizens of the woods, which rush or fly off at the first sign of anything or anyone strange. They sense danger in everything unusual.

However, I had no compunction about eating my share of the partridges the next day for lunch, when Fan served them fried with slices of sowbelly. Their pure white flesh, so tender and juicy, was a real dainty morsel.

Fan was always at her best and most efficient when surrounded by men, and particularly if there were an admirer among them. She was certainly wonderful on the scow. She has always loved to feed people and the bigger the crowd, the more she showed her capability. She had taken first prize in England for bread making at one of the big Agricultural Shows, and her bread was always really delicious. The oven of our cook stove was too small to bake the batch she used to make, so she devised the following scheme for baking a large batch:

When we tied up for the night, usually about sundown, she would have all the loaves ready in a large covered bake pan. We would make a good big fire, on the sand, and leave it until the sand was red hot, almost. She would then rake out sufficient to allow the placing her bake pan in the hollow thus made. Then she would rake the hot sand back over the top of the pan and keep a very low supply of embers on top of the replaced sand for about one hour, at the end of which she would take out the bread - beautifully brown and deliciously sweet smelling. With six adult men and four women to bake for, she kept very busy, but she really loved and enjoyed it.

That first evening, after supper, we saw on the opposite side of the river something that looked like charred wood sticking out of the bank. Two of the boys got in the boat and rowed over to investigate, and found it was a seam of coal. We went the next morning before starting off and filled four or five sacks with the coal and it proved to be very good fuel in the cook stove.

Dad was always first up and rarin' to go, so soon after daylight each day we started out. The girls would soon have breakfast ready and we always ate this meal on the scow.

Each evening on the trip, some of us would climb to the very top of the riverbank to see if there were any farms in the country, but never once, after leaving Fort Saskatchewan, did we ever see any sign of habitation, human or otherwise.

Before leaving England, Gilbert, who was always on the ball for attending to details, had procured maps of the Saskatchewan River from the Department of the Interior at Ottawa. These maps were topographically true in every detail and we navigated by identifying each rivulet, stream or creek with those marked on the maps. Gilbert and Fan of course, attended to this duty.

On the second day out, the pilot boys rowed back and reported that there were half-a-dozen scows tied up on the South side of the river, the Indian pilots averring that the river was too low to admit of the scows passing through the rapids some distance further downstream. We listened and could hear the roar quite distinctly. We could also see at a distance the splashing of foam and the rise of the waters as they dashed over the boulders forming the cataract.

97

Part 2   It's a Dry Cold

We enquired from the Indian pilots how long we might have to wait. They said, "Maybe a day or two - maybe a week or ten days." We asked if other scows had gone through. They answered, "Yes, when the river is higher."

After a family conference, at which we all expressed our general distrust of the Indian pilots, we decided to shoot the rapids. Looking back now, I can't but think what an awful chance we took, but we had faith in our pilot boys ahead and in their ability to direct us through.

The pilot boys got their boat through without any portage, and looking up stream they could then direct us where the river was deepest, and with our heavy sweeps we navigated the zigzag course of the channels between the boulders, and thus came through without mishap.

All those whose scows had been held up, some of them for as many as six days by their pilots, were on the banks watching our progress and cheering us on. This helped and we were very thankful to have got through safely. And those Indian pilots had been getting $4.00 per day and their food!

We afterwards navigated several other rapids, but none of them offered the challenge now that our first encounter with them did. Several times throughout the journey, we came to islands, idyllically beautiful in colouring and setting, but a tremendous hazard in our course, as we did not know on which side to steer our barque. However, the pilot boys would rush ahead and direct us to the deepest water, so that we never encountered any danger worth recording from the presence of these islands, and they always lent worthwhile beauty and charm to the scenery. Taking everything into consideration; we were certainly lucky. We had perfect weather - I think it rained just

98

one day, but we had shelter. We were all young and gay, and
eager for adventure. Even Mother, who was ever sweet
tempered and encouraging, and when we sang, as we often did,
she joined in happily and cheerfully. Drifting along on the river
Molly would play on the piano and we would all sing such
popular songs as:

> "Oh. Flo why do you go
> Riding alone in your motor car?
> Everyone says you are singular, singular peculiar.
> There's room for two, for me and you,
> In your elegant motor car."

> "Lottie Collins' lost her drawers
> Will you kindly lend her yours?
> For she's going far away,
> To sing Ta, ra, ra boom-de-ay."

> "Won't you come home Bill Bailey,
> Won't you come home?
> I'll do the cooking darling,
> I'll pay the rent,
> I know that I'm to blame
> Oh Bill Bailey, won't you please come home?"

> "You are my honey, honey, honey-suckle,
> I am your bee, etc., etc."

Also, George Robey's song about the girl falling off
her bicycle:

> "Oh, I sawr 'er fall
>
> I sawr hit all,

Couldn't 'elp it.

'

Ad to."

These were among some of the Music Hall hits of those days. Molly knew them all. Several years later, I went as George Robey to a masquerade at Stretton School and sang this song, thereby shocking the modesty of a worthy matron with two marriageable daughters, and marriageable daughters were as scarce as hen's teeth in those early days.

On the evening of the eighth day, when we tied up for supper, Gilbert said, after perusing his maps, "Well, we should be nearing the mouth of the Vermilion soon now and sure enough, he was right. About an hour after we started next morning, the pilot boys came back and reported that there was a wide mouth river entering the Saskatchewan from the South less than a quarter of a mile ahead. We were then in mid-stream, sailing gaily along, when the command, "Pull to the South" rang out. Then both sweeps fully manned with both girls and boys swung round to the South side, through the swelling waters of the Vermilion River, into the eddy. Here we tied up as near to the bank as we possibly could. We had arrived at the goal of Barr's vision! The first Barr Colonists to reach it!

Throughout the entire journey of over two hundred miles, the Saskatchewan River had been beautiful and interesting. The varying colors of the water from grass green to pure azure blue were, each day, a source of wonder and conjecture to us. What color will the lady wear to-morrow? this evening? or in an hours time? The girls would ask each other, and "Do wear your lovely turquoise, please".

Her moods, too, were variable and unpredictable, and always wonderful, while around each bend, as she swerved and curved her way to the sea always with new delights of scenic grandeur to awe us and fill us with enchantment. For natural and unspoiled scenery, her beauty and variety are unsurpassed by any other river in the world.

So farewell, O Saskatchewan River

We all apostrophize you in love and gratitude. You have borne the burden we placed upon your ample and lovely bosom, faithfully and elegantly. Each one of us will often return, in memory, to you and re-live the enjoyment, the fun, and the pleasantries of these past eight days. We have had our tense moments, our periods of alarm, our narrow escapes, but throughout you have been to us a gracious and beneficent lady.

Farewell!

CHAPTER 7

Breaking ground

Now we began the unloading.

For this purpose, we built a platform, to reach from the scow to the riverbank, with some two-inch planks we had brought with us from Edmonton. Having completed the job we brought the horses off first, and that was the first time they had been taken off the scow since they were loaded. We had got oats for them as soon as we had reached Edmonton, and we had also brought back a good supply with us, so they were in really good shape, nevertheless, they seemed mighty glad to graze on the fresh green grass of the prairie.

"We won't have to rush with the pail anymore". Sighed Molly, with relief, and Ted amplified this remark with the following ditty:

"Thank heaven for the pail, to catch the obnoxious stale."

As we all looked at him in wonder he added, chuckling,

"When Frank or Nellie lifts a tail."

"Shades of Shakespeare!" Quoth Gilbert.

"Now I call that a purty poem." said Bill. "Can't you give us another verse, boy?"

Part 3   Breaking Ground

"Poem!" said Fan. "People have been hanged for lesser crimes than making up a thing like that," but everyone laughed all the same.

While the rest of us worked at the unloading, Dad and Gilbert went to map out a road up which we could haul our effects. The banks here were very high and steep and heavily wooded, and they had to find the easiest route. They came back after some time and reported that some ploughing and digging would have to be done, and that from all appearances this would be no easy task. But we all fell to with a will, and by using the team and plough, with pitchforks, hoes, shovels and axes, we ultimately accomplished something by way of a road, the traces of which may still be seen when crossing the ferry at Lea Park. Frank and Nellie hauled our effects up this trail, a few at a time. Even with a light load, every one of us had to push at the back to help the team up the steep incline. Mother only was exempt. She sat in her chair encouraging us as far as she could see, and laughing when something amusing happened.

When the unloading was completed, they all went to the homestead taking with them enough bedding, provisions and other items to supply their needs until the morrow. I remained behind at the river, alone, and began to pull the scow apart.

Early in the morning, Dad, Bill, Harry and Ted came back. I was glad to see them for at daybreak, the rooster began to crow, lustily filling the startled silence with reverberant challenge. I was afraid he might attract the unwelcome attention of wandering coyotes or other wild animals of prey. In later years the memory amused me when I learned that the coyote is the most cowardly of all wild animals.

103

Part 3   Breaking Ground

That day Harry, Bill and Ted took the small rowboat and left to go to Prince Albert by river, a distance of over two hundred miles, to work in the brickyard. They took some provisions, food, blankets, the tent, and Gilbert's map. They took no gun! Itner's warning, it turned out, had proven to be only too true!

Over the next four or five days, Dad and I hauled the rest of our effects, including the lumber of which the scow had been built, to the homestead. Then we began to build a house sufficiently large to accommodate the family.

"Come and show us where you want the house built". Dad called to the girls one morning.

They all came running, full of excitement. A real house of our own with no rent to pay! Wasn't it marvellous!

"Fancy no rent collector coming and knocking on the door on Monday morning any more." said Molly, quite wistfully.

"You are not going to cry about it, are you?" Fan asked her.

"No, no," said Molly, "but won't it be funny to wake up on Monday morning and not have to wonder if Mother has the rent, or what excuse she will give him for not having it?"

"Do you remember that time at Cockowlets, when we all sat in the house all day with the door locked and the shades pulled down, because the bums were outside waiting to get in?" recalled Rose, and they all shrieked with laughter.

104

Part 3　　　　　　　　　　　　Breaking Ground

"What happened that time, Mother?" asked Fan.

"Your uncle Ben Wright happened to come to visit us, and when he knocked at the door we thought it was the bailiffs and dared not open it until he called through to us who he was," Mother told her.

"Oh, yes, I remember now," said Fan. "He gave them some money and they went away."

"And now there's only one thing in life that's sure." said Molly.

"What do you mean? Only one thing in life that's sure!" We all asked her.

"Well, Daddy has always said 'there are only two sure things in life: death and rent day'. Now there's just death."

"For pity's sake, what's the matter with you, child? You sound broken hearted. Were you in love with one of those despicable rent collectors? I believe you must have been." said Fan.

"Yes, that one with the dangling eye, at Cockowlets". Said Rose

"Come on! Come on!" Dad interrupted the laughter that followed Rose's remark. "Let's get on here. Why can't you think of something pleasant, if you must bring up the past?"

"Well, where's the road going to be?" asked Fan. "We must have a long winding driveway through the trees. I think it would be nice to have that little rivulet running along at the bottom of the back lawn."

"That creek floods in the spring. We were afraid the barn would be washed away last April." I cautioned her.

After a lot more lengthy discussion, a site was decided upon and we began to dig the cellar. The three girls helped with wheeling the soil and rocks up an incline we made for them with planks as we dug it out in the bottom of the hole. One day a neighbour came along and saw the girls working, and he afterwards told how Dad, who, he said, looked like an old army Colonel, was making his girls work like slaves. This amused us all.

We made the house thirty-six foot square, with our original shack tacked on to the back for a lean-to kitchen. We built it of the logs we boys had got out during the winter, and chinked them with a clay mud. I think it was the second day on the homestead when the girls first heard the meadowlark. What a thrill they all got. He came and sat on a broken tree stump, at a little distance from us and gave forth his full-throated rollicking song, as if he were giving them a hearty welcome to the country. No illuminated address could have given the whole party more pleasure.

"The darling little bird," they said.

When the June rains came, the sod roof that we had put on our shack proved to be both unsatisfactory and inconvenient. We had utensils of every description everywhere to catch the ubiquitous drip and Mother sat in her rocking chair with an umbrella over her head. Even after the rains had ceased,

106

Part 3   Breaking Ground

the drip continued for days, but we were pioneering and
discomfort and hardship were only part of the game.

We made the floor for the new house out of some of
the lumber we had used in building the scow. First, we had to
cut each plank up into suitable thicknesses for joists for the
floor. This presented some difficulty, at first, but we solved the
problem by digging a pit six feet deep. I stood at the bottom
while Dad stood above me on the plank to be sawn, and then by
pulling a buck saw that we boys had bought in Prince Albert,
back and forth we ripped each plank in two parts, each two by
six.

Then we fixed up a barn for the livestock. We banked
it with beautiful sweet smelling hay and pile hay on the roof.
That made the barn warm and comfortable for the winter

Our next achievement was the acquisition of a cow.
One day on the way from Lloydminster, we heard that a family
named Roberts had one for sale. They lived about six miles
south of our homestead, in the district now called Millerdale.
They had been farming in that area about three years before the
'Baa lambs' arrived. Dad and I set out next day to find the
Roberts homestead, and to make a deal for the cow. When we
drove into the yard, one of the boys, there were three of them,
came to enquire our business. Dad told him we'd heard he had a
cow for sale.

"Yeah, for sale," he said. "Not for trade."

We assured him we wanted to pay cash. This seemed
to please him, though a tear ran down his cheek and his doleful
voice became even more doleful, as he told us how he had set
out from Wetaskin, one year earlier, with a good team of black

mares, a wagon, a plough, and a good milk cow. He began trading on the way and after several trades, all of which he swore he had got the best of the deal, he eventually arrived home with one old 'knacker' of a horse, and a buggy. "That's it," he said, pointing to a dilapidated old buggy standing on one wheel and three props and with the stuffing exuding from all its cushions.

He was very funny. One side of his face was always crying and this, combined with his slow doleful manner of speaking, made one think he was a very sad person, yet at every dance or social evening, he would be there always surrounded by a group of young men, laughing hilariously at his jokes. I remember one evening, at a dance, some years later a few of the young bloods among us were in the cloakroom of the school discussing girls, the usual topic in a gathering of that kind, he said, "I don't care how stiff or prudish they are, I can always, get what I want."

Someone asked, "How do you do it Ben?"

He said. "Just take her hand and hold it tight, and look into her eyes and start to weep, and by the time, she gets her hand free she has surrendered. It never fails."

We all roared with laughter.

We spent that summer making the house habitable for winter, laying in a supply of firewood from the surrounding bush, and making hay. We also dug a well and got good water close by the house. We boys, who knew what it meant to melt snow in the winter, were delighted with this amenity in our advance towards civilization. We put up about fifty tons of hay and could easily have put up three times as much within a radius

108

of one mile from our home. This hay was beautiful feed, consisting of grass, wild pea-vine, and wild vetch, about knee deep. I still maintain it makes the best stock feed in the world.

In later years, when we began to break the virgin prairie with oxen, at first we turned them out at night to feed. Very often, we had a lot of trouble finding them in the morning, as sometimes they would be miles away. One morning we decided we would keep them in the barn that night to avoid wasting time next day looking for them, so one of us spent the whole afternoon mowing hay and carting it to the barn where we filled the stalls, piling it to the roof., and packing it as closely as we possibly could.

"Do you think that will be enough?" Ted asked.

"I should think so," I said, and Harry said, "Why there's enough there to do them for a week."

Next morning, when we went for them, they stood gaunt and empty. Their sides that on other mornings, had been bulging away out, now were sunken right in. They looked terrible, and they had eaten every spear of the hay we had piled into their stalls. No one would have believed it without seeing it. We had to turn them out to feed before we could hitch them up to the plough. After this, we turned them loose every evening.

Don't ever try to work with oxen if you can possibly help it. They are the most stubborn of animals, and the most stupid and proverbially the strongest.

Flies!

Part 3   Breaking Ground

Egypt was well off having only ten plagues. In Canada, I'll swear we had ten times ten. There were the heel flies that attacked the heels of the cattle. This small wasp like fly worked in the afternoon in the bright sunshine. We would hear the cows and other animals come running with their tails straight up and bellowing terribly. If there were not a strong door on the barns, they would break in. They rushed to any shelter they could find. The oxen, too, panicked when they heard the fly. Off they would go - plough and all - to the nearest slough and stand right in the middle, where the water was deep enough to cover their heels. This fly was one of the most dreaded nuisances when breaking with oxen or bulls.

There was the nose fly that bothered the horse's nose. These we could frustrate to some extent by putting on nose guards. These cost fifty cents each in those days, and did not last long, as they were easily crushed. We soon began to make our own out of screen wire. We kept two bought ones for "their Sunday best", as Rose said.

There were chin flies that pestered horses in the pasture. The horses would stand, rubbing their chins up and down each other's backs to get relief from the irritation. The bulldog fly attacks both man and beast. He would grab a chunk out of one's arm or leg and leave a bleeding wound. He worked with speed, and usually got away with his spoil before a person could kill him. The mosquitoes were terrible. They came out in the evenings, when we were feeding the stock for the night. We always made a smudge by lighting green or damp grass or hay, and the horses and cattle would stand in the smoke arising from this smouldering grass. The mosquitoes could not live in the smoke. How the stock suffered from these abominable pests!

Part 3   Breaking Ground

These are some of the plagues we had to contend with, but believe me the other ninety-odd existed, and pestered in their various ways.

When the autumn of 1904 came, Dad, Gilbert, the girls and I had the house fixed up so as to be fairly cosy. We had made a warm barn and cow shed for the winter and had dug a well and got good water. We had also planned the yard and by dint of digging, hoeing, and ploughing, had a nice sized patch ready for a garden in the spring.

We had bought a brand new John Deere walking plough in Edmonton for twenty dollars. Ten years later walking ploughs could be picked up all over the district for a dollar or two each. We tried ploughing with Nellie and Frank, but they could not move the plough in the tough prairie sod. We gave up until one day Jack Fleming came along and saw we had made an attempt and questioned us about our efforts

Dad said, "How do you get this damned turf turned over?"

Jack laughed, and then explained the "breaking" process and offered to lend us his team, consisting of one small pony and one mule to break enough for a garden. He even came and helped us.

That was the spirit among us all in those early days. Every man felt he was welcome to the use of anything his neighbour possessed. There existed a true communal spirit among us, a real feeling of brotherhood that was both delightful and helpful, without which the settlement would not have progressed as rapidly as it did. However, as prosperity grew among us, this communal spirit of fraternity declined in proportion. This was to be greatly lamented, because it was a grand and beautiful feeling. At that time, we were all socially and financially on the same plane. Perhaps some of us had come from better or more prosperous homes than others, but we had all come to seek escape from the fettering narrowness, and limitations of over-populated England, and in the hope of finding freedom and happiness in a new beckoning land.

Dad had brought out some roots of horseradish and artichokes. These he planted and the horseradish grew so prolifically that it eventually became a noxious weed. Even to this day, horseradish can be found in the fields surrounding the spot where we then had our garden. The girls had also picked up some seeds in Winnipeg and these; chiefly lettuce, radish and onions grew quickly and made a very enjoyable addition to the menu in the late summer.

We had brought a good supply of provisions from Edmonton, and these supplemented with the wild fruit Saskatoons, strawberries., raspberries and cherries, and the game - partridge, prairie chicken, duck and goose, all then in profusion, constituted our bill of fare all that summer, and well into the cold weather.

F an and Gilbert now began the landscaping of the yard. They were both so enthusiastic, especially Fan. All of us felt her invigorating influence. It was decided there were to be a lily pond, a rockery, a birdbath, terraces, hedges; all the appurtenances of "Ye Stately Homes of England". We were all obsessed with the "Hestite" idea in those early days. That fall the weather was ideally Indian summer weather, one of the nicest Indian Summers I can remember. We all exulted in the wonder of the climate--the warm brilliantly sunshiny days with their hazy, bluish horizons, and the crisp,

Part 3   Breaking Ground

pleasantly cool evenings that always brought with them a
delightful sense of wellbeing and fatigue and desire for rest and
sleep. We all enjoyed every moment of that summer and fall
and all the work that settling had entailed.

Then suddenly out of the blue, Fan and Gilbert
announced they were going back to England! This
announcement struck a desolate note in the melody of our living.
I believe each one of us felt it. They had both been so efficient,
so go-getting! They had become indispensible in the new life
we had embarked upon, but we all assumed they were going
back to be married, and we rejoiced that it should be so, because
we all loved Gilbert.

I drove them to Edmonton. The team was in really
good shape and we made the trip in six days. We took along a
tent, hobbles for the horses while we ate our noon-day meal so
they would not wander off, also a tethering chain for them at
night. We took a grub box and frying pan, a gun and
home-made shells to shoot wild duck, prairie chicken and bush
partridge, all of which were very plentiful. We seemed to lack
nothing and the trip, for all three of us was most enjoyable, so
different from our trip in the spring, when each day we
wondered if the team would live through it.

One night it rained very heavily and the tent blew
down. Neither Fan nor I woke up other than to hear the rain and
go to sleep again. When we woke up in the morning, Gilbert sat
holding up the tent over Fan and me.

"Why did you not wake us?" we asked.

"Oh, I wanted you to get your sleep." he answered.

113

Part 3   Breaking Ground

When we reached Edmonton, I purchased a good supply of provisions for the winter, the items of which were similar to those we had brought down on the scow in the spring. I then said "Good-bye" to Fan and Gilbert and wished them luck, and we all three seemed very happy, though I hated to see them go. That was the last time I ever saw Gilbert.

Billy Shaw rode back with me. I ran across him on Jasper Avenue, and we were mutually glad to meet each other; he was glad of the ride back to his homestead and I was glad to have his company. We had seen quite a lot of Billy during the Summer as he often came to our place and often had meals with us, while we had been over to his homestead borrowing or lending - "neighbouring" as it was termed. He always seemed anxious to be friendly and helpful. We were to find out later that his motive was not strictly just "neighbouring"!

Billy was a shrewd woodsman, and absolutely at home camping out. There was little or nothing about camping that he did not know. He had also done quite a bit of gold prospecting.

On the way back home, we shot dozens of prairie chicken and wild duck on the trail. There was a definite trail across the prairie now. It led to Beaver Creek where a ferry crossed the river. It was quite a novel contrivance, as well as convenient. Travelers drove onto the ferry and pulled themselves across by a rope which stretched from one side to the other. It was a good substitute for a bridge. When we reached home, we dug a hole about six feet deep into which we put all the game we had shot, which had frozen during the night. It stayed frozen all winter, at least until such time as it was used up.

114

Part 3   Breaking Ground

Dad said to me the day after I had arrived back from Edmonton, "Have you heard those deer calling?"

"No," I told him, "Where have you heard them?"

"Just listen," he said.

I listened and sure enough, I could hear them out in the hills to the South-west.

"Let's go out tomorrow and get one," he suggested.

"Right-o," I told him,

"Did you remember to get some shot when you were in Edmonton?" he asked me.

"Why no, was I supposed to get some?"

"Well, you knew it was all gone." He said.

"No," I told him. "I didn't use the last of it."

"Oh, well. I guess we can't go then if we have no shot." He said as he turned away.

I could see he was disappointed, so I got Frank in from the pasture and rode over to Billie Shaw's to see if he had any.

"No, darn it," he said, when I asked him. "I meant to get some in Edmonton but forgot all about it."

Part 3   Breaking Ground

When I got home again, I began to look everywhere for some forgotten or mislaid shot and in doing so came across a large bundle of hobnails that Harry and Ted had brought out from England for repairing boots. In a flash back, I remembered when we were kids, cutting the tops off hobnails to use in our home-made rifles, so I took them out to Dad and said, "Why not cut these up and use the slugs for shot?"

"Ah," He said. "That might be a good idea. Let's try it."

We had lots of powder and shells, so we got busy and made quite a number of cartridges using about six tops, or slugs as we called them, in each. Next day we, Dad and I, sallied forth, he riding Nellie and I Frank, and each with his gun and hunting knife. We rode along in single file for some distance and then Dad reined up along side of me.

"Is that Ted's gun?" He asked me.

"No," I told him, "it's my own."

"Oh, you bought one too."

"Yes, I bought it as soon as I knew we were coming out to Canada."

"It's a sixteen, isn't it? You should have taken Ted's. You'd have had a better chance," he said.

Dad then went to the North of a fairly large stretch of heavy bush, which seemed a likely spot for a game hideout. I kept to the East and soon came to a depression thickly clothed with red willow. Here I dismounted and tied Frank up to a

poplar tree and then walked noiselessly into the willows. I heard
the deer start and move north. Soon I heard them coming back
and I stood ready to fire. They came to where the bluff thinned
out; I could see them through the trees. Then, sensing my
presence, by some deer instinct, they slowly sank to the ground,
where they seemed to flatten out with only their antlers showing.
These looked so much like the surrounding broken dried sticks,
that no one looking around and not knowing deer were there
would have recognized them for antlers.

Soon I heard Dad coming and at the same instant, the
deer sprang to their feet. I fired and got a beautiful young buck.
That was quite a thrill, I assure you! I have shot quite a few
since, but not one of them has given me the thrill or pleasure of
that one, my first, shot with slugs I made.

The meat was delicious.

A few days afterwards, Jimmy Hyland came to me
and said, "Say, Fred, I wonder if I could persuade
you to come to Edmonton with me to bring home some cattle
that I have bought and left there?"

"I've only just been to Edmonton," I told him. "I just
got back a few days ago."

"Well, I have no money to pay you, but I tell you
what; I'll give you this rifle and three boxes of shells for it if
you'll come."

He held out the rifle to me and I took it and examined
it with the eye of an expert, or tried to make him think so. He
said, "It's a damned good one. I'm sure you'll like it. It looks a
little ragged," rather ruefully "but it sure polishes up nice."

117

I was about to hand it back to him when he added, "I'll pay all your expenses" and looked at me hopefully.

I had nothing much to do at the time so I told him I would go.

When we reached Edmonton and went for the cattle, we found that two of the cows had freshened, but no one knew what had happened to the calves. On the way home, those two cows were one problem. They were two quiet old 'bossies', but Jimmy hadn't expected milk cows to be among the herd.

"Can you milk, Fred?"

"No. Can't you?"

"No. What in God's name will we do with them?" he asked me.

"We'll just have to try. They should be milked right now." I told him.

"We'll get them out of the town first," he said.

We got them to the outskirts of the town, but the cows were by then so restless and were bawling so plaintively that we decided to stop and milk them. We dismounted and tied up our horses to a tree. Jimmy said to me, "All right. You go first."

"No, you You go first. They're your cows," I said.

"I wish to God they weren't just now," he laughed, as he gingerly took hold of a teat and began pulling on it for all he was worth. The cow kicked and began to bawl loudly, and he ran away.

"Here, let me have a go. You'll pull the damned thing off of her if you pull like that," I told him. "Besides you are on the wrong side of her, aren't you?"

"Does it matter?" he asked me. "I didn't know they were so pernickety about which side, so long as they got milked."

"Well, they are". I said as I went bravely up to one "Bos" and patted her on the side, as I had seen Dad do.

"That's the way, Fred. I remember now," Jimmy cried out, joyously. "You've got to get friendly with them first."

"Come on then," I told him. "I'll attend to the friendly part if you do the milking,"

"All right." he said, stepping forward briskly, but still on the wrong side of her. She turned her head towards him and regarded him suspiciously. He jumped back about three feet, "My God," He said, "don't she look fierce?"

"Fierce nothing," I told him, "They are quite quiet. She just doesn't like you on that side."

He detoured round her to where I was standing and said, "You know I think they should be milked with both hands. Cows like this are always milked with both hands, aren't they?"

Both cows were now very nervous and restless, and bawling continuously. It was getting on my nerves. "Well go ahead. Try with both hands. Do something." I told him.

119

Part 3   Breaking Ground

He bent down and bravely grabbed hold of two teats, but jumped back immediately and said. "My God, Fred, her bag's as hard as a rock."

"Why sure it is." I told him. "It's full of milk. Go on, get busy."

He tried again, his hands shuttling back and forth, and he pulling with all his strength. I had watched Dad milking quite a number of times and he seemed to do it quite easily and without effort. I said, "Let me have a go." I tried, but not a drop could I get either.

"Well, isn't that a corker! The darned things look as if they have been milked twice a day since they have arrived at the use of reason. What will we do with them? I'm afraid their bags will burst." He said.

I thought for a while. Then I said, "Let's drive them into the next farmyard we come to, and ask someone there to milk them".

Jimmy thought that was a good idea, so at the next farmyard we drove the two milk cows in. There was a lad about twelve year's old standing near a barn.

"Say, Son, can you milk?" Jimmy called to him.

The boy glanced at the cows with an appraising eye. "Naw, can you?" Jimmy went over to him and quite confidentially told him that neither of us could milk,

"Well, gee williker's, if you aren't two dunderheads." He said. "Goin and buyin' a bunch of cows an' you can't milk.

You must be some farmers all right." And, he laughed loudly.
His loud guffaws brought a woman to the door of the farmhouse.
"What do the men want, Peter?" she called over to him.

"They want me to 'drig' these two old 'mooleys'." He
called back.
"Well, go an' do it. The hogs can stand the milk."
And, as he made no attempt to move, she said, "Go on now. Get
a pail."

"Aw, gee, mom, I've milked six this evenin'. Can't a
fella -"?

Jimmy produced a dime. "Look here," He said. "I'll
give you this dime if you'll milk them."

Action! He ran for a box to sit on and a pail and soon
the milk was pouring in a steady stream into it, while the cows
stood quiet and motionless, pure enjoyable relief beaming from
every bovine line of their faces. Three pails full he emptied into
the pig troughs and in less than half an hour we were on our way
again.

At one place where we called there was a nice little
pony standing in the yard. "That will make a nice riding horse
when it grows a bit more," I said to Jimmy.

"When it grows a bit more?" he repeated
questioningly. "I think it has grown all it ever will grow."

"But it's only a pony." I said. He was silent.

Part 3   Breaking Ground

The farmer then came up and I asked him if he wanted to sell the pony. His whole face lit up with pleasant surprise. "He's yours for twenty dollars."

I bought the pony.

When I got home, Dad came out laughing. "Where did you pick that thing up?" he asked me.

"Pick him up?" I said. "I bought him. What's the matter with him? He's only a pony."

"Pony!" he said laughing. "I bet he's twenty years old if he's a day."

"Why is he so small?" I asked him.

"He's what we always called a 'Runt Horse' on the farm. We always destroyed them. They are no good for anything."

"I thought he was a young pony, and that he would grow." I said.

"No" Dad said, "There's too much in-breeding in him. The horse tribe can't stand it."

I sold the "Pony" some time later to a neighbour who wanted him for a pet for his children. I got ten dollars for him, so got out of that deal a sadder but wiser judge of 'ponies'.

I was still smarting over the loss of the ten dollars when one afternoon Mr. Humphrey and Ray drove into our yard in a buggy drawn by an ox. That was the most grotesque looking means of transportation I have ever seen. The ox was a huge fellow, enormously proportioned even for a bull, with two horns of fearful length and potency. At first sight, one got the instant impression of the massiveness and strength of the brute, and the fragility of the buggy and its two toy occupants. He halted immediately at Mr. Humphrey's "Whoa," and both men got out of the buggy. Mr. Humphrey asked me almost at once, "Are you busy just now, Fred?"

"No," I told him, "At least not for a day or two."

He said then, "I've lost two bulls. They have been gone now for over a week, and we can't find hide nor hair of them. If you'll find them for me I'll give you thirty dollars."

"Have you any idea which direction they would be likely to go? Where did they come from originally?" Dad asked him.

"I bought them in Lloydminster last fall. I don't know where they were raised" he told us.

I had heard many people talk about looking for lost animals and had heard them say, "Lost animals always follow the watershed". There was no other immediate prospect of earning thirty dollars in view and winter was setting in, especially at night, it was getting very cold and frosty. To be quite honest with myself our home seemed to have lost a whole lot of its brightness and gaiety since Gilbert and Fan had gone. I missed them tremendously that winter. I told him I would try. He seemed delighted that I would undertake the job, and wished me good luck. They went out through the yard on their way to Jack Fleming's. They had not been gone long when they came

123

back, Mr. Humphrey pulling the buggy with the shafts in
fragments piled up in it, and Ray leading the ox.

"What happened?" I asked them.

"Just as we got out of your yard he turned right round
and looked at us." They told me.

I drove them home, tying the ox and the disabled
buggy to the back of my wagon.

Next day I started out on my quest for the missing
oxen, and arrived at Inkster's three days later. Inkster's farm and
ranch would be somewhere in the Gully, North and West of
where the town of Maidstone now stands. I reckoned if they had
followed the watershed that they would have arrived at the Gully
by this time. I asked Inkster if I might camp there that night and
having got his permission to do so, I then enquired about the
oxen.

"Yes," he said, "they've been coming up with our
cattle every evening, and that first evening they had brand new
halters on them, but I haven't seen them since."

"You haven't seen the halters?" I asked.

"No," He replied, "I fancy the Indians have stole
them."

I formed the impression while he spoke that he was
feeling a little guilty about those halters. I thanked him and he
called after me as I drove out of his yard the next morning,
"Them bulls have not been coming up with ours these last two
or three days." Something about Mr Inkster's manner that made

me think, he knew more about the halters than he cared to let me know.

I travelled north meaning to turn east when I reached the river and circled back to Inkster's. It was a real, sharp, frosty morning with every blade of grass and every leaf of the underbrush bejewelled with diamonds of every size and color gleaming and twinkling in the bright morning sunshine.

As I drove along, keeping my eyes peeled in every direction for any sign of the oxen there suddenly appeared ahead of me a beautiful young buck. He turned at once to run, but like lightning, I picked up a rifle I had borrowed in Lloydminster, and got him just behind the left shoulder. He dropped like a stone. I rushed out, cut his throat, took out his stomach and put him in my cutter. I certainly felt elated at this piece of good luck. I then continued travelling North and East till noon, and then swung round to travel West and South. After a mile or two, I came to a farm belonging to a Mr. Waters, I believe the name was, and just near this farm were the two oxen of my search grazing with a herd of cattle. This Mr. Waters was driving a bunch of cattle into Lloydminster the next day to sell them, so I arranged that the two oxen should run with his cattle, and I would drive behind with the team and cutter, and help the two boys who were driving the herd. We arrived in Lloydminster late that night. I left the bulls in the corral with Waters' cattle, and next morning got up very early and started out for home with them tied behind the cutter. It was late when I arrived home so after making sure they were fed, and safe for the night, tired out with the driving and sleeping on the ground, I sought a real night's rest in a good comfortable bed.

Early next morning I set out for Tring, the oxen tied behind my cutter, and reached Humphrey's yard about ten o'clock. Mr. Humphrey and the two boys came running to me, and you never saw such fond and lavish affection and endearments as the three of them bestowed on those two dumb brutes. No prodigal son or sons could have been the recipient of more loving and extravagant rejoicing. Mr. Humphrey wrung my hand in gratitude. I believe if he had been a little taller, he would have reached up and kissed me. He pulled his purse out of his pocket and paid me my thirty dollars, and this I relished much more than I would a kiss, as much as I have always liked Mr. Humphrey.

It was now nearing the end of September and I set out with the team and wagon for Prince Albert. It was still beautiful Indian Summer weather and the whole country seemed to be ablaze with shimmering gold, relieved by the yellows, greens, browns and reds of the wild cherry and Saskatoon trees and the colourful rose bush undergrowth. I remember one balmy, dreamy afternoon, as I was driving along, singing almost at the top of my voice. As I went back in thought over my life up to the present, the feeling of sadness that suddenly assailed me for people I had known well, in that part of London where I had worked with my brother, Bert, in the butcher shop. People who had lived all their lives in dire and unrelieved poverty; people who had never seen a country scene at all comparable to the one which I now beheld and which stretched for miles and miles, around me, away into the hazy horizons. I thought, "Why cannot some philanthropic person give his money to bring out those inhabitants of the city slums of England, and settle them by the thousands, in this beautiful, beautiful country, where they could breathe cool, clean, fresh air, and look away into the distances. Their minds could be cleansed of the sordidness of housing congestion, with its attendant unclean, foul odours and surrounding proximity. What a godsend it would be for many of

126

them! I vowed that if I ever achieved wealth, and I could see no reason why I should not, that I would do just that.

How that stimulating Indian summer air goes to one's head!

Part 3   Breaking Ground

CHAPTER 8

> They ploughed him up and ploughed him down
> Put clods upon his head,
> Then they swore a solemn oath
> John Barley corn was dead.
>
>   Burns

I arrived at Prince Albert without adventure or
mishap of any kind. Not so was the experience of
Harry, Bill and Ted, when, as you may remember, they set out,
by row boat, for Prince Albert the morning after our arrival at
the mouth of the Vermilion River, by scow, from Edmonton in
June of 1904. They took with them provisions, blankets, maps,
etc. for the journey. Each night they pitched the tent at sundown
and cooked supper. They had a good supply of homemade
bread and beans and sowbelly, but they had no rifle and shells.
They just took along the fundamentals, as the boat was small.

The weather was very sultry and they moved along
with the stream at about three miles per hour. It was really too
hot to row from about 11:00 a.m. to 4:00 p.m., so they made
these hours their period of rest and relaxation. They decided to
cook breakfast before starting in the morning and then take turns
at rowing until their rest period. They ate lunch on the boat and
afterwards took it in turns to sleep.

It was in the afternoon of the second day
that they saw an animal leap off the bank into the water. Harry
and Ted were on watch at the time and Harry asked, "Did you
see that dog jump?" They both thought it must be an Indian's
dog and for a few minutes gave no thought to the incident, as
they were nearing a couple of small islands in the river and their

attention was fully occupied by the question of which channel to take. Discussing the whole experience afterwards, they found that the undue size of the animal, for an ordinary dog, had registered with both of them, but neither one had spoken of this fact at the time.

Having decided which channel, they turned round and simultaneously let out a yell of terror and astonishment. The animal was just a few feet away from them, and swimming vigorously towards the boat. It was a long, catlike animal with a huge head and open, rapacious jaws. Its large, bared cruel teeth and the look of fiery malignance in its eyes left the boys in no doubt as to its intent. The commotion and shouts woke up Bill and he saw the animal, just as it reached out a paw with protruding claws towards the boat and, seizing an oar, he hit it with all his strength on the nose. Blood spurted out and the cat shook its head for a moment, but soon came at them more ferociously and seemed to try to climb into the boat. Harry said, "Get its eyes", and at the same time gave it a terrific blow right across the face. It fell back, again for a moment, and now thoroughly enraged - renewed its efforts to get hold of the boat, reaching out with its powerful and terrifying claws, each of which seemed to be almost as thick as a man's finger. Time after time both Harry and Bill beat the beast off by hitting with all their strength, while Ted, sitting in the bottom, blanched with fear, tried to keep the boat steady. Several times, it almost capsized and they feared the oars would break. At one time Bill shoved the blade of the oar into the animals' mouth, while Harry, at the same moment, reached out and gave it a tremendous blow across the eyes. That must have been the K.O., and lucky it was as the boat almost went over and Bill just saved Harry from going overboard.

129

Soon after, they saw the cat-like animal floating a few yards from them, but they kept at a safe distance away from it until they were sure there was no life in it.

The whole episode had taken about twenty-five minutes, but to those three boys, surprised and terrified as they were it seemed to be hours. Ted at the time was seventeen; Bill was around twenty-two and Harry twenty-four. They have never been able to identify the creature. When they became sure it was dead, they steered it to an island where they landed and pulled it ashore. They thought the pelt would be no good so they hung the carcass up in a tree. It was definitely of the cat family, in that they all concurred. They measured it by spanning and found it was at least six feet six inches from the point of its nose to the tip of its tail. It was not a lynx. It was too large and had a tail. Whatever it was, the boys surely were unnerved by the occurrence. [1]

At sundown, they pulled to shore for the night, but supper was out of the question. Food had no appeal for them. As we had done on our trip from Edmonton, they climbed to the top of the riverbank but there was no sign of habitation, just vast solitudes of prairie and parkland with considerable bush stretching away into the distances. They had no axe or they would have cut down good strong poles for defence, in case of a recurrence of the cat experience. They felt very unsafe and defenceless, isolated and terribly jittery. They were afraid to go to sleep and, after some discussion, decided to make a fire in front of the tent and that two should sleep while the third kept the fire going. They had heard that no wild animal would come

[1] (Editors note: From the description and behaviour I believe this animal was most likely a wolverine, a skunk-bear.)

near fire. However, there was not much sleep for any of them as, at the least noise or disturbance in the undergrowth, whoever was on watch called out and immediately two of them seized the oars, while the third stood ready to hurl a firebrand at any intruder. They were all glad when the first signs of daybreak appeared in the East.

They ate a hasty breakfast, made sure everything was ready to push off before putting out the last embers of fire, and as Ted said, "Rowed like blazes," to get as quickly as possible away from the scene of their gruelling experience.

The next day, their third day, was not as hot as the first two had been. There was a slight breeze and they put up their oars and put a blanket on them for a sail, and really made some headway and with less effort. They could take it in turn to get some sleep. Towards evening, the river seemed to be studded with islands and sandbars, and navigation became more exacting and precarious, also they thought, more fraught with danger from wild, rapacious animals. The scenery, in the shadowy glimpses of the departing sunset, was magnificent, but they were too scared to comment on or enjoy the beauty of their surroundings. Harry says, in telling of the trip, that their necks ached from the continual turning of their heads from side to side and looking back, always on the alert for the imminence, of danger. "We looked just like owls with our heads always on the move," he says.

That night they again lit a fire and took it in turns to tend it throughout the hours of darkness. They made and ate a good supper, the first real meal since the lunch of the previous day. It was a beautiful moonlight night and apart from the usual noises of wild bird life, there was nothing to disturb the peace and serenity of the stillness. With the first light of morning, they

were all three awake and up and soon were ready to push off.
After rowing for about two hours, they came to where a
wide-mouthed river ran into the Saskatchewan and decided,
from a perusal of the map, that this was the Battle River and that
they must be near Battleford. This brought some greater sense
of comfort and tranquility, as they knew the country from then
on was more settled and they were not quite so far from
civilization, with all its attendant fellowship and helpfulness.

Soon after passing the mouth of the Battle Rivers, they
heard singing, just a few notes and then it died away, but those
few notes had the effect of a soothing palliative to their taut and
harassed nerves. They seemed to relax, and Harry says they all
three smiled when they heard it and that was the first time any
one of them had smiled since the fight with the cat. Then, as
they neared a bend in the river, the song came to them lustily
and clearly in a pleasing baritone:

> "John Barley corrn was a herro bold,
> Of noble enterrprise,
> For if you do but taste his bluid
> T'will make your courage rise;
>
> T'will make a man forrget his woe;
> T'will heighten all his joy:
> T'will make the widows hearrt to sing
> Tho the tearr werre in herr eye."

Rounding the curve, they came upon him - a big,
raw-boned, red haired Scotchman drunk as a fiddler. He was
drifting very slowly close to the shore in a small boat, and when
he saw the boys he hailed them with,

Part 3   Breaking Ground

"Come overr herre laddies." They rowed towards
him.

His small boat was laden with bottles of moonshine.
One bottle, half full, was in his hand and this he held out to them
saying, "Hae a drink, laddies." They thanked him but said they
dared not. They thought the stuff he was offering them would
not help in a fight with a cat, should another emerge out of the
near future.

They asked him, "What wild animal, very like a cat
but much longer and bigger is there in the bush here that will
attack human beings?"

He laughed, "Weel now, I dinna ken a cat o' them
prroporrtions. Is this a riddle ye are giving me?" and he
chuckled with amusement.

They assured him, "No, indeed, but a large animal
attacked us in the boat the day before yesterday."

He looked enquiringly at them now, the bottle held
half-mast and said confidingly, "Whaur had ye stoppit the nicht
afore?"

They told him in the tent on the river shore.

He asked them, "All by yersels?"

"Yes, certainly" they told him.

He lowered the bottle now and enquired slyly, "Who
sold ye the moonshine?"

Part 3   Breaking Ground

They told him that they had had no moonshine or alcoholic drink of any kind, and went on to describe the animal more fully.

He seemed very nonplussed and asked them several questions about their encounter with the cat, listening carefully, but with an incredulous look on his face all the while. They felt quite exasperated.

He volunteered the information, "I see things too when I take a tassle o'er muckle, but not cats," then ruminatively, "no, never cats".

Harry asked him, "What wild animals are there round here?"

He said, "Hoot mon there's nary a one that will attack you unless you interfere with their private or sex life," his eyes twinkling. "There is the lynx, but it has no tail and would only be aroon thrree feet long. Arre ye surre ye werre no dreaming?"

Bill said, "We could not all be dreaming and here is the oar with the blood still on it to prove what we are telling you."

He shook his head and took a long swig., "Verra odd, but hae a drapple laddie. It's guid and will hearten ye. Mind ye, I'm no dooting yer wurrd, but I've been aroon these pairts for most twelve yearrs and I've niver seen a cat as beeg as ye say."

They declined his offer and prepared to pull into mid-stream.

He said, "Ye dinna ken what ye are missing laddies. It's guid, I hae distilled it mae sel'." Then, as they still refused his offer, "Ye will be seeing ma frens mebbe - they will all have their flags oot to gie me welcome. Tell them Alex McEttrick will be along verra soon."

Bill was amused at the name and the way he said it. He asked, "Is that your real name?"

"Alex McEttrick at yer serrvice," He said. "An' neither wife nor bairns to fash me heid aboot."

Harry asked, "Are you not afraid the police will catch you?"

"Catch me", and he took another swig, "O' course they catch me, but what is a $50.00 fine? I'm tellin' ye, there's gold in it. Look, ye can see it - see the lovely golden color? Ye can taste it - there's not a cat in a barrel o' it," chuckling again "a few snakes mebbe in oer muckle, but narry a cat," shaking his head, "Well, so lang. Tell them a' am comin'. Alex has never let them doon yet" and holding up a bottle.

> "Then let us toast John Barrly corrn
> Each man a glass in hand;
> And may his grreat posterrity
> Ne'er fail in auld Scotland"

The boys had put the sail up again and were moving away from him down stream, but his cheering and heart some song followed them on the breeze, until looking back they could no longer see him. As they went along, right enough, on each side of the river and spaced at irregular distances, flags of all descriptions and made of every conceivable shape and color, like Joseph's coat, were floating welcomingly and beckoningly on the light wafting wind.

135

Part 3   Breaking Ground

They soon came to the elbow where the river turned sharply north, but after their encounter with the Scotsman, they felt much safer and more courageous. John Barleycorn seemed, indeed, to have entered their blood.

In two more days, uneventful and enjoyable, but still charged with vigilance and alertness, especially at night, they came to Prince Albert situated right on the river flats. Here they got work right away, Bill and Ted working in the brickyard and Harry worked at bricklaying. He worked for Frank Spore – Itner's Uncle from St. Louis - and helped to build many of the brick buildings still standing in Prince Albert today.

Harry is now seventy-six years of age, and when I asked him, a few days ago, about the fight with the cat, he shuddered and a look of pain crossed his face at the memory. He told again the same story I had heard from the three of them when I arrived in Prince Albert, and which I have heard from all three countless times since, and which has never varied in even the most minute detail. Harry says that of all the people to whom he has told the story few have believed him, and of those who have, fewer have agreed entirely on the identity of the animal. The most feasible suggestions have been that it was a cougar, which had strayed from its native habitat in the mountains, and, following the course of the river came to grief at the hands "Of us three strangers". He says, jokingly, "Maybe it smelled our rich red blood and, like all natives, thought three green Englishmen would be easy prey."

"Aw," says one of his boys, now in his forties, "It was a lynx just trying to scare you. They do that you know if they think you're timid or scare some."

"Lynx, nothing," says Harry showing annoyance. "I tell you it had a tail, and was much bigger than any lynx I have ever seen."

"I wonder if the skeleton's still hanging from the tree on the island?" says Alice, his wife, a little too innocently.

"Ah," says the boy, "what island, Dad?"

"Hanged if I would know now," Harry says, giving Alice a quick, searching look, "and I'm damned sure I'll never go to see".

Prince Albert, that Fall, in all its Indian summer glory, was the prettiest town I have ever seen. On the North side of the river, the high thickly wooded banks that feature the Saskatchewan River throughout most of its prairie course, have here disappeared and given place to a vast seemingly illimitable stretch of heavy and very beautiful timberland, at that time unspoiled in its primeval beauty. On either side of the river, the flats stretched back for as much as half a mile on the North and more than a mile on the South side. On these South-side flats the town had been built, and had expanded, and was still expanding, in terraces up the gently sloping face of the high bank.

Between the North and South shores of the river, a ferry similar to those everywhere in operation on rivers throughout Canada to-day, plied back and forth, daily, through the hours of daylight.

When I arrived at the end of September, I was surprised to learn that the three boys, Harry, Ted and Bill, were ready to go home.

Part 3   Breaking Ground

"What the dickens are you going home for?" I asked them.

"Because we are sick of the place," they told me. "There's a whore house started up just near the yard, and it's impossible to get to sleep till after daylight every night."

"You'll do as we did last winter - spend all you've earned and in the spring have nothing again." I warned them.

"I don't give a damn," said Harry. "I'll never set foot in the place again." So they took the team and went home, where they again spent all the money they had earned that summer. I began to work for Itner, getting logs out of the bush, for firing the kilns the next summer. This work lasted until the end of February and then I could find no regular employment. There were hundreds of men out of work. I purchased a bucksaw, and with this over my shoulder, I would go round to those houses where I would see a pile of logs, and having rapped on the door,

"Morning Ma'am.," I would say "would you like your wood sawn?"

"Well, I don't know. How do you charge for sawing it?"

"One dollar per cord, Ma'am."

"Oh, yes. I think we'll let you do it. When can you start?"

"Right away, Ma'am, and I'll guarantee that every stick will be the proper stove length."

Part 3   Breaking Ground

I would invariably get the job, and I should think so, too. It took me a whole day, sawing from 9:00 a.m. till dark at night to saw one cord. Soon I got more work than I could handle alone, so I hired Foss Heathcote to be my assistant. Foss was the saddest investment I ever made. He was obsessed with a mortal fear of working himself to death, and the passage of the sun across the sky was so deeply imbued with interest for him that he watched it continuously. One day I asked him, "Why do you stand gazing at the sky all the time?"

"I have pawned my watch." He told me.

He could tell the time by looking at the sun, more exactly than anyone I have met. He was seldom more than a minute or two out.

In the cold weather, when we finished in the evening, my back would often have a sheet of ice over it from the frozen sweat; his was always dry and warm.

"You'll kill yourself, Fred. You'll work yourself to death." He would tell me.

"Well, isn't that better than starving to death?" I'd ask him.

"God, no!" he would say. "Rather let me starve to an honourable death, than work to a craven death for the bloody 'Plutes'."

Foss was too slow and could not earn what I was paying him so I had to let him go. Itner had also hired Foss to work for him in the brickyard.

"He's a very willing boy," he said. "He's always willing to let other fellow do the work."

Like most of the men in the unemployed ranks, during that winter and spring, I lived on two meals a day: dinner at noon and supper at six in the evening. We ate those meals at the Chinamen's restaurant. So every day at the stroke of twelve, there would be a mad rush of hungry men to the Chinamen's restaurant, and that little Chinaman surely helped out the unemployed that winter. For twenty-five cents, we would get a plate piled high with good substantial food, two cups of tea or coffee, and all the bread and butter we wanted. As soon as we were finished eating he would come, laughing, "Belly full?" he would ask. "Then take your toothpick.'" he would laugh, and we would each take a toothpick and go and stand or lean against the wall of the Prince Albert Hotel and pick our teeth. The ritual never varied.

One afternoon I met Itner and his wife on the street. They were both dressed up to dazzle, and he was carrying her music case. They both stopped to say hello and Mrs. Itner told me they were going to a tea and musicale at the home of one of the business magnates of the town, and went on to enlarge on her many and various social commitments. Itner stood by looking thoroughly ill at ease and bored. He kept tugging at his collar, moving from foot to foot and changing the music case from one hand to the other, and as they said goodbye, he gave me a very revealing wink.

Next day I met him alone on the street. He stopped me and said, "For God's, sake, Fred, never marry a school marm."

"Why?" I enquired.

140

"She'll want to eddicate you and make a gentleman of
you." He said. "You mustn't spit or chew. You must put your
collar and hames on, and step out with her in the afternoons,
when there's your work sp'iling. You mustn't say ain't or tain't.
Now just tell me, Fred, how an American can talk without
saying 'ain't? It just tain't nacheral." and he walked away
laughing boisterously.

Just at this time, I had made the acquaintance of a
school "Marm". I often ran into her in the morning when I was
going to work, and it wasn't long before we began dating each
other for walks in the evenings. One evening she suggested,
"Let's hire a rig from the livery and drive out to my uncle's farm
next Sunday afternoon."

"How far out is it?" I asked her.

"It's about eight miles, I believe, but it's a real good
road all the way. You'll enjoy it I'm sure. Aunt Stella is a
lovely cook and I know we'll get a good meal."

After having eaten at the restaurant for so long, the
thought of a good home-cooked meal had great appeal for me.
Besides, I felt I couldn't very well refuse her invitation so
though the thought of the four dollars, at least, that the rig would
cost me, caused chills and fevers to run up and down my spine, I
told her I would get the rig and pick her up on the Sunday.

That night I scarcely slept. "What a stupid, gallant
fool I am," I thought. Towards morning, I had a brain wave, and
then I slept.

Itner, at that time, owned the swankiest turn-out in
Prince Albert, a handsome well-accoutered driver, and a brand

Part 3   Breaking Ground

new rubber-tired buggy, the very latest in buggies, resplendence shining from its every inch. I told myself, gaily, "I'll borrow it for Sunday." as I fell asleep. The next day I made it my business to meet him on the street and stopped to chat. After a few minutes, I asked him, "Will you be using your driver and buggy on Sunday?" I thought that would be my most tactful approach.

"Why do you ask?" he questioned me. He seemed disquieted by my question. I could tell he was, because he began to spit furiously and his mouth twitched at the corners, always a sign that he was troubled.

"I've got a kind of a date with Miss Anderson for -"

"That fat slob," he spat in disgust. "Now, Freddy, I'd like to see you do better than that red head Jane. She must weigh at least one hundred and sixty pounds."

"I'm not thinking of carrying her." I reminded him.

"No! No! But do you know who she is?" he asked me.

"Sure! She lives with her grandmother on--Street. They both seem to be quite nice people." I told him.

"Did you know that her uncle is a squaw man, and that most whiles he just keeps one hop ahead of the law?" he asked me.

This was really disturbing news, but I wouldn't let him see that it made any difference to me. I told him, "No, I didn't

know that, but it's all right. I'll get a rig from the livery barn for
Sun --"

"Now damn it, Fred, I can't let you do that. Take the
damned horse and buggy, but I'm telling you right now, there's
not another son of a bitch in Prince Albert that I'd loan them to.
Now I'm mighty perticular about both horse and buggy--", and
as my face straightened, and I was on the point of saying
something very impolite—"now don't tell me to put them where
the monkey put the nut." Then as if speaking to his self, "I wish
the missis was to home so I could have said I was taking her out,
but she ain't."

As he stood spitting, swearing, and the corners of his
mouth twitching, I suddenly got the full impact of his position.
He was finding it very hard to lend me his horse and buggy, but
he was finding it still harder to refuse me. I realized, almost
with a shock, just the gall I had had to make the request, so I
said, with all the sincerity and warmth I could put into the
words, "I'm sorry Itner, I know just how you feel about them. I
would feel the same, myself. I'm ashamed of having asked you
for them. Forget it. I'll get a rig from --."

"By God, you're a man, Fred." He grabbed my hand
and shook it. "But I'm damned if I'll let you hire a rig. Take
mine and I'm proud you've asked me for them. I know you'll
take good care of them, but er, - er -," spitting, the corners of his
mouth twitching –"don't get too mixed up with that red head
Jane." Then he laughed, winking knowingly.

"You needn't worry." I assured him winking
knowingly back. I left him, feeling the genuine interest he had
in my welfare.

143

Part 3   Breaking Ground

On the Sunday, I felt very gallant as I clopped up in Itner's outfit to get Miss Anderson--Mabel, if I remember rightly. She exclaimed when she saw it, "Isn't that a lovely turn-out. You must be favoured of the little brick god." From this and other remarks on both sides, I soon sensed that a deep animosity existed between "The red head Jane", and Itner, but I never got to the bottom of it.

I really enjoyed that Sunday. The roads were dry and good-- it was about the second week in May. The drive both going and coming back was very pleasurable. I liked both Uncle Jim and Aunt Stella. We arrived in time for lunch and we had two good, well-cooked meals while we were there, to both of which I did full justice. On the way home, Mabel asked me, "Would you think Aunt Stella is a full Cree?"

"No," I said, "She has the Indian look in some of her features, but she's the nicest looking Indian woman I've ever seen."

She said, "Yes. I always envy her lovely slim figure. No one would ever think she's the mother of twelve children."

"Twelve!" I exclaimed. "Were there twelve?"

"Yes, and from the way things are shaping up, there are liable to be twelve more. Uncle Jim is thirty-four and she isn't thirty yet."

"She must have been married very young."

"Yes. Granny has told me she was sixteen, and that's another thing -- are they married?" and the deep color mounted up from her neck to suffuse her whole face.

"Well, it looks very much like it." I laughed.

"Yea," she said. "I wanted to tell you, because if you haven't heard it already, you will. Itner will tell you. Uncle Jim picked her up in Little Chicago. Did you notice I didn't call her aunt when I spoke to her?"

I told her I hadn't.

Little Chicago was an Indian and Breed settlement on the North side of the river. It was sometimes referred to as the "Pink Light" district of the town, for here, quietly and without effrontery, a brothel business was carried on right under the noses of the police, but so unobtrusively and exclusively, as not to attract interference by the authorities.

"You can tell she's a good mother, and an excellent housekeeper. She works like a Trojan: her hands are never idle--washing, cleaning, baking, mending. She's certainly thrifty; I wish I knew they are married."

"Is he your mother's brother?" I asked her,

"Yes and Granny's son. Both the Simpsons and the Andersons felt so badly when he brought her to his home. That was when Granny moved out and came to live in Prince Albert. My mother died of consumption a few years after and I have lived with Granny ever since."

"They seem very happy." I said. "Those children all look so happy and healthy. They're a really good looking family."

"Yes, there's two sets of twins - the two eldest, and the two little girls of six. They all four have red hair, and yet there's something 'breedy' about their looks. Oh, well --" and there were tears glistening in her eyes.

I had begun working again in the brickyard when it opened up in the spring. Itner had made me overseer and now I was earning more money. The brickyard was situated about a mile beyond the south bank of the river. Nearby was a new red-light district. As the boys had told me, the noise from the new brothel was very disturbing to one's sleep. Night after night, the "Business" operated chiefly by Negroes, and some white trash kept me awake. Here the lumberjacks and other such rough elements sought solace and companionship. Each evening, about eight o'clock, the revelry began and always lasted well into the daylight hours of the next day. The place was brilliantly lit up by coal oil lamps, which shed a warm and welcoming invitation to its patrons. The piano, stridently out of tune, banged forth all the popular songs of the day, hilariously and uproariously. Dancing, singing, brawling, fighting all were intermingled, while moonshine flowed freely and audaciously, catering to every taste and desire. The business flourished like the green bay tree. When the town coffers required replenishing, a police raid was a never failing source of revenue.

In the early spring, I had roomed in the home of a Claude and Mrs. Aston, and had become quite well acquainted with them. Claude was clerking at Philion's General Store, and one night this establishment was broken into and a quantity of merchandise stolen. This caused quite a sensation in the town, and, for some reason, Philion expected a recurrence of the burglary, so he hired another lad and me to watch in the store at night to try to catch the culprits. We kept vigil for several nights but nothing happened, so our services were discontinued.

That first night how scared we both were! Every little sound sent our hearts palpitating. What we would have done if the burglars had made an appearance I don't know. Run for our lives, I believe. However, we drew our pay and had a good feed of chocolates and biscuits each night into the bargain.

Apart from this little diversion, and a few dates with Mabel and a few visits to her Uncle Jim's home, where I was always welcome, the summer passed uneventfully, and when the brick yard closed down in the Fall I set out for home - for the last time, though I didn't know it then.

I have never had any contacts with Prince Albert since. I have often wondered what became of Mabel. I hope she married some good man. One not so thickly coated with convention as I was; who recognized her worth, and her admirable courage in clinging to her Uncle Jim and Stella and their young family, when all his other relatives, even his mother, had cast him out. That she eventually realized her intense yearning for a home and family of her own--a yearning that manifested itself, always and delicately, in conversation with her. For when I remember those glistening tears in her eyes, I know she was a good girl.

I traveled home by train to Saskatoon and from Saskatoon to the siding where Kitscoty is now situated, by construction train. The promised railway from Saskatoon to Edmonton was, indeed materializing. I remember when we reached the siding I jumped off onto the track and only just missed landing in a deep slough. Then I walked home.

147

Part 3   Breaking Ground

CHAPTER 9

First a wedding and then a chivaree!

I was surprised at the number of new settlers that had
come into the district in my year of absence; also at
the advances toward civilization that began to appear. Most
surprising of all was that Rose (Floss) had a beau. Shy, demure,
and retiring, she was the first of the three girls to be married.

Among the new settlers were Alwyn Bramley-Moore,
William Ashworth, James Burke, the Addison boys, and the
McDougall's. Bramley-Moore and William Ashworth took
homesteads south of us, the others settled on land to the north.

Mr. Bramley-Moore took up a homestead on the ridge
to the south of us and was soon joined by his wife and two
children. Hearing that there were two adult girls in our home, he
came to ask if Rose might go and work for Mrs.
Bramley-Moore. Rose was delighted to have the opportunity of
earning a few dollars, so she went. She soon afterwards made
the acquaintance of William Ashworth (Billie he became later to
all of us), a retired sea captain, whose homestead was about half
a mile from the Bramley-Moore home. A mutual attraction
sprang into being almost from their first meeting, but they were
both so shy that their furtive attempts at courting were pitifully
inadequate. For some time they were not getting anywhere.

One day Bramley-Moore came to Bill and me and
asked us, "What are we going to do about this couple? They
both want to get there, but they haven't even got to first base yet.
I think something should be done to help them."

148

"Ah," said Bill, laughing. "That first base is a bugger to get at. After that, the rest is easy; now at least that's what I'm told. I haven't got to that first base myself yet."

"Well, I think something's got to be done." Bramley-Moore said laughing.

His home on the homestead was the usual pioneering shack; sometimes just a frail partition separating the bedrooms, often merely a curtain. That night, soon after the family had retired, he called out, "Miss Marfleet".

"Yes?" Rose, who was just dozing off, woke up to ask.

"Billie says, 'Barkis is willin'," he called back.

"Who's Barkis?" asked Rose.

"Why, Billie, of course. Good-night"

This became quite a joke among us all, and it bucked Billie up to the point of proposing. So they were married soon after, and we gave them a rousing wedding reception at our home, and a few nights after people came from far and near to chivaree them. Theirs was the first wedding in the new Streamstown St Patrick Anglican Church. That was the first time any Barr Colonist of that district had ever heard of, or taken part in, a chivaree.

A few days prior to the wedding Jack Fleming came to me and said, "I hear Rose and Ashworth are getting spliced."

"Yes," I said. "They've made up their minds at last."

149

Part 3   Breaking Ground

"How about a chivaree?" he asked me.

"A Chivaree? What's that?"

"Have you never heard of a chivaree? Say, do you people ever have any fun over there?" He asked, laughing

"Oh yes, we have in our own way." I told him dryly. "I've just never heard of a chivaree. Is it a drink or something?"

"No," he laughed, "It's just a noisy gathering of the neighbours. They all gather around the groom's shack after they've gone to bed, and make such a hullabaloo that he has to get up and give them a drink and lunch. Then there's usually a sing-song and then everyone kisses the bride, wishes the couple much happiness and goes home."

"On the night of the wedding?" I asked him.

"Oh, no, we wait a night or two till they've got thoroughly married."

"Aren't they married in church?" I asked with pretended innocence.

"Tut-tut, they're just churched there. Will you all come?"

"Oh, sure thing! When does it start?"

"The second night after the wedding, we'll all congregate near Billie's shack and hide in the bushes till their light goes out, and soon after we'll break loose. Bring something to make a noise with."

Part 3   Breaking Ground

When I got home, I told the family all about the impending chivaree, ending up just as Jack did with,

"Everyone then kisses the bride."

"Kiss, the bride!" screamed Molly with laughter. "Good Lord! Our Rose!" and she almost convulsed with laughter.

"Yes, that alone should be worth going to see." said Bill.

So on the appointed night, we all collected near Billie's shack. The light was still burning in the kitchen when we arrived, but we hid in the bushes and waited. Once Rose came and looked out, and called to Billie.

"Come here, Will. I'm sure there's something moving in those shadows."

Billie came and put his arm round her and the two stood silhouetted in the open doorway, looking. We all stood as still as death. Then Billie said, "Oh, come in. There's nothing. Let's get to bed." And the door shut. Our subdued tittering rippled through the shadows. Soon the light went out and about ten or fifteen minutes later, Jack Fleming called out softly, "All right boys, let her go." and such a pandemonium as burst forth. Cowbells were ringing in every tone and key that were ever invented and in some that never were invented, tin cans and old wash boilers were crashed together or beaten with sticks. The weirdest noise of all came from old ploughshares beaten with iron rods, and intermingling with all this was the clackety-clacking of what seemed to be hundreds of pairs of bones. One party was singing--singing? "He's a jolly good fellow." discordantly and rowdishly, while another almost out vied them with, "She's my sweetheart, I'm her beau".

After a little time the light went on and Billie appeared at the door and called out, "Is hell let loose out there?"

"It is. It is. Oh, he's a jolly good fellow."

He beckoned us so we all dropped our "Musical instruments" and began to troop in. Molly whispered to me, "I bet Rose is under the bed". Imagine our surprise, when we got inside to see her standing, smiling, and looking quite unperturbed.

"Wait till they begin kissing her." I said to Molly.

"Yes," she said. "I bet she'll make a dive for under the bed then."

Rose then said. "You are late aren't you? We've been expecting you these last two nights." And everyone gave her a resounding clap.

She had the coffee pot on the stove already, and while the ladies took possession of the chairs that the newly-weds owned, the rest of us sat on the floor, tailor fashion, and like bumps on a log. Billie produced a bottle and all the glasses and cups they had received for wedding presents and poured drinks. However, there were not enough of them to go round, and this caused a lot of fun and gaiety, and shows of mock modesty and some real modesty, until ultimately, everyone had had a drink and all were feeling young and gay.

Rose then, assisted by some of the ladies, served
coffee and sandwiches and after all had been 'dined and wined'
the call came for a singsong. The first to be called upon was
Dan Moore. After a little hesitation, he stood up and said,
"Being Irish, I think the best tribute I can give to this very
memorable occasion is to try to sing an Irish "Come All Ye". I
am not good at it, but I'll do my best." He was a good singer
and he began:

> "Come all ye good people and list unto me
> While I tell you about the big chivaree,
> When Rosie and Billie decided to wed
> And we came, all us rascals,
> To get them out of their bed -"

It went on and on. He mentioned the name of
everyone present and made some pertinent and witty comment
on each one of them. I thought it was very cleverly done. I
remember the ovation that burst forth at the end:

> "Och sure and we all had an illigant spree
> While Aaron sat playing the fiddle-de-de."

"Write it out for us. Write it out for us." They all
begged him. Rose and Billie later got a copy of it, and I
wouldn't be surprised if Rose has her copy among her most
treasured possessions to this day.

There were several other songs and recitations, and
last, but not least was Billie's song about the "Birds and the
Breezes and sweet scented Treeses" which received lengthy
applause. Then we all sang, "He's a jolly good fellow" once
more, and swarmed to kiss the bride and wish them both much

happiness. Then everybody shook hands with everybody else, some two or three times over and so to home and bed.

That was the first chivaree in that district!

I have written at some length about that chivaree, principally because I believe all the real good times, and they were real and many and good, that followed in those early days, had their beginning in that event. It was our first real insight into the Canadian way of creating fun and frolic out of the merest pretext. Many of us, now in the eventide of life, can look back fondly and nostalgically, to those long drives to a chivaree or a dance or just a party, on the cold winter nights, with a realization and appreciation, leavened with maturity, of the part they played in our lives. The good part that kept the spirit of youth and hope and the will to do, aglow in our hearts and souls, despite the isolation, the hardships, the struggles, and disappointments that made up our daily lives.

"What did you think of the chivaree?" We asked Rose and Billie, when they next came for their mail.

"I thought you were a pretty tough looking bunch of people." Billie said. "I've only seen one tougher in all my life."

"Where was that?" We asked.

"It was on the screen in the days of silent pictures. The picture showed a Negro being lynched, and by heaven, I can remember seeing each one of your faces in that lynching crowd."

We laughed and let it go at that.

154

Part 3   Breaking Ground

It was the next spring that we lost Nellie and Frank.
At that time there were no fences anywhere and the
horses roamed at will all over the open sections of lend. Jack
Fleming's pony and mule, and our team usually stayed around
on the section north of us. The four horses were great pals and
when we wanted them, we knew they wouldn't be far away.

"Hadn't you better go and look for the horses?" Dad
asked me one morning, after I had remained at home a week or
so.

"There's lots of time," I told him. "We'll wait till the
first crow comes. That will be time enough."

"Tupper says he heard one last week," he told me.
"Of course, there's always those who must be first."

"Ay," I said, "always".

He looked at me then, twinkling, "But I don't think
you'll ever be one of them."

"Well it's too early." I said. "I can get the yard and
garden all cleaned up."

The creeks were filling up and there had been water
a-plenty around everywhere from-the melting snow, but this was
now rapidly drying up. The Chinook winds that blow down
from the Northwest each spring had begun and were quickly
licking up all surface water and thin skiffs of snow remaining in
the open, despite the lengthening days of sunshine. I finished
cleaning up the yard and then began to look for the horses in a
desultory kind of way, but could see nothing of them.

155

Part 3   Breaking Ground

"Do you know if Fleming's pony and mule are with ours?" I asked Dad.

"Yes" said Molly, who was then at the age when there's romance in everything, even in a gelded mule. "They went through our yard a day or two before you came home, to keep a rendezvous with Nellie, I imagine."

"And you think they are still rendezvousing?" I asked her.

"Oh, they could have gone back, of course, but I didn't see them."

Next day, I went over to Jack's to enquire if his team had come back. He said. "No, they have been gone over a week now."

I told him. "I'll go over to Billy Shaw's tomorrow. They may have wandered over around Stinking Lake."

He said half reluctantly, "I'd like to come with you but my footwear is completely worn out. So is the boys'. I just have nothing I could wear on my feet, and this prairie grass is terribly hard on footwear in the spring."

I said quite nonchalantly, "I will be all right – mine will stand it".

Next morning I looked my footwear over. The collection did not offer much in the way of variety or elegance, but I decided to wear a pair of moccasins that I had bought in Prince Albert in February, which I had not worn a great deal. Over these I tied, with strong strings a pair of well-worn heavy

rubbers, packed up a good lunch and sallied forth. I made North
across heavy hay land for maybe three or four miles, and seeing
no sign of horse or any other animals, I turned, traveling in a
north-easterly direction. I had now discarded what was left of
the old rubbers after walking for about one hour or better, as I
could no longer keep them on my feet. This I was to regret
before I reached home. The string with which I had tied them
was all cut up and worn and the rubbers themselves were
hanging in pieces. I went on with just the moccasins for another
couple of hours then sat down to eat my lunch and was horrified
to see that much of the stitching in the moccasins had been cut
by the sharp prairie grass. I reckoned I was about ten miles from
home then. I cut the makings off my plug of Macdonald's,
rolled it into a cigarette using a piece of the brown paper
wrapping of my lunch, sat down and enjoyed the smoke. Then I
decided I would go home and try to borrow a horse, and start out
again tomorrow. I had not gone far when I saw a stranger
coming towards me. I hailed him with the usual greeting in
those days.

"Hello! Are you homesteading around here?" It was
Clutterbuck.

He said, "Yes, about six miles East o' 'ere. I'm
working for Dr. Jordan at the present." indicating Jordan's shack
with a jerk of his thumb.

"Who's he?" I enquired.

"Haven't you met him?" he asked.

I told him I just had gotten back from Prince Albert
the past winter.

He said, "He's a rum, owd cuss. I dunno rightly wat to make o' 'im. 'Ee 'as brought in some lovely Hereford cattle and I'm just 'elpin 'im with them for a few days."

At the mention of the cattle, I asked him if he had seen anything of the horses.

He said, "About a couple of miles back I saw where some 'osses 'ad been layin' down, but that musta' bin two days ago. Their dung was quite dry."

I handed him my plug, knife, and brown paper, and we sat down and each rolled and smoked a cigarette. He told me he thought the horses were traveling in a North-easterly direction, but he was not sure. I thanked him for the information and sat out for home.

How that grass ripped those moccasins! My feet began to ache and really hurt. The moccasins soon were all unstitched, so I undid the deer hide lacing and tied the pieces, which were now apart, to the soles of my feet. This did not last long. My feet were scratched and bleeding, and in this condition, I hobbled along for two or three miles. Never had I been so glad before to see the old time-stricken poplar, stricken by both time and weather inclemency that always stood out, brave and undaunted, flaunting its green flag each spring. It was an ever a welcoming landmark, towering, high and handsome, above the surrounding growth of young brush, on the bluff north of our home. I hobbled to the creek that ran just north of our house and bathed my bleeding feet in the cool stream. I wished now I had kept a bit of the rubbers and some string to tie them to my feet, but I had not. I would have to make it to the house barefoot. I stood up to do so, but nearly fell into the creek, the pain in my feet was so excruciating. It was just as if I were

walking on sharp swords. I crawled on my hands and knees to
the house

Next morning Dad was up early, with sunrise as usual,
and wanting me to get up and go over to Billy Shaw's to borrow
a horse to go after Nellie and Frank. I got some boots on but
was still so very lame that Dad walked over and rode back on
Sinbad. That animal was the most homely looking bit of
horseflesh I have ever seen. One leg always looked and acted as
if it were an afterthought of the Creator or as if it had been
added by an amateur, or as if it were a fifth leg, there to supply
in an emergency. There seemed to be no co-ordination with the
other three. He was quick enough and of great endurance, but of
most grotesque appearance and ungainly gait. I shall never
forget how comical Dad looked as he rode up the lane on
Sinbad's back. Yes, by this time, we had acquired a lane or what
we called a lane, which later became a real lane, leading from
our front yard out to the graded road, which ran North and South
just east of us, the future driveway of Dad's "Hestite". Dad, all
his life, had ridden on horseback in England, and when the
Englishman rides, he rises up out of the saddle and drops back
into it at each step of the horse. As Dad rode up on this
awkward, ungainly mount, with his aristocratic style of riding,
we all stood outside our house just convulsed with laughter.
Then he dismounted, he seemed quite peeved at us for laughing
at him. He threw me the reins and said, "Here, take the dammed
old quadruped".

I knew I would be in for some pretty tough riding, but
it had to be done so we set forth, 'Sinbad' and I to find the
horses. That was the first time I ever saw a badger. We were
traveling a rather open part of the prairie when I saw a heap of
soil with what I have since learned was badger bush growing in
a circle around it, and on top of the pile sat a badger.

159

Part 3   Breaking Ground

I was curious about the creature, a curiosity that he seemed to disdain. I rode quite close to him but he never moved or batted an eye. I thought, "I'll make you move, you son-of-a-gun", so I dismounted and stooped to pick up a rock when he came for me with teeth and claws bared in the fight. I clutched the reins, mounted Old Sinbad, and beat it. Then, not having had enough, I dismounted again, picked up some small stones, and hurled them at him. He sat looking at my futile efforts to hit him, with a supercilious sneer on his face, and then very deliberately went down his hole.

I rode all that morning and soon after noon picked up the trail of the horses. I followed this for at least twelve miles, traveling along the bank of the river in an easterly direction until a heavy thicket of young growth rising from the river's edge right up the bank to its top, forced me to follow the narrow opening between this thicket on the North and the heavy, almost impenetrable, bush on the South. It was getting near sundown and I had proceeded less than one mile on this narrow opening when suddenly I came upon an Indian camp.

There were about ten or fifteen tepees scattered around the edge of the clearing. At least twenty horses of various descriptions hobbled and grazing in seemingly perfect contentment. It would be just about directly South of Fort Pitt on the south bank of the Saskatchewan River. I have often since thought of that scene. It opened before me so suddenly and without warning. It was an ideal camping site, a large wide-open space, well sheltered and shaded by trees. The terrain here was beautiful parkland, without undergrowth and covered with a thick carpet of the verdant young grass of early spring.

The braves were all sitting round in a large circle smoking. Dozens of children it seemed running around, with

160

almost as many dogs. The squaws all sat a little distance apart many of them smoking, some of them preparing the evening meal, but all seeming to be carefree and un-harassed and remote from worldly cares. Surely a pastoral scene worthy of any artists brush, I thought.

I approached the braves to enquire about the horses, but not by word or sign did they show any awareness or my presence amongst them, though I guess they had been quite aware of my coming for some time. I began to feel quite nervous. Had I had a fleeter steed, I would have turned tail and run for it, and more particularly so if I had known then that that very spot almost, was where the Indians had made practically their last stand only about ten or twelve years earlier in their rebellion against the British. The event is now known in history as the Rebellion of the Northwest Territories, the Riel Rebellion. I had heard in a nebulous kind of way of the Riel Rebellion and its extension into the Northwest Territories. This was near the scene of Poundmaker's surrender. However, I was blissfully ignorant of all this at the time.

I smiled and said, "Good evening".

I could not tell if they had heard me. They gave no sign whatever.

I proceeded slowly, "I have lost four", putting up four fingers, "horses, mule, pony, horse, mare. Have you seen them?"

I looked around at the squaws and the children. They were all smiling and their small black eyes were glinting amusement, and I thought, hoped maybe, friendliness.

161

The braves sat silent a second or two longer. Then one of them grunted. "Uh, uh." This seemed to be the cue for the others to talk. Then partly by words but mostly by mimicry at which I think they are very clever, they gave me to understand that the four horses had gone through three days ago to "Big Gully".

I asked. "How far to Big Gully?"

They told me about sixty miles. Holding all ten fingers up and shutting them six times. I mistrusted those Indians. I thought they know more English than they pretended too.[2]

As I have said, there were at that time no fences and quite a number of horses had been lost. Some were saying the Indians were stealing them. I rode on towards the Gully, that is East, for about two miles and dismounted and settled to sleep for the night - cowboy fashion with my head on the saddle. However, sleep was impossible. The mosquitoes by the million were chewing me up. I waited for daylight when I got up and rode back through the Indian camp, looking carefully at all the horses and satisfied myself that not our four, nor any one of them, was amongst the Indians horses. I headed home determined to borrow a team and follow the trail next day to the 'Big Gully'.

---

[2] Editor's note: Since it was highly unlikely that the native people of that time would have understood the meaning of an English 'mile', it is more probable that the Indians were signifying how many horses they had seen going by three days ago.

Part 3   Breaking Ground

It was two days later before we were ready to start out.
This time Jack Fleming and the two boys came with me. Jack
had borrowed Old Tupper's big floundering team, each as balky
as only a horse knows how to be balky. We took a good supply
of eats with us. Jack brought his rifle and a quantity of
homemade shells, but in the busy-ness of getting ready, I forgot
mine. I took along a fifty-pound sack of mouldy rolled oats,
which I had bought for dog feed, since I now owned a dog,
faithful old 'Ruff'.

By noon of the second day, we only got a few miles
East of Lloydminster. At least one, the other or both of those
ill-conditioned brutes was baulking all the time, so I suggested
to Jack that we return to Lloydminster and try to hire a fast team
at the livery barn. We neither of us had any money, but when
we arrived back in Lloydminster, I made a deal with young
Palling, at the livery barn, to borrow a good, quick team, and
during the summer I would deliver to him at Lloydminster, three
loads of good prairie hay. He seemed very glad to make this
deal, and he lent us a team of mules. We set out. That team was
quick. This time my dog did not follow us from Lloydminster
for some reason, but stayed with Tupper's team, why, I don't
know.

By sundown, we had again picked up the trail or the
horses, still apparently traveling east. What climbing those
horses had done! Two of us would wait in the wagon while the
other two would climb the steep banks and slopes. By the end
of the third day (fifth since we left home), we came to a
dead-end where the Gully enters at the Saskatchewan River.
Then we traced the horses along the banks of the Gully for
miles, taking us three days, we had so much climbing to do.

Now, we were out of food, or practically so. We
subsisted the next day on a couple of bush partridge shot with
our last two shells and eight wild duck eggs we found in a nest.
These we ate raw with pepper and salt from our grub box. With
the addition of a little vinegar, which we did not have, raw eggs
with pepper and salt and a dash of vinegar are called "Prairie
Oysters", Jack told me. Then perforce, we had to make porridge
for ourselves from the mouldy rolled oats. That was the most
unpalatable fare that I, or any one of the four of us, had ever
lived on. We were starving, but the idea of another meal of that
porridge nauseated us. In the afternoon of the seventh day since
leaving Lloydminster with the mules, we were all sick and
weary with disappointment, fatigue, and hunger, and we sat
debating whether we should turn back and go home and give up
the search, or continue. We were just about to turn round to go
home when there, standing looking at us, was the most perfect
specimen of young buck I have ever seen. Jack reached
involuntarily for the rifle, and then drew back his hand. Never
have I seen such chagrin, such despair and disappointment on a
man s face. It convulsed with pain for a moment and I thought
the boys would weep, but they were two very manly lads. No
one spoke and the buck stood, beautiful and graceful, eyeing us
up and down.

I exclaimed. "Watch me catch him", and jumped out
of the wagon. I knew, of course, I would never do it, but he
leaped into the bush and I ran after him, followed by guffaws
and peals of laughter from Jack and the two boys. I thought I
would give them a real laugh as I chased him. I followed him
right through the heavy bush into a clearing and there, not two
hundred yards away, were about sixty horses, among them the
four we were looking for, all as fat as moles. I rushed back and
told Jack and the boys, and he and the younger one came back
with me. I called Nellie and Frank and they came running to

164

me, Jack's pair followed them. We soon had them tied to the wagon and started for home.

Now all sixty or more of those horses were most probably lost by Barr Colonists but it never occurred to us to rescue some of them, as many as we could, and advertise them, which is what we should have done. No doubt, the owners would only have been too glad to recompense us for any expense we would have had in doing so. I often since have wondered what happened to them. The rightful owners, no doubt, may have found some of them.

Our delight at finding ours was so great, that when we made some of the mouldy porridge for supper, it did not seem quite so distasteful.

On the way home next day, we all enjoyed the scenery. The cherries and Saskatoons and the red-barked dogwood covered with their bursting, creamy flowers were all in bloom. In fact, the whole underbrush seemed to be a riot of blossoms. The banks of the river were heavily clothed with spruce, silver birch, some pine and Tamarac, It was beautiful, but we did not dwell too much on the beauty of the scenery. Our belts were tightened to the very last notch. It was four very hungry, very delighted, and very thankful individuals that reached Lloydminster next day. Never did food taste better to us who had lived on mouldy porridge all those days.

However, the Big Gully is beautiful in both spring and fall. In spring with a wild undisciplined beauty of flowers and trees, in fall with the riotous gold or the shimmering quivering aspens and poplars, interspersed with the brilliant, clamouring reds, magentas and roses of the cherry and wild rose. At all times the joyous and gay bird life, is everywhere: a perfect

165

paradise for all who find rapture in the untrodden wilds; and always there is that rare, resinous, aromatic scent of "The Pathless Woods".

Part 4   Homesteading Marches On

CHAPTER 10

Homesteading marches on

During that first winter on the "Hestite", Harry and I had made several trips to Hewitt's Landing to freight lumber, which had been rafted down the Saskatchewan River from Walter's Mill, to the lumberyard in Lloydminster. Those were always trips of hardship. Often we slept in a snow bank at night, as there seemed to be few homes on the trail. Besides we still had the Old Country feeling of timidity about trespassing deeply embedded in our bones, and "The Englishman's home is his castle". So very often we detoured round a well-lighted shack rather then risk being unwelcome if we asked for shelter. The frozen, slippery boards of lumber, too, were hard to handle, and often when coming up the bank of the river, which was here shelved in natural terraces, when the sleighs tilted the entire icy load would slip, board by board, back down to the shelf below. Then we would leave the team on the upper shelf, walk down, and carry those sodden icy boards on our backs, up the incline and reload them, often to meet the same harrowing experience at the next ledge. That really was asses' work, but we got twenty-five dollars per person per trip.

Soon after Rose and Billie's wedding, Harry and I again set out for Hewitt's Landing, a distance of sixty miles, round trip. The weather was still mild when we left home, though a slight snow had fallen which made sleighing possible. When we reached Lloydminster, we got a chance to go to Battleford for provisions for Hall's Store. We embraced this opportunity to earn a few extra dollars. The trip took two weeks and when we arrived back in Lloydminster, the weather had become very much colder. However, we bought two good,

heavy horse blankets, filled our grub box anew, and after having
rested the team, we set out for Hewitt's Landing. We arrived
that same night, and early the next morning got our sleigh load
of lumber and started out for Lloydminster in a temperature of
forty degrees below zero. We had no difficulty in climbing the
bank, much to our surprise and delight. Nearing nightfall, we
saw a dim light shining from the window of a log shack, so we
pulled in. We had more knowledge of the Canadian ways of
hospitality to wayfarers.

They were an English couple with two small children,
who occupied the shack, and I have never seen such dire poverty
in other than an Indian home. There was a dirt floor and most of
the furniture was made from logs from the surrounding bush.
Even the table leaf was made from split logs. We asked if we
might sleep on the floor for the night and in the voice of a
cultured Englishman, he told us we were welcome. So we
unhitched the team, tied them up in the bush, fed them, put their
blankets on and went back to the shack. We were both very
hungry, but we waited till the lady began to get supper before
making any attempt to get ours. Imagine our astonishment when
she put on the table just some terrible looking bannock, and four
broken cups filled with melted snow.

Never shall I forget the look of starved longing on the
faces of all four of them when we began to fry our home cured
bacon, and thaw out our food. Harry whispered to me, "Let's
give them some". So we shared all our food with them, and how
ravenously they ate it. After supper, we sat and talked with
them. Harry asked, "Did you come out with the colonists?"

"Yes," he said, "to my sorrow".

"We have found it pretty tough, too." We told him.

168

"Tough?" He said. "It's hell."

We smiled at this. It must have been nearly fifty below at the time.

"Why did you come away up here to homestead?" We asked him.

"Why? Why, indeed?" he said bitterly. "I didn't know--had no idea of what it would be like. I filed on board ship, from that map Barr had. It was just a red spot on the map, but Barr assured me it was good farming land, and I took his word for it. The damned place is nothing but rock and fenland. So here, I am; stuck in the mud, and I can't go out to work because my wife won't be left alone; she's scared of the Indians. So I'm just tied hand and foot, as it were."

His wife then spoke for the first time. "Oh, Hector," she said beseechingly. "Why won't you let me write home? I know they would send us the money, at once, to go back. These boys could post my letter in Lloydminster, I'm sure." and from her voice I would have judged her to be a cultured English lady.

"Sure we will." We assured her.

Then Hector spoke impatiently. "What have I to go back to? I gave up my job in the bank and you know I'd never get it back. Besides, your people would hold it against me for the rest of my life. I'd never hear the end of it. You know that."

Then he turned to us and said, "No, I'll get my patent in another year and then I'll get a mortgage on my homestead and clear out."

169

Part 4   Homesteading Marches On

"Will you go back to England?" We asked him.

"No. I'll go to either Winnipeg or Edmonton. I feel sure I can get a job in a city."

He then spoke to his wife very affectionately. "Don't you think you'd better get to bed my dear?" and immediately turned out the lamp, and the three of us sat by the stove and talked in the darkness. After a minute or two, he called over to her, "All right?"

"Yes" Only a monosyllable.

He then lit the lamp again, and we talked for some minutes longer until we said we had to make an early start in the morning, and spread our blankets and rolled in. He then again turned out the light and went to bed.

Next morning he would accept no money for our night's shelter, so we left all our remaining food with them and started out. It was very cold but the sleighing was good and we had soon left the shack behind. We traveled along in silence for some time and then Harry burst out, "What in hell does he expect his family to live on for the next year?"

"I was just thinking the same thing." I told him.

"I think we had better report the case to the police when we get to Lloydminster." He said then.

"Or to Reverend Lloyd." I suggested.

So when we reached Lloydminster, after unloading the lumber and putting the team in the barn we went to the North

West Mounted Police barracks and asked the constable there, "Do you know a family living about ten miles north on the trail to Hewitt's Landing?"

"Yah," he said. "Hector Cosgrave. What of them?"

"They are in a desperate plight there. They're starving." And we went on to tell him what we had seen.

"Gee whiz, that's bad. They seemed to be really well off, when they first came in. I'll have to run out there in the morning, I guess. I'll have a talk with Mr. Lloyd this evening. We'll have to get them in here. Perhaps we can get him a job in the town." He told us.

"Don't split on us. We want to keep out of this." we told him.

"No, no, that's fine. I'll just pretend I'm on the trail of duty, which I am." He laughed.

We came away feeling much better about that woman and the children.

Early the following spring, Bill asked me one Saturday evening, "Are you coming fishing tomorrow, Boy?"

"Sure," I told him. "Where to?"

"The Vermilion. Jack Smith says the river is full at this time of year."

"Yes," said Molly. "Muriel was saying yesterday that she and Hazel got two pails full last Thursday - just the two of them."

"Two pails full!" I scoffed. "How big were the pails?"

"Yes, I can quite believe it. They say there's lots of fish down there." Bill confirmed.

"Then let's go by all means."

So, on the Sunday morning we set out; Molly, Bill and I, taking the team and wagon, as the Vermilion was about four miles from our house.

"We'd better take this bucket to hold them." Suggested Molly.

"We'll never get the full of that. This dish will be big enough." I told her.

"Oh, I think I'll take the bucket, and don't you think we'd better take a bite along with us?"

"I should say so, if we are going to catch that bucket full." Said Bill, laughing.

When we were ready to start, Bill said, "I think we'd better throw in a couple of rakes. Jack says the trail's pretty rough in places."

"Wouldn't hayforks be better?" I asked him.

172

"I guess they would if we have to fill up holes." He said, as he went to get them. When we reached the river, we tied the team a little distance from it and walked, through the thick bush that fringed its shores, to the water's edge. There we stood in amazement! The stream looked like a leaping, moving thing of life! Fish! Fish by the million, swimming madly, resolutely, deliriously up the river to some instinctive encounter with survival.

"Jiminy Jeepers!" Exclaimed Bill. "I've never seen so many fish in my life."

"I've often dreamed of finding lots of fish in a river, but this beats anything I've ever hoped to see." I said.

"What shall we do?" asked Molly, "We can't use our tackle in this. They'll just drag it away with them."

"Let's get the forks." I said, starting off on the run.

When I returned with them, Bill and I stood just at the edge of the water and, with the forks, flipped those fish out by threes and fours, onto the bank, which was soon strewn with them. Molly asked us, "How many more do you want? We must have a wagon box full now. What are we going to do with them all?"

We halted then and looked at the bank. We could scarcely believe our eyes. It seemed incredible that we had forked so many out in such a short space of time. We carried them to the wagon box in buckets full, and got the wagon box at least half-full. Next day we put the jackfish in brine and afterwards dried and smoked them, and they surely made

173

delicious eating while they lasted. The suckers we fed to the pigs and chickens.

This may read like a "Fish Story" but that it is true any resident of that part of the Vermilion Valley will testify. For, even to this day, this phenomenon occurs each spring at the spawning seasons.

L ater in the spring, just as we were ready to sit down to dinner one day, my dog, Ruff, came yelping to the door and banged into it as if in terrible fear. We all rushed to look out just in time to see a huge, black bear charge through the yard, closely followed by two horsemen, one of whom was popping at it with a revolver. The other was armed with a twenty-two rifle. We rushed outdoors but both fugitive and horsemen were over the ridge and hidden by the bush.

"Well, I'll be darned." said Bill. "The wild and woolly West!"

"Did you know the horsemen?" Dad asked.

"The one with the revolver was Guildemeister." Molly said.

"And the other was that new man down on 16 (section 16 of the township) I believe." Bill said, "His name is Smith, I think."

"That's right", said Molly. "Muriel was speaking of him yesterday. He goes to their house quite often."

174

Part 4   Homesteading Marches On

"Another new homesteader! They do keep coming, don't they?" I said.

"You're right boy," said Bill. "Here they are, right on the doorstep." and at that moment the two horsemen entered.

"You're just in time." Molly told them.

"We were hoping we would be", Guildemeister laughed. He then introduced David Smith, who seemed a little abashed by our easy informality.

"Well let us sit down", said Dad. "We mustn't keep the damask waiting."

So we all got seated round the dinner table and began to eat.

"Where did you run across the bear?" I asked them.

"Just North of Lloyd," Guildemeister told me. "We've been chasing him since nine o'clock this morning."

"And a merry chase he's given us." Smith said. "I only hope he's feeling at least half as tired as I am. At least." he added.

"Has he got away on you?" Dad asked.

"We hope not," said Guildemeister. "He went into that thick bluff on the Hudson's Bay section, just north of the creek. He must be just about played out, so we thought we'd come back here and beg a bit of dinner and a cup of English tea, and rest our horses awhile before we resume the chase."

Part 4   Homesteading Marches On

"Did you feed your horses?" Dad asked him.

"No. We just tied them to a tree outside."

Bill said, "I'll put them in the barn and give them some hay." and he went out.

"Isn't the bear dangerous?" asked Molly.

"He would be if he weren't so scared." laughed Guildemeister.

Both he and Smith seemed really tired. They sat and talked for about an hour, and then Guildemeister said, "How about it, David? Shall we take up the chase again?"

"Sure thing," Smith agreed. "It's a habit with me now.", but I thought he didn't seem too keen on it. He looked very tired.

"Do you think you'll find him?" asked Dad.

"Oh, I think he'll be resting in the bush, so let's get before he gets rested too much." Guildemeister told him.

So the chase was on once more: they two on horse back and I went along on foot armed with my trusty forty-four.

When we reached the bluff where the bear had disappeared, the two horsemen went to the West of it and began hollering and shouting, while I waited on the East of it some little distance away. Soon they warned, "Look out, Fred, he's coming," and at the same instant the enraged animal rushed out, his eyes glinting yellow, with either fear or anger, and charged

176

right for me. I dropped on one knee to take aim, and immediately the two horsemen emerged from the bush behind him. I dared not shoot then for they were directly in line, so I stood up wondering if I should run for it. I think the bear then saw me for the first time, for he reared straight up on his hind legs and I fired straight into him, but instead of his dropping down dead, as I had thought he would, he rushed back into the bush. The two horsemen rushed round to the West again and again began hollering and shouting, as before the bear rushed out, but when he saw me, he turned to go back. I fired and saw him stumble and waver so I knew I had hit him, but he kept on going. I called to the others, "Look out. I've hit him. He's going back into the bush."

They came round from the West then and we followed where the bear had gone and soon saw blood on the snow that still lingered among the trees. We soon found him. He lay as if he were dead. I said, "I'd better put another bullet in him to make sure."

We then went home to get Nellie and Frank, and a buckboard to haul him home, but when we came back, we could not get the horses to go near him. He smelled just like a polecat. After a lot of difficulty, we got the carcass on the board and got him home. Dad, Molly and Bill came out to look at him.

"Who'll get the brush?" Dad, an old English huntsman, asked laughingly.

"The brush?" queried Guildemeister.

"Yes, in England when hunting the fox the first lady in after the kill gets the 'brush' - the tail." Dad explained.

177

"It won't matter much who gets that brush." Bill joked.

"Who owns him now?" Dad asked.

"Fred shot him." said Guildemeister.

"But you brought him from Lloydminster." I told him.

"Let's flip, and whoever wins shall choose first." Guildemeister suggested.

"What are you choosing about?" asked Molly. "He's no good now."

Guildemeister said. "The meat's good. Bear steaks are considered a rare delicacy."

"Pooh!" said Molly, holding her nose. "There's nothing delicate about that."

"Then you'd better take the meat." I offered.

"I don't want it. What would I do with all that meat? You'd better keep it." He said generously.

So Gil, as we spoke of him, took the pelt and we each thought the other had got the better of the deal.

"You'd better come over on Sunday and have a feed of bear steaks." Dad called after them as they rode out of the yard.

178

Part 4   Homesteading Marches On

The next day the odour had evaporated, or abated, or whatever odour of wild animals does. So Bill and I skinned the beast and found that the pelt was so mangy and riddled with revolver pellets as to be valueless.

On the Sunday, Gil and Smith arrived for the 'feed', and when they entered the kitchen; they both sniffed anticipating the delicious, tangy odour of cooking game that permeated the whole house. However, when it came to eating the steaks, they were so tough that not one of us could get either a knife or fork into them. Never did anything in the way of meat so defy all the arts of culinary skill to tenderize it. We tried boiling, stewing, roasting but all to no avail. We threw it out into the yard where it lay for a few days untouched. No domestic animal would go near it. David Smith rode into the yard on the following Wednesday. "What are you going to do with the 'Rare Delicacy'?" he asked, when he saw it.

"Nothing seems to appreciate," we told him.

"Let's bury it." He suggested.

So we dug a hole and dumped it all in and at the end of the obsequies, Smith, a Scotsman, quoted gravely. "Woe worth the chase, woe worth the day."

Here ended the story of the first and only bear we ever shot.

Guildemeister! I never heard him called by his given name, Walter. He was always either Mr. Guildemeister or Gil. He came in from the States about three years after the arrival of the first Barr Colonists, and brought with him a large herd or Hereford cattle. He never homesteaded

179

but leased a section of land for grazing. However, his herds
roamed over all the surrounding open country and were almost
as fat as moles. He always seemed to have lots of money, and if
ever a man was gifted with the Midas touch, he was. He was
always in the midst of a deal either of trading or selling and
while, he invariably got the best or the bargain he had the happy
knack of seeming to have conferred a favour on the other party.

He came to Dad one day and said, "You know, Mr.
Marfleet, you and the boys could easily handle a thousand head
of cattle here. Don't you think so?"

"I suppose we could if we worked together." Dad
replied.

"Well, if you ever think it is worth trying, I'll give you
a thousand head, or any number you wish, on half shares. Think
it over."

Dad discussed the offer with us boys, but we were all
so very scared of involvement in indebtedness of any kind that
we refused the offer. In later years, we realized what a godsend
the acceptance of such an offer would have meant to us, but we
were too green to realize it at the time.

Yes, we surely had our moments!

He sold out after having been among us for about
seven years and departed, having made more money during
those few years than most of us have made in a lifetime of hard
work. The marks of his trail, back and forth to our house, the
old Guildemeister trail, could still be seen years after he was
gone.

Part 4   Homesteading Marches On

I have mentioned that I came on a construction train from Saskatoon to where Kitscoty now stands. The Great Northern Railway, now known as the Canadian National Railway, was indeed materializing. The train carrying passengers and mail usually ran three times a week between Saskatoon and Fort Saskatchewan, where a bridge spanning the Saskatchewan River was in course of construction, and at this time the West-bound train stopped on reaching the South end of this bridge. Then passengers got off and walked across to the North side, the mail was carried across by the Postal clerk, and all entrained again for Edmonton. Trains did not proceed across the bridge until a year later.

With the advent of the railway, we thought our pioneering days were over and done with. Soon the town of Kitscoty came into being--just twelve miles to the South of us. A mere stones throw!

New settlers and land seekers kept pouring into the district, and invariably they were directed to our home, where, they were told, they would be sure of a good meal and accommodation. By this time, we had abundant milk, butter, eggs, our own home cured bacon, and in winter fresh meat and fish. Sometimes these new comers paid for this service, but often it was gratis. Then too, they would enquire about getting their mail, and when we told them it was brought from Lloydminster, they would ask us to get theirs and hold it for them until they were settled, and we were glad to oblige them. However, this mail soon reached such proportions, and demanded so much more time, and responsibility that we decided to let each settler get his own. When the news of our decision spread through the district, a petition, signed by every resident, was brought to Dad begging him to apply for a Post Office to be located at our house as being most central and most

181

easily accessible to them all. After due consideration, Dad
decided to accede to their request.

Homesteading Marches On

Chapter 11

Marwayne

W hen Fan and Gilbert arrived back at his home in Tunbridge Wells, purportedly to be married they had found a cousin of Gilbert's entrenched in the Nicholson home as housekeeper. There arose some disagreement between them concerning the tenability of this housekeeper cousin and Fan's status in the future Nicholson ménage, so Fan came back to Canada, unwed. Though Gilbert came out very soon after her and tried to restore their former betrothal, Fan would have none of it unless on her own terms. He returned to his home in England, where he is now a very old man, still a bachelor, and completely blind.

I was working in North Battleford at the time, which I have always regretted, as I believe that if I had been on the spot when Gilbert came back to Edmonton, I could have affected at least an amicable understanding. That might have lead in time to a complete reconciliation, as I loved them both very dearly, and I know they were at that time, very warmly attached to me. We were all sorely disappointed as well as greatly distressed at this turn of events. However, Fan's happiness was at stake and we all recognized that she was the one to make the decision.

Fan was, at that time, housekeeping for four young bachelors, including Billie Griesbach, who later became Brigadier General Griesbach, and a Federal parliament Senator but was then just starting a Law practice in Edmonton.

183

"Say, Billie, how are you for thinking up names?" Fan asked.

"Great. Boy or girl?

"It's not a child, Billie."

"That sets my mind at ease. A dog then? What's the breed?"

"I'm not getting a dog, silly. Dad has applied for a Post office and the Department at Ottawa has approved his application, and asked him to submit names relative to the origin of the settlers in the district."

"Why is your family thus favoured?" asked Billie

"We were the first settlers in there, and almost from the first summer new settlers coming into the district have come to our house to enquire about land and locating and—"

"Ah. You have sisters, I understand." Billie said with a laugh.

"That's got nothing to do with it. I think it's because we can always give them a good meal and usually Dad can advise them about vacant land."

"I see, and the Post office?"

"Well, when any of the boys goes into Lloydminster, he always brings out the mail for all the settlers in the district, and they come to our house for it; and when a neighbour goes to town he also brings everybody's mail and leaves it at our house.

184

So it's just a kind of assumed by the residents that we'll look after their mail, and it really takes a lot of time and care, so we might just as well get a Post Office if we can."

"Where did most of the residents hail from?"

"From the British Isles; they're nearly all English and
_"

"Gee whiz! All English! What a –"

"Yes? 'What a 'what'? What's the matter with the English?"

"Oh, I don't know." he said, laughing. "They've all so much green in the eye."

"Helpful ass!" Both laughing. "Why can't you be serious?"

"I am serious, Fan. Terribly serious. Let's see now, an English name. Why are they all English, by the way?"

"Have you ever heard of the Barr Colonists?"

"No. What did they do, sack Rome?"

"Oh, all right", and Fan flung out of the room.

Later that evening, Billie came to her looking quite contrite.

"Have you thought up a name yet, Fan?"

"No."

185

"Well, I've been thinking."

"Oh, please don't. The strain might be too great. Water on the brain, you know."

"No, no, not at all, I'm quite a brainy fellow, eat lots of fish. Eh, what? As you British say."

"You haven't got what it takes."

"Yes I have. I think. I'd make a very good Englishman."

"Don't flatter yourself."

"Anyway, Fan, about this name. You were the first settlers in the district you tell me."

"Yes."

"Then the post office should be named either after your name or the place you came from. Where do you say your farm was?"

"At Wainfleet, St. Mary in Lincolnshire."

"We'll write that down. Wainfleet, Mary, Lincoln, Marfleet, Wainfleet, Marfleet," then singing, "Oh, I am a pirate bold and I sail – "

"Say, are you going batty?"

186

"No, no, I'm just going to scuttle those two fleets and what's left?

"Wain? Mar, Mary –"

"We'll scuttle Mary too. Then we have Wain Lin—not too bad. Wain Coln – putrid. Wain Mar? Mar lin? That's fair, Marcoln? No."

"Oh, I don't know. I rather like both of those. Marlin? Marcoln? I think either one would sound nice.
"

"What about Marwain?"

"Oh, I like that. Marwain? I like that best of all."

"Yes, I think I like it best, too."

"But we'll spell it M-A-R-W-A-Y-N-E. It looks more aristocratic spelled that way. Don't you think so, Billie?" Fan said.

"Oh, you English and your aristocracy!"

And so it was that Billie Griesbach, later General Griesbach of World War I fame known throughout Canada helped Fan choose a name for the impending Post Office.

The Post Office Department at Ottawa accepted the name 'Marwayne' and it still endures.

Therefore, the Marwayne Post Office came into being and gave the name Marwayne to the surrounding district. Dad was appointed Postmaster at a salary

187

of twenty-five dollars per annum. As yet, there was no town of Kitscoty, so the mail had to be hauled to and from Islay, a distance of fourteen miles. I applied for and got the contract for hauling mail at a salary of one hundred and twenty dollars per year, and that was considered a princely income in those early days. Besides, I could augment it to some small extent by purchasing and carrying home merchandise for patrons who would give me their lists. Usually they waited for me as I passed their house on my way to Islay.

"Say, Fred, would you bring me these few things?"

'Few' was right: tea, sugar, salt and coal oil, with very few variations.

"Sure, Mrs. B — just .."

"Oh, and Jack wants a plug of baccy and two boxes of snoose."

"Just a minute. I'll write that down. A plug of baccy and two boxes of snoose and coal oil did you say?"

"No, no. What in the name of all that's wonderful, would he, a bachelor, want with coal oil? Just the baccy, and snoose for Jack."

"Is that all, Mrs. B--?"

"No. Mrs. S—said for you to call and get her list. She said she hadn't got it ready, but I guess she didn't want me to see it. They are that secret she's afraid I'll find out something about them. Not that I'd ever want to bother my head about them." And then, whispering, "She says she wrote home to her

188

people last week for money. She says they are awful rich in Scotland." Now, dropping into a lower whisper, "Did you see a letter from her last week?"

"I don't know, Mrs. B--I really must be -"

"Ah, now, aren't you the mealy mouthed one. Pete wants a pad, envelopes, and stamps. He must be writin' to that girl again. Now would you have noticed any letters in his mail from her?"

"No. Giddap there"

"Don't forgit Jack's baccy and snoose. He's chewing the ashes out of his pipe till he gits some, and his breath smells like a back house."

"Well, keep away from him and—"

"Ask Joe to charge all that up." I was on my way.

I made no charge for carrying this merchandise, but sometimes, if the list were long and I had a large, and varied quantity to purchase and haul home, a generously disposed "Patron" would give me a quarter or even fifty cents. One dear old soul gave me ten cents once. It was funny the way she gave it to me. She had it in her fist closed tight and she took hold of my hand, put the dime in it, shut my fingers tight over it, as if she were ashamed to let me see it, and said, "Taint much, Fred, but it will buy a plug. I know you are not supposed to do all this for free." and winked at me. Oh, people were poor then. They just couldn't afford to be generous.

During the following winter, I certainly made some arduous trips. In winter, I used a home-made cutter, built from planks, remnants of the lumber, which we had used for building the scow. There was neither regular road nor beaten path to Islay, and often I had to break the trail all the way. Many times the horses got into drifts so deep that they could not extricate themselves. Then, I would get out and dig the horses out which meant shovelling away what seemed like tons of snow. Then I would pull the cutter, which, of course, would slide over the snow quite easily, over the crest of the drift and into a place where the horses could get a foothold. Usually in such instances, the harness would be broken, so I would have to repair it, which meant tying it together with binder twine. By this time, I would be in a "muck sweat" and soon after I got started up again, I would be shivering and my teeth would be chattering as if I had an ague. Such misadventures did not occur too often, fortunately, but when they did, I assure you they were real hardships. I always earned my two dollars on those occasions.

Another and more pleasant way whereby I could supplement my salary was by carrying passengers to and from Islay. For this service, I made a definite charge of fifty cents per passenger, per-trip. The capacity limit of my vehicle for passengers was two, but if there were three and one was a good-looking girl, I could always make room for her on my knee. The fact that she was good looking lent a little interest to, and tended to alleviate the discomfort of nursing her all the way home. However this, regrettably, did not occur very often.

A very frequent passenger was a Miss Gilchrist, who was then teaching at Stretton School, about four miles Southwest of Marwayne. All during the term, she went each week-end to visit her brother who was farming just outside Islay. On these trips, she always wore her nightgown under her dress. Long skirts in those days I would have you know. How do I know she wore her nightgown under her dress? Why of course, she told me so.

It happened in this way:

We were traveling along one bright, frosty morning towards the end of February, enjoying the good sleighing, the good weather for that time of the year, and the clear, musical, reverberant tinkling of the bells, that I always kept on the harness in the winter, when suddenly a rabbit, dressed in his winter coat of white, hopped out of the bush right into the path of the team. Frank reared up in fright and then jumped sideways, thereby breaking his bellyband.

"Darned son-of-a-bitch" I blurted out as I got out of the cutter to mend the harness.

"Who's the 'son-of-a-bitch'?" Miss Gilchrist asked as she, too, began to get out. "I think I'll stretch my legs a bit."

"There's a good place behind that bush." I told her.

"Smarty - guess again!" However, she went!

When she came back and was about to get into the cutter, there was a sudden, screeching tear!

"Gee whiz!" she said, "I've torn the hem almost completely off my nightgown, and it was a brand new one, too." She added ruefully.

191

"I'm sorry." I said, but I was laughing.

"Yes, you look heart broken."

"Well, I'll cry with you if you like."

She was almost weeping as she stood at the side of the cutter holding up the torn hem of her nightgown, and thereby catching her skirts up in front.

"I think you'd, better tear it right off." I said. "You can't hold it up like that in Islay, or the people will be thinking I've been a little rough with you."

She stooped down, tore it right off and folded it up.

"Why did you wear your nightgown under your dress?" I asked her. "That isn't usual. Is it?"

"No, I guess not, but at my brother's I sleep on a camp bed in the kitchen. They have three young children and there's just not any privacy, so I go prepared to tumble into bed as soon as I take my dress off."

"I see, I see, said the blind man, and he couldn't see at all."

"Oh, shut up."

It was some short time after the nightgown episode that I really got in wrong with Mrs. Bonnet. There was still quite a lot of snow on the prairie, but the roads were soft, slushy, and miry in the early spring thaw. I decided after some thought to take the cutter on my trip to Islay and try a new route through the bush. Mrs. B. was on the lookout for me and waved when she saw me going around her place and not on the usual trail. I pulled up as near as I could to her yard, which was a regular bog.

"Do you think you'll make it?" she called to me.

"Oh, I think so. If I can keep on the prairie." I told her.

"Well, you might. There's just that ravine on Huntley's place, but if you'll keep to the North—"

"Were you wanting something from town?" I cut her short, as I wanted to get going.

"Yes, I'm right out of sugar. I loaned Bob half of what I had two weeks ago, and I wish now I hadn't. I don't suppose I'll ever—"

"How much sugar did you say you –?"

"Oh, it must have been three pounds, but he'll never -"

"I mean how much do you want me to bring you?"

"Oh, bring me a twenty pound sack; I always use the sack for a dish cloth. Ask Joe to charge it. We'll pay him in the fall if ..."

"Oh, he'll charge it, all right. He's very good, I don't-"

"Good, my parson's nose! Don't talk to me about that old bugger bein' good. He's mintin' money, so he is; an' Jack wants a plug an' two boxes of snooze, an' he told me to ask you to ask Joe to charge it up, too."

"Is that all?" I asked as I finished writing the list.

"Yaa, Oh, maybe you'd better bring me a pound of tea. Unless I miss my guess you won't be able to make it next week."

I wrote it down, started up, and was well on my way when I heard her, calling, calling after me. I turned round and went back.

"Bring Dick a sweat pad." She called to me, with her two hands forming a megaphone round her mouth.

It was quite a bit later than usual when I arrived in Islay. I went at once to the livery barn but there was no one around, so I put my team in and fed them myself. I thought Mike was over at his home, and that I would see him when I went back for the horses. Then I went to get the mail. Joe Finnegan, besides being Postmaster, owned the only grocery in the town, so I always got my orders filled when I got the mail. There was no one in the store. I went outside and looked around. Not a soul was on the street except some children playing in a pool of water away at the other end of the town. I hung around for a while but no one showed up. I went to the hardware next, - there was no one there either. Then I tried the blacksmith's shop--the same thing. 'What the Sam Hill has happened to all the people?' I thought. I then made my way through the mud and slush of the street to within hailing distance of the children, who were all having one heck of a time, playing in the water, and really getting most delightfully dirty and soaked through.

"Where's Finnegan?" I called to them.

"Dunno, dunno" in a chorus.

Then I saw Mike's two children standing up to their knees in the muddy slough.

"Where's your Dad?"

"He's in the beer parlour." The older one told me. "Shorty's givin' everybody beer for free today. He's opening the new hotel."

So that was it.

I went to the beer parlour. It was so full I could scarcely push my way inside. "Here have a drink, Fred." Shorty, the hotel proprietor, said to me as soon as he saw me. I took the drink and as soon as I finished it, Shorty refilled my glass. I drank that also, but refused to drink any more as it was getting late. I made my way through the crowd to Finnegan, who was sitting with his arm round some woman and seemed to be quite plastered,

"Say, Joe, what about the mail?" I asked him.

"Aw, to hell with the mail." He spat. "Here have a drink, Fred."

"No," I told him. "I've had enough."

"Aw, you never have enough, you never have enough. Here, here tomorrow we die. Tomorrow we die." raising his glass.

195

"That's right, that's right—so let us be merry. Here's to Dougherty - the best Irishman that ever left the auld sod."

"Ya, ya. Ireland's loss is Islay's gain, Ha, ha!" from the crowd.

"But you're not Irish, are you Shorty?"

"No. I was born and brought up in Aberdeen." He told them.

All this time I had been trying to get Finnegan listen to me. "I must get the mail, Joe, and some groceries." I told him.

"A' right. A' right. Go to hell and get them yourself."

I went back to the store. Everything had been left wide open. The till was unlocked, with all the money in it. I made up the mail, got the groceries, ate some crackers and cheese, went to the hardware, got the sweat pads, and went back to the hotel to get Finnegan to sign my time sheet. With his arm still round the lady, who kept jiggling up and down on his knee, he made some hieroglyphic, doodling scrawl across the sheet, but that was the best I could get from him. So I went to the livery barn and got out my team and drove out of the town, followed by the strains of "Waltz me around again, Willie." from the hotel, and the screaming mirthful shouts of the children.

I don't know which had the worst hangover, the adults from the free beer, or the children from their wet, muddy, soaked clothes. One thing I'm certain of, everyone in Islay that day, had one whale of a time!

196

I followed, as nearly as I could, the same route home. When I reached the Bonnet's farm, she came to the fence to meet me. I handed her the sweat pad and other small commodities across the fence and then went to reach for the sugar. The cotton sack lay on the bottom of the cutter gaunt and empty! A sharp stick had stuck through between the planks, and had ripped a hole about four inches long in the bag. When I reached it to her, empty, she snatched it and hit me between the eyes with it. "You dirty son-of-a-bitch." she said, "What kind of a fool are ye? Ye might a knowed. Why didn't ye put it on the pad?" 'Why indeed?' I thought. I was glad the fence was between us or she would have torn my eyes out, I believe. "Get goin', ye dirty bastard or I'll -"

Oh, but she was eloquent!

"I'll report ye! I'll report ye!" she screamed, then suddenly she asked me calmly, "Well, what are ye goin' to do about it? Ye can just pay me for it."

Just then, her husband, a quiet, inoffensive little man, appeared on the scene. "Oh, no, my dear, it was an accident. Fred's not supposed to haul your groceries for you. He only obliges you." He told her.

"I'm awfully sorry, Dick." I said, and taking advantage of this lull in her vehemence, I drove away.

I could understand her anger. The loss of twenty pounds of sugar in those days would be a near calamity to most homesteaders. On my next mail run, I talked Finnegan into giving me a twenty-pound sack of sugar and delivered it to Mrs Bonnet.

Part 4   Homesteading Marches On

A t that time, most of us had our own milk and
butter and our own home-cured bacon. In
addition, as soon as winter set in, each householder butchered a
steer, to provide his family with fresh meat during the winter
months, and always when the warm spring weather came, the
left over beef was cured or corned. Then fish from Cold Lake
was hauled to our doors and sold for four or five cents per
pound, and we bought it by the hundred weight, each family
always purchasing two or three hundred weight, and kept it
frozen throughout the winter months. This same fish is now
very scarce as most of it is flown, commercially, direct from
Cold Lake to Chicago. It sells now in Edmonton at thirty-five
cents per pound when we can get it, which is rarely.

As well, each fall we took wheat to the gristmill in
Lloydminster, and got it ground or milled into flour, cream of
wheat and wheaten flour for breakfast cereal. Rolled oats were
then a luxury to us, and so it was that the usual orders entrusted
to me, on my trips to Islay, were for sugar, salt, tea, coal oil and
tobacco.

That year (September 1, 1905) all that large expanse
of country, then named on the maps of Canada, the North West
Territories, was divided up into the three autonomous provinces
of Alberta, Saskatchewan and Manitoba, and for the first time
we had all the excitement of an election. Bramley-Moore
became our first member of the legislature representing the
electorate of Alexandria. He retained his seat until 1915, when
he was killed in action in World War I. He was, everywhere he
went, a very popular man.

I have said that our good times seemed to start from
that first chivaree for Rose and Billy. It was soon afterward, that
one evening at a "Party" at the Roberts home we began dancing,

198

and from that night all the young people went dancing crazy. It was a welcome outlet, I think, for their craving for amusement and excitement. That evening we all sat around playing games. There was always a program drawn up by the hostess for these parties, and the games varied from "Spilling the fruit basket", through charades to "Old Mrs. McGinty's dead," and "The wee Maloney Man." Aaron sat in a corner playing the fiddle, but no one took much notice of the music or tunes, till he struck up, "The Captain with the Whiskers". Then we all began singing and Hughie, in a moment of exuberance, grabbed a girl and danced around the large kitchen with her. That magic spark touched off the fervour for dancing in all of us. Soon we were all up, each with a partner, and Hughie began to call off. Square dances became the favourites with all of us, and every Friday night, from then on, for years, there was a dance in someone's home.

"You'll not be goin' out tonight?" Mother would ask us pleadingly.

"Oh, but we must, Mother." We would answer her.

"Well, you'll get lost in this blizzard, I'm afraid. Where is it tonight?"

"At Blake's."

"At Blake's? Why that's the other side of Islay; it must be over twenty miles to it?" Dad would say discouragingly.

"Serve you right, if there's no one there when you get there." From Mother, "I hope there isn't. You're just crazy."

Part 4   Homesteading Marches On

Crazy was right; but nothing the elements could devise would daunt us. We would arrive almost frozen to the marrow, when it was too blustery to get out and run, as we always did when it was clear and cold. We always took Frank and Nellie, and the sleighs with the wagon box and by the time we reached our destination we would have picked up five or six other devotees of the terpsichorean arts. Then it was great fun running to keep from freezing, or often just for running.

All the homestead shacks consisted of just a kitchen and bedroom space, which was partitioned off by curtains, or by gunny sacks sewn together to make curtains and papered with the sheets of "The Family Herald", a weekly to which we all subscribed and which we devoured from the title page to the very last line of each advertisement. Everyone loved this paper for both its splendid reading matter and its duality or even tri-ality of purpose. It was our only contact with the outside world. We always danced in the kitchen and as many of these were very small, it took a whole lot of manoeuvring to dance under the stovepipes and not knock them down. However, we usually engineered this 'hazard' quite successfully, but on a few occasions a "mooning" couple would forget and then—woops! --a shower of soot and a cloud burst of smoke! On one occasion, Hughie called out warningly, "Look out there, Mary. Calm down. You're steppin' too high." But, too late. Mary's exuberance had got the best of her and down came the pipes. Then—"Open the door! Open the door!" And we all stood shivering till the soot was cleaned up and the smoke cleared away. Then, 'On with the dance! No sleep till morn!'

The dance always lasted until well past daylight the next day. When they took place in the Islay district, I often took the mail with me, and waited at the home of the dance until Finnegan had the incoming mail ready. In this way, I saved

200

myself a trip, when those whom I had taken to the dance could find other means of getting home.

One day Mother enquired, "Did you dance with Jenny last night?"

"Naw, George got ahead of me."

"Was Tressa there?"

"Yes, but she danced all night with the townies."

"Who did you dance with?" Mother pressed me.

"Oh, Jackie and Mary and Elsie, mostly. I did have a couple with Jenny. She says I'm the best dancer in the crowd."

"She says that to everyone, I bet." Mother laughed.

Then I felt deflated.

Molly spoke up on my behalf. "He is, too, Mother. All the girls like to dance with him. I have heard them say so time and again." Then I was puffed up, and must have looked it because Molly warned. "Now don't go around looking like a bloated ox."

Trust a sister to take it out of a fellow.

"Wasn't that a good one on Jimmy?" Molly asked me after one dance.

"Yeah. That took the biscuit."

"What was that?" Mother enquired.

"Jimmy went yesterday evening to get Tressa, with his team of bulls and wagon box, and just as they were setting out for the dance, Peter drove up with his buggy and driver to take her, and Tressa got out of the wagon box and got in with Peter and came to the dance with him. Jimmy didn't get there till two o'clock this morning."

"Well, I would call that a pretty mean trick", said Mother. "Wasn't Jimmy mad?"

"No, he's too soft. He's as soft as grease," said Molly.

"He told me he was glad for her to ride with Peter, because she had a more comfortable ride." I told her.

"Yes, she did have two or three dances with him after be got thawed out." Molly then said as if that verified the fact that Jimmy was glad.

Hughie, though a rattling good dancer, rarely danced, He seemed to get more enjoyment out of "Calling Off" and directing the rest of us. I have seen him laugh till the tears streamed down his face at the capers some of us cut, and the mix-ups we often got into. He always insisted that everyone dance.

We always had a good time when we went to Gildermeister's ranch. His was the largest kitchen so there was plenty of room, and Gil was always popular with the girls. Indeed, he was popular with everyone. This practice of going to the homes kept up till the school districts were formed. Then there was more room in the schools. Then, also, led by the

202

school marm, as a rule, we became more elegant and fastidious in our style of dancing. This elegance manifested itself more particularly in our manner of asking the lady for a dance. Now, instead of going up to her with bugging eyes and either giving her a backward nod of the head, or thumbing over the shoulder towards the centre of the room, we went forward and bowing elegantly we would ask "May I have the pleasure?" At the end of the dance, we elegantly held out the arm to her and led her back to the seat, whereas formerly at the last note of the music, partners stopped short, and each went to their own side of the room, with never even a "Thank you". I have seen some of the rougher element among us give his lady a slap with his flat hand on her rear as she turned to take her seat. The first time this happened I thought an Irishman, newly arrived in the district, would die of laughter. "God's truth," he gasped between convulsions. "He just gave her a clap on the ass."

Now if the school marm were young and good looking, we all modeled our dancing manners on hers. The rivalry between the young men for her favour was terrific. She invariably married one of the swains at the end of her teaching term. We certainly had some real good times, but though the dances were now more refined, maybe, they never were more enjoyable than were those of the very early days on the homestead.

I certainly loved dancing in those days!

CHAPTER 12

Button, button, who's got the button?

A bout the year 1906, there came to Streamstown, the district adjoining Marwayne on the East, the Reverend Smythe, an Anglican Minister, his wife, and a large family of girls and one boy. The Reverend Smythe, like the rest of us, had come to homestead.

At this time, there was no church, of any creed, nearer than Lloydminster, and the Reverend Smythe, with true apostolic zeal, set out to revivify the district with religion and love of the Creator, which lies, dormant or otherwise, deep in every human heart. Soon after his arrival, he came to visit us at Marwayne and finding that we belonged to the Anglican Church, decided with our full consent and support, to hold services every Sunday at our house. We put up a large announcement in the Post Office, and were agreeably surprised at the pleasure this announcement seemed to give to all the patrons. Almost from the very first service, the house was full every Sunday. People of every denomination came for miles and miles, to worship with us, all joining, reverently in the prayers and the singing of hymns. The service was a great satisfaction to all of us, but, perhaps, more especially to Mother, who had always been deeply religious at heart. I remember how clearly and with what great and reverent enjoyment, both she and Dad always sang the hymns.

The Reverend Smythe held the services faithfully every Sunday. Not even the severest weather kept him away. He was an elderly man and the long drive with his wife and family each Sunday must have taxed his strength often, especially must it have been hard on him in the very cold weather. We ultimately arranged with him that when the temperature fell to fifteen degrees below zero or lower we would not expect him. His faithfulness to what he considered his duty brought solace and comfort to many of us, and we appreciate to this day, his work in reviving religion among us at that time.

Any stranger coming into our yard on a Sunday morning, when the service was being held, would be astounded at the number and variety of vehicles and beasts of burden assembled there. We used some of the planks left from the scow to build benches and seats. We always got these ready after breakfast on Sunday morning. Dad always saw to it that the room was ready. Very often there was an overflow into the kitchen, however many, Dad made sure everyone had a seat. For two years the Reverend Smythe held these simple, but always reverent, services, and many of those who came will still remember the zeal and fervour of those early Sunday morning devotions at the Marfleet home.

Meanwhile the Reverend Exton Lloyd, who had been successful in establishing a church in Lloydminster, was very sensible of the need of religion in the outlying districts. He worked constantly and indefatigably to raise funds for this purpose, meeting with but limited success. He at length went to England, where he met with a zealous lady who gave him five hundred pounds with which to build ten churches in the districts surrounding Lloydminster. On his return, five of these were built west of the town, one of which was at Marwayne, right on Dad's homestead just near our house. This made it very convenient for us to attend the services. We always carried Mother to and from the church on Sundays.

In the spring, of 1906 my brother, Bill, and I worked together in putting in our crops. When the seeding was completed, we decided to go to Edmonton to get work for the summer. At this time there was work to be had fencing the new C.N.R. track, so we got on a fencing crew. After working there for a couple of weeks, we both suffered terribly with itch, and upon investigating, we found we were lousy! We must have got the lice from the bunks in the boxcar where we slept. We quit work at once, got our pay and went into Fort Saskatchewan where we bought new underwear. We then came back to a good, clear creek running into the Saskatchewan River, just near the new bridge now spanning it. This new line from Saskatoon to Edmonton had not as yet been taken over by the railway company, so the only trains running on it were still construction trains. These also carried passengers, but there was no fixed schedule. A train might come through at anytime, perhaps twice a day, perhaps not once a day--but we had forgotten all about trains in our anxiety to rid ourselves of the vermin. We jumped into the creek, swam around until we were satisfied we were thoroughly clean, then we got out and began running around to let the sun dry us, exuberant in our sense of cleanliness and well-being. We were quite a distance from the creek when we noticed the train coming. Then we made a mad rush for our underwear, - but, too late! The train came puffing over the bridge, with the passengers, men and women, at the windows calling and waving to us. What could we do but wave back? Even in our wild and woolly west, that would be an unusual sight--two nude, prairie dryad standing on the brink of a creek, waving and blowing kisses to the passengers of a passing train!

We got into our clothes and felt really comfortable and well. We then walked into Edmonton along the track, and on arriving there, we looked up Harry Alsop, who was working in Edmonton at the time, putting concrete floors in basements of private homes. He was glad to have us work with him. Harry was one of the fairest men, also the hardest, for whom I have ever worked. He was one of those men who do not know what it means to spare oneself at a job. In addition, he could never do anything but a perfect job, as far as he could make it perfect, and he was a clever workman. Both Bill and I found him very exacting, but fair to the last cent. He, at that time, worked on contract, and whether he was in the black or the red, we got our pay. He was a man of sterling qualities and very likeable, but very short-tempered. His temper, however, was always over and forgotten in a moment.

My sister, Annie, and her four children, were then out on the homestead, and Harry was living in a little shack in the town, just at the back of the present Cecil hotel. Bill and I lived with him in this shack, and every evening at the moment of six o'clock, we dropped tools and went to the shack where Harry always fried beefsteak for supper. I have never met anyone who could fry beefsteak as well as Harry. It just melted in one's mouth. Of course, we were all young at the time, and each one of us had good, strong teeth and we were all three hungry, and these three factors, I know help greatly in tenderizing beefsteak, but it really was good.

Every Saturday evening immediately after eating his beefsteak, Harry started out to walk to Onoway to his homestead and his wife and family. This was a distance of thirty miles. He always carried on his back, usually in a gunnysack, the groceries and other needs of his family for the coming week. He must have had the strength of an ox at that time. One Saturday evening, I saw him put a bottle of brandy into the sack. When he saw me look at it he said, with a wink "That's the doctor. Annie's expecting any time now." In truth, those were pioneering days.

Part 4   Homesteading Marches On

In winter Harry and Noel arranged to cut strong
Tamarac fence posts at 3¢ each and hauled them home to erect a
fence in the spring. By May, 1907 Harry was in a position to
cultivate and seed the first crop of oats on their homestead. In
December 1907, and for the next two years Harry hauled freight
for the Hudson Bay Store at Lake St. Anne at 75¢ per
hundredweight. He also was hauling supplies west for the
railroad crews and for others in need of his services. In
February, 1908, Harry contracted to haul the first thousand ties
on the right-of-way for the Grand Trunk Pacific Railway west of
Edmonton at a price of 6¢ each. In March of the same year
Harry and son Noel cut down and hauled 118 logs to the Rich
Valley Sawmill; sawing 5000 feet of lumber and hauled it home
to build a larger home and farm buildings.

While freighting, it was not uncommon to see pack
trains of twenty horses or more, in charge of three or four men.
It was quite a picturesque sight to see. One rider on the lead,
and the pack-horses strung out single-file at his heels, without
bridle or a thing to restrain them but their pack-saddle and load
of anything up to two hundred pounds tied on with the diamond
hitch, known only to experienced packers and from which they
rarely escaped until taken off by these men, who ride at the rear
to keep the laggards in line. There were also "Mule Skinners"
driving four mules each, who were often troublemakers on the
trail.

The railways began hauling the freight west of
Edmonton in the summer of 1910, and contract hauling was no
longer a steady employment. So, Harry had more time to
dedicate to his farm and family, as there were two more babies
now, Leonard and Marjorie.

208

Homesteading Marches On

On February 10th, 1910, the Onoway branch of United Farmers of Alberta was organized with seventeen charter members. Harry was one of them. On January 31st, 1911 pioneers of the region attended the funeral of Mrs. Rimer, the first settler to die in Onoway to be buried in the Mission Anglican Church graveyard. This little church was eventually abandoned and a new one built in the village. The original building raised by the hands of early volunteer settlers was discarded by less experienced newcomers.

An Agricultural Society was formed and on September 7th, 1911, the first of many Fairs was held in the district. How Annie and the children worked to raise and collect the perfect specimen from the garden and field to display at the Fair. During this time, work was also being done on the Mission House hospital. On January 15th, 1912 the C.N.R. steel gang laid track through Onoway. In July 1912, Noel filed on a homestead two and one half miles from Harry's home and began improving the land. The next winter Harry and Noel made a contract to cut telephone poles to be used through Onoway and District. They were erected by June 24th, 1913

In the spring of 1913, building commenced on the Mission Hospital erected by the English Church Mission on a very pretty site overlooking the Sturgeon River one mile north of Onoway. August 7th, 1915 the new Hospital was opened. Two nurses arrived from England to take charge. All the letters that Annie and her English missionary friend had written had finally born fruit.

In June of 1913 there was a church meeting at which the building of a new church was proposed, the location of which caused a great deal of contention. A large majority voted to retain the original site, where the land had been given and consecrated by a Bishop in 1911. However, the log church and mission house built by the spontaneous efforts of the first settlers was deserted and stripped of its contents which were taken to the new church one mile away. The building of which, no one objected but to destroy the work of others seemed quite unnecessary and not in keeping with church principals. The deed of gift of the land stated a church should be built thereon and not used simply as a cemetery which is what it is today.

On August 24th, 1915 the first passenger train from the east to Vancouver passed through Onoway. Dorothy left home to become a nurse, Harold joined the 151st Battalion of the Army In 1916, while Harry was away in Calgary training with the Army, Noel, Sid and a neighbour cut the timothy and placed it in the hayloft. It was July, and perhaps not quite dried enough. On September 12th, 1916 it combusted and destroyed the barn completely. Luckily no livestock was killed. Harold was killed in the war at Vimy Ridge January 3rd, 1917. It was a sad and disastrous winter.

In September, 1918, Noel purchased land near Kitscoty and left Onoway. Harry and Annie made plans to join him, but it was April 1927 before they were ready to do so. From Kitscoty, they moved to Cold Lake, Alberta, where their son Leonard had a homestead. Annie took over the post office at Bank Bay and operated it for about ten years.

All of this came later but during that summer in 1906 we worked for Harry. One day, both Bill and I together did a piece of work rather carelessly, I admit. When Harry saw it, he let out a yell! "You two damned young buggers! You don't care what your work looks like so long as you get your pay."

210

"Oh, stick your damned, old pay." Bill, who was just
as short-tempered as Harry, and more impetuous, flashed back.
"I'll go where I can earn more, and not have an old bugger like
you nattering at me all the time." and he dropped his tools and
ran up the steps and into the street.

Harry was immediately repentant. He asked me to go
and find Bill, and ask him to come back and say he would raise
our pay. I went at once, but Bill already had a job, working on
the Cecil Hotel, which was, then in the course of construction.

Then Harry decided he would go home and remain till
after Annie's baby was born and she was up and around again,
so I too, went to work on the Cecil Hotel. That was a
man-killing job if ever there was one. We carried hods of brick
and plaster, on our shoulders, up ladders, from seven in the
morning till six o'clock in the evening, for twenty-five cents an
hour, top wages then. The sun beat down on us, unmercifully,
during the heat of the day, and soon we both had blisters on our
shoulders so badly that we couldn't bear even our underwear to
touch us. We stood it for three weeks and were glad to work
with Harry when he came back. This work was now much more
agreeable after our experience at the Cecil Hotel. The
basements were always cool and there wasn't any ladder
climbing.

Edmonton, at this time, was suffering from growing
pains, expanding in every direction. The wonder of it awed
everyone! New businesses came flocking into the town and
building construction was going on everywhere. It no longer
looked the little, scattered village, it had looked a few years
before when we came to Edmonton, and built the scow. People
were saying, "It will have to stop soon. There's not enough
wealth in the district to support a much larger town than we have

now." However, it kept on growing, and when I came back to it in 1912, after an absence of six years, and walked out of the big, new CNR Station, I stood bewildered at the immensity of the place. For a time, I was lost and had to ask my directions from people on the street.

Harry quit his business in the late fall, and went to his homestead, and Bill and I went home to Marwayne, and again we found that a great number of changes had taken place during our absence. There were a great many new comers, all settled on homesteads, and getting their mail at our Post Office. But of greatest concern to both Mother and Dad was the new church that had been established about six miles to the South of us. They claimed we had lost quite a few of our congregation to it, - a Baptist Church, I believe it was. Dad was quite vocal about the depletion in the attendance at our services. Speaking of the worshippers we had lost, I remember him saying, "Ah, a new broom sweeps clean. These who have left us are the black sheep of any congregation. They know no religion in their hearts, so can't stay with any church. You wait and see, in ten years time both churches will be standing empty, and no church service, no religion, it will be just like it was before the Reverend Smythe came." His words came true.

I was surprised at Dad taking it all so much to heart. I had never considered him a religious man, but looking back I now think, he was perhaps, voicing Mother's sentiments.

"Who are the people who are responsible for establishing this new church?" I asked him.

"Oh, this damned bunch of newcomers that are so very religious; they don't play cards, and don't go to dances, but they

212

don't hesitate to break up an established church and its
congregation to further their own religious ends. They—".

"What are their names?" I asked him, more to stop his
flow of rhetoric than from much interest in the newcomers.

"There's a large family of Springford's, and a
son-in-law, named Aston." He told me.

"Aston?" I thought. Then I asked, "Is the name
Claude Aston?"

"'Yes, do you know him?"

"Yes," I said, "I roomed with them in Prince Albert,
the last winter I was there. They seemed nice people. I liked
them."

"Oh." he said, and that "Oh" conveyed to me both his
disapproval and his dissatisfaction with me for knowing them
and liking them, I thought.

I soon renewed acquaintance with the Aston's. In
fact, Bill, Molly, and I all became friends with them.

One Christmas, soon after their advent among us,
Mrs. Aston, Ada, as she became familiarly
known to us all later, asked Molly, Bill and I to go there for
Christmas dinner. At that time she "boarded the school marm",
a lady named Miss Anne Bresnahan, who though not much older
than any of the rest of us, behaved in austere, and spinster like
ways. She was staying over the holidays at her boarding house.
Molly and I had been to a Christmas tree and dance on
Christmas Eve, and when we arrived home, Molly, who seemed

very tired, said, "If anyone moves in this house before eleven o'clock in the morning, I'll scalp them."

"Yes," I agreed, "I want to get a good sleep, too. I just can't work all day and dance all night any more."

"Poor, old man!" Commiserated Molly, sarcastically, "but we have been, going the whole hog lately. Last night's dance was the third this week, and two last week, but" she added gaily, "I've enjoyed them."

"And so have I, for that matter, but I'm going to make up for all my lost sleep when I finish hauling these logs for Harry. I believe I'll sleep for a week." I told her.

"What about mail day?"

"Oh, I'll have to get up for that, of course."

"Harry's getting a lot of logs. Whatever size is his house going to be?" she asked me.

"I don't know. I think he must be planning on building a barn, too."

We were speaking of my brother, Harry, who had not yet arrived home from Prince Albert, where he had been working since spring with Frank Spore, Itner's uncle, and who, with Harry, built many of the brick buildings still standing in that city today. Harry was planning to build a house on his homestead in the coming year, and, we assumed, also getting married.

214

Part 4   Homesteading Marches On

The next morning, Christmas morning, Bill got up bright and early, and seemed to contrive to make a lot of noise. About ten o'clock he poked his head into the little cubicle where Molly slept, which was partitioned off from the living room by a "Family Herald" curtain, whitewashed to give it body, and asked her, "What time is that shindig at Aston's today?"

"About two o'clock, Mrs. Aston said." she told him.

"Tell Fred to pick me up at Jack's. I'm going over there now."

"What are you going over there for?"

"I promised him yesterday that I'd go over and give him a hand this morning."

When Molly and I called to get him on our way to Aston's, he was unusually lively and full of laughter.

"Have you been drinking?" Molly asked him.

"Ya, I did have a drink about an hour ago." merrily, "but that's all steamed off, evaporated, gone, but a sweet memory," laughing, and hugging Molly boisterously.

"Behave yourself!" Molly chided him. "Who had the drink?"

"Sam had a couple of crocks of his "Blind Pig" and we all had a drink or two."

"Sam!" Molly exclaimed. "He's the last one I'd – ".

"Ah, you always want to keep your weather eye on that last one." he laughed roguishly.

"I'd watch keeping an eye on that s – ".

"Now, careful. You are not fooling us, you know." putting his arm around her affectionately.

We all three laughed then for we knew that Molly had quite a warm place in her heart for Sam Rogers.

"It's a corker what a drink will do to a fellow," Bill mused. "You'd never think Sam was tender hearted, but when he saw the blood running from those pigs he blubbered like a kid."

"Oh, that's what you've been doing." Said Molly.

"Now, you're not supposed to know anything about that." he told her, tweaking her ear.

Soon after our arrival at the Aston's home, dinner was served, and Mrs. Aston warned us, principally for the children's sake. "Now don't anyone choke over this pudding, chew it very carefully."

"Wonder what's in it?" Claude said, winking at the eldest boy.

"Oh, of course, you'd have to give the show away." Ada reprimanded him.

"Not at all, my dear. I merely wondered, what's in the pudding?" He told her.

216

"Well, there's raisins and - " she began, but the boy interrupted her. "But Mommy, I saw you – ".

"Oh, what's the use? There's a dime for the one who will be the richest, a nickel for the poorest and a button for the old maid or the bachelor," she told us.

"But won't the one that doesn't get nothing be the poorest?" the boy asked brightly, and we all laughed heartily.

Almost in his first mouthful Bill got the button, quite a large one, it was. He held it so that just Molly, Claude, and I saw it and motioned us not to say anything, and then, waiting his chance, he popped it onto the school marm's plate and covered it with her pudding. He then assumed an air of innocence and began talking, while we three waited for her to say she had it. She finished her pudding and never said a word. I thought Bill's eyes would pop out of his head. Claude, who had the dime without letting on, now opportunely, popped it into the boys helping and we all laughed loudly. Miss Bresnahan too, seemingly, enjoying it as much as any of us. Bill laughed so much that I felt sure she would guess what he had done.

When the boy exclaimed that he had the dime, Ada asked in surprise. "Did no one get the button or the nickel?"

"Yes, here's the nickel," said Molly, taking it out of her mouth.

"Oh, you'll be the poorest." we all told her.

"Well, wherever is, that button?" said Ada, looking very carefully at the small portion of the pudding still left on the serving dish, "It just isn't here."

217

"Maybe someone's swallowed it."' Claude suggested, innocently.

"Oh, they couldn't," Ada said, "It was that button that you gave Sonny, to make a buzzer with, Miss Bresnahan. I'm sure no one could swallow that, could they?"

"I would hardly think so," Miss Bresnahan agreed.

"Maybe it will turn up in somebody's pocket." I suggested.

"Oh, sure, sure," agreed Bill, and Molly laughed till the tears ran down her face. Indeed, we all laughed, Miss Bresnahan included.

Later in the afternoon, we played games, Tiddley-winks, and Snakes and Ladders, and had lots of fun.

"Let's play something new." someone suggested.

"Yes," agreed Bill, very willingly, "let's play 'Button, button, where's the button'?" and all except Ada, laughed till I thought we'd collapse.

What added to our amusement was that Miss Bresnahan laughed just as heartily as we did.

"All right," said Ada, still looking quite perplexed, "You choose sides, Bill, as you suggested this game."

"I'll take Miss Bresnahan." said Bill, standing up with alacrity.

218

"Oh, let's play charades." said Claude. "I like charades."

So, we played 'dumb' charades. Bill, Miss Bresnahan and Ada were on one side, and Claude, Molly and I on the other. Our side went out first and we chose the word 'Rainbow'.

We came back, Molly with an open umbrella over her head, and Claude and I with our coat collars turned up, our shoulders hunched, and picking our steps. The other side got 'Rain' immediately. At the next act, Molly came in with a large bow on her hair, and they got 'Rainbow' without even giving us a chance to play the whole word. Then they went out, and soon returned, Bill began to caper around as light on his feet as a dancing master bunting Ada and Miss Bresnahan with his head, while they ran everywhere to get away from him. We got 'Goat' from that act.

When they next came in, they all three carried hats, which they first put on their heads, and then took them off and changed them and put them on their heads again. Then they went out to return to act the whole word.

We thought that might have been either 'Hat' or 'Change', but we couldn't get it.

When they came back to act the whole word I thought we three, Claude, Molly and myself, would die of laughter. Miss Bresnahan had the enormous button sewn on the front of her blouse, 'Butt-On'.

Going home that night, Molly Bill and I discussed the whole episode, and many times after, we discussed it with Claude and Ada. We have never been able to decide whether

Bill had played a joke on Miss Bresnahan, or whether she had turned the tables on us and had had a good joke to herself out of us all.

"But how did she dispose of that button?" We asked ourselves again and again, but never got an answer.

In 1907 the hamlet of Kitscoty, twelve miles directly south of us, mushroomed into being. One day we heard that the lots at the 'siding' were being surveyed and that people were already buying them. About a week later, there were already a railway station, and station agent, a grain elevator, a hotel with beer parlour and dining room, the bank of commerce, with operating personnel, two grocery stores, a restaurant operated by a china man, a blacksmith shop and various other business places. Soon thereafter I was "Advised" by the Post Office inspector that henceforth the mail for Marwayne was to be carried from Kitscoty and I was "to govern myself accordingly".

Accordingly, I began to carry the mail from Kitscoty.

There were now two schools operating in the adjoining districts - Stretton School, four miles South-west of Marwayne, and Streamstown School, ten miles to the South-east.

That meant two school marms!

Part 4   Homesteading Marches On

CHAPTER 13

Lucille

Very often, a teacher only lasted one term. There were always homesteading bachelors by the dozen hot on their trail. She then either married or folded her tent and departed. So usually, twice a year there was at least one new school marm to come out from Kitscoty with the mail. The duty of meeting her in Kitscoty, and having her company at our home, where she always had supper, conveying her thence to her boarding house, always made a pleasurable interlude in the otherwise rather monotonous job of mail carrying. The anticipation of such an interlude brought thrills of pleasure. Sometimes, alas! The realization betrayed the anticipation but taking it high and by they were young and interesting. The collection and delivery of the school marm was a pleasant little diversion from the humdrum of the usual routine.

Passengers for Marwayne usually enquired from Alex, the hotel proprietor, about means of transportation out to their destination, and, having been advised, they would wait in the hotel until I notified them of my time of departure.

One bitterly cold day in early January, I was in the restaurant talking to Jim, a bank clerk, and Barney the blacksmith, and one or two others just getting thoroughly warm before setting out on the return trip.

"Gosh, Fred, I don't know how you take it on days like this. Aren't you afraid of freezing?" Jim asked me.

"I'm pretty darn near it sometimes," I told him. "I would, of course, freeze solid if I didn't get out and run."

"But you can't run when it's as cold as this."

"Yes, I do. I have run nearly all the way home from Islay more than once." I said.

"How far was that?"

"All of fourteen miles".

"Good God! You must have the endurance of an ox. I'm darned if I would turn out on a day like this for anybody. Why don't you wait for a break in the weather?" Jim said.

"'His Majesty's Mail' you know. Besides, how would I feel if I stayed home because it is cold and some poor devil came four or five miles expecting some important mail?"

"Well, of course, there's that to it. But I don't believe I'd turn out and drive twenty-four miles on a day like this for anybody's mail, important or otherwise I just couldn't do it."

"Couldn't do what?" Alex asked, coming towards us and grinning all over.

"Drive out to Marwayne today in this damned cold." Jim told him.

"Oh, I've some news for you, Fred that will warm the cockles of your heart. There's a nice young lady, upstairs in the parlour, waiting to ride out with you."

"Young lady." they all chorused!

"School marm." I yum-yummed to myself and I felt a glow of warmth infuse my body even now at the thought.

"Where's she going?" I asked Alex.

"Oh, just to Marwayne, I think."

"But to whose house?"

"Gosh, I never asked her. Clean forgot to ask." the old rook lied.

I continued my preparations for the home journey and about fifteen minutes before I was ready to start. I went bounding up the stairs to the parlour in the hotel, eager anticipation resounding from my every step.

There she sat, as pretty as a plum, and black as the ace of spades!

So that was why Alex was grinning, and why he had forgotten to ask to whose house she was going. I vowed I would get even with him, but I never have.

I hoped I had hidden my surprise from her. I said, smiling, "I'm the mail driver. I understand you're riding out to Marwayne with me."

"Yes," she said. "I'm going to my uncle's. I guess you know him, Matthew Brown. He's farming there."

'Farming' was a little pretentious, I thought. Matthew Brown, 'Nigger Brown', as we called him, had only come into the district the preceding fall and had settled on a homestead. He didn't have a square inch of his land broken at the time.

"Oh, yes, I know him well." I told her. "My people keep the Post Office where he gets his mail. We see him quite often."

I then told her that I would be ready in a quarter of an hour and that I would pick her up at the front door of the hotel.

When I came back, to get her she appeared wearing low strapless shoes with very high heels, a light flimsy overcoat, and a white, lacy, transparent scarf, which Molly told me afterwards was called a fascinator, over her head. Such an apparition to behold on such a cold day!

"Will you be warm enough?" I asked her, rhetorically, knowing darned well she would freeze.

"Oh, I can take it if you can." she answered me with a bright, engaging chuckle.

I stood regarding her dubiously and wonderingly until she seemed to be a little embarrassed under my gaze. What could I do? I thought of several suggestions I might make, but discarded them all as being unfeasible or possibly even offensive to her.

I had a good, heavy, woollen robe, that Mother and Molly had patch worked out of the good parts of worn out suits and overcoats, and lined, with a new, dark, flannelette blanket. This I put on the seat, and when she got into the cutter, I tucked

224

this blanket well in all around her and under her feet, giving her my share of it. I had a foot warmer and this I pushed over to her side. I then took a horse blanket; I only had one and put it over both our knees and under our feet. However, I just could not do anything about her head and that fascinator. As we passed the restaurant she was chatting quite lively, and there stood Alex, Jim and Barney and several others waving and blowing kisses to us. I smiled and waved back, as did she, but I was feeling really perturbed. I had an uneasy foreboding about that trip home.

"Are you a Canadian?" she was asking me.

"I guess I am now." I told her. "But I came out to Canada in 1903 and took a homestead in the Marwayne district."

"You keep the post office?" She said.

"No, my father is the Postmaster," I told her. "But my sister looks after the mail."

"Where is your home town?" was her next question.

"It was in Lincolnshire, in England."

"Oh, you're an Englishman!"

This she said with that same suspicious fear that some people have in their voices when they say, "Keep away, he bites. He's a bull dog." I felt sure she expected me to snarl at her.

I asked her then, "What part of the States do you come from?"

"Oh, from Oklahoma!"

225

"Oh, from Heaven," couldn't have been said with more bliss and pride in her tone.

"Yeah", I said, "I believe Mr. Brown told us that he came from Oklahoma too."

"He's my poppa's youngest brother." she volunteered, "When Poppa died, Matt Brown looked after us. There are four of us. I have three brothers. Matt Brown paid for our schooling, and we all love him just like we loved our own Poppa.'"

After that, we drove in silence for some time. I was beginning to feel cold so I was sure she was feeling it too. As if in answer to my thoughts, she said, "Uncah Matt did not tell me that it is so cold here. It is much colder than in Oklahoma."

"Is he expecting you?" I asked her.

"Oh, no," she chuckled. "I'ın his favourite niece, and I wrote to him to tell him I was coming to visit him and Aunt Mamie. He wrote back and said I shouldn't come till spring, but I'm just giving him a surprise."

"Yes." I thought, "I bet it will be the surprise of his life."

I noticed that she had begun to put her hands over her ears but with just light silk gloves on, she soon put them under the blankets again. I kept looking at her ears and face but, being black, I couldn't tell whether she was freezing or not. I had been toying with the idea of giving her my woollen inside mitts that Mother had knitted for me, but was afraid my own hands would freeze if I did so. However, she now seemed to be really suffering with her ears and when she put her hands up to protect

226

them, they too, seemed to pain her. I drew off my mitts and taking out the inside ones, I told her, "Here put these on over your own. They will keep your hands warm."

"No, no," she said quickly, "I can't take them. Your hands will get cold."

"I'm only loaning them to you till your hands get warm." I told her.

Still she showed some reluctance about accepting them, so I insisted. I was beginning to feel the cold, myself, so I knew she must be nearly perished, for I was well and warmly wrapped, but even so, I could feel the cold creeping in – penetrating!

I was scared for her.

I moved closer to her, but felt her flinch and draw away.

"The snarl" I thought.

My feet were now quite cold, so I reached over and, insisted on sharing the foot-warmer.

That day the cold seemed a solid thing. It was one of those days, 38 degrees below zero, when one just can't breathe through the nose. When the moisture in the nostrils and eyes forms ice, and when the breath becomes an icy cloud as it issues from the mouth. The horses, which trotted briskly all the way, moved in a white frozen cloud, and were thickly encrusted in a coat of hoar frost. How do horses stand it? I have always wondered.

| Part 4 | Homesteading Marches On |

My feet were now quite numb, so I got out of the cutter, took the lines and ran with the horses. However, my hands, in the cold unlined leather outer mitts soon began to lose grip, so I had to get back in and put them under the blanket.

Seven miles out from Kitscoty, we came to the Bonnet farm. I drove into the yard, helped the girl out, and half carried half supported her to the door of the Bonnet home. Mrs. Bonnet seemed appalled when I entered supporting a 'Nigger Gel' as she afterwards spoke of her, with my arm encircling her, nevertheless she made us very welcome. She made some hot tea and gave us cookies and Christmas cake. The poor girl could hardly eat for crying. We stayed for about an hour, till we were both thoroughly thawed out. I asked the girl if her ears hurt, and she answered with a bright smile, "No. I'm quite warm now."

When we got up to go, Mrs. Bonnet, whose manner during our stay had at times indicated that, she realized the gravity of that poor girl's predicament, and mine. Yet at other times had betrayed a kind of levity in her eyes and voice came to me as I was putting on my mackinaw and whispered, "I'll never breathe a 'wahd' about it, Fred, an' I hope you'll both be happy."

"Good God," I wondered, "Does she really think I am planning on marrying or eloping with this black girl."

We set out for home, another five miles. Either it had gotten colder or we felt it more. When we reached home, the girl could hardly speak. I carried her into the house. When I flung open the door, and entered the kitchen with this black girl in a light summer coat, ridiculous slippers, and white fascinator in my arms, both Mother and Molly stood speechless with surprise. I went out without giving any explanation, to put the

228

team in the barn. When I returned, Molly had supper on the table, and Mother, she, and the girl were conversing like old friends. We kept her till she was thoroughly warm and seemingly happy again, and then she and I set out again for Mr. Brown's home.

Molly had lent her a warm fur-lined winter overcoat, a good warm wrap for her head, and some overshoes, which were much too large for her. She now looked so warmly wrapped up that I had no qualms about delivering her to her uncle's home, a distance of four miles. I knew that Nellie and Frank had had enough, so for the trip to Matt Brown's I took a young, black team that I had recently broken to harness. There was, at that time, a well-beaten trail between the Post Office and the Brown's home, but no one had been over it for several days so it was completely obliterated by drifted snow. However, I knew it so well; I thought I could follow it without any trouble. In fact, I anticipated no more trouble whatever.

When Mother asked, with much concern, "Do you think you'll be all right, Fred? Perhaps we'd better keep her here for the night?"

I answered confidently. "Oh no, I know that trail so well I could follow it with my eyes closed." This, as it turns out, might have gone better if I had tried it with my eyes shut, saving my mother a lot of fear and anxiety

That was a most beautiful night, a night whose beauty is begotten of the calm, stern, solid cold. The sky was a very dark sapphire blue, and so deeply inverted above, with the stars bright and twinkling. One could clearly see the empty space between them and the arching vault above. The moon, our only illumination in the entire world, hanging it seemed, almost

229

frighteningly, suspended between earth and heaven. Neither of us spoke and I mused on the beauty of the scene. The poplars and birch, gaunt spectral and unlovely in their winter nakedness, their shadows etched over the surface of the brilliantly white snow underneath, in a beautiful lacy pattern in deep dark blue.

I looked at the girl, she was sound asleep.

I knew there was a short, steep ravine about a mile this side of Brown's but thought I was well to the west of it. However, I had miscalculated, and now filled with snow level with the prairie, it was impossible to see. The horses suddenly plunged into it. They began, at once beating about, struggling to get a foothold, and breaking the harness and cutter all to pieces. The girl pitched out and in fright, lost her overshoes, and began sloshing around in those ridiculous slippers, screaming frantically at the top of her voice. This added to the horse's fright. I also had jumped out and was trying to quieten the horses and undo the harness – what was left to be undone, and get the team out of the ravine. The girl was still running around and screaming at the top of her voice.

"Uncah Matt! Uncah Matt! Oh, my lord! Uncah Matt! Help me, uncah Matt!"

Never have I been in such a quandary. I tied the horses to a bush and waded back into the ravine to retrieve her overshoes. The girl was still crying and wailing as she put them on.

I seized her by the arm and commanded her to stop screaming. I told her, "I'll run to Mr. Brown's with these horses. I can't let them go. You must walk after us in the tracks we make. You must not sit down; keep walking!" and I left on the run. After some minutes, I looked back and she was lying in the snow, so I turned the team round and ran back and picked her up and stood her on her feet.

"You MUST walk!" I told her. "You MUST keep going. I'll be back in a few minutes." I left again, running with the team. I dared not look back this time. I felt sure she would be lying in the snow, perhaps on her face. I soon reached Matt Brown's yard, and tied my team securely to a post and started back again on the run.

When I came up to her she was sitting in the snow, weeping. I picked her up, got her on my back, piggyback, and carried her to Matt Brown's home. They were in bed, but when I banged on the door and called his name, he came robed in a white night gown that reached from his head to his toes, a white night cap, and carrying a lighted lamp held high above his head. He reminded me of Holman Hunt's famous painting "Light of the World". The girl clung to me with both knees and arms, when I tried to unload her on the doorstep, had begun again to call out, hysterically, "Uncah Matt! Uncah Matt!"

"Lucille!" he exclaimed, "Ma po' Lucille! Come in out de col', chile. Ma po' lamb." However, Lucille wasn't moving until we got indoors, so I carried her in and dumped her on the kitchen floor.

I then went out, put my team in the barn, and fed them. When I came back, Matt Brown, still in white nightgown and cap, and Mamie Brown, also completely enshrouded in white, had Lucille's slippers and stockings off and were examining her feet. "Do you think they are froze?" they asked me.

I examined them, just to be polite. They were very petite and as black as jet, but I couldn't say if they were frozen or not.

By this time, I was just about played out, and was very glad when Mrs. Brown, still in white, made some very excellent cocoa, which she served with delicious homemade bread and butter and cake. I was so tired that I dozed off after drinking the hot cocoa, so Matt Brown asked me to stay the night, and I accepted very gratefully. He showed me to a room lighted by a coal oil lamp, with sheets, white as snow and spotlessly clean, turned down. I undressed quickly, got into bed and stretched my legs, luxuriously restfully, down to the bottom, but I immediately let out a yell and jumped out. Matt Brown came running to the room and I asked him,

"What have you got at the bottom of that bed? Puppies?"

He laughed heartily and said, "No, Fred. I have some hot rocks wrapped up in sheep skin."

"The woolly side out" He said, as I got back into bed,

That night I slept with Mr. Brown - not with Lucille.

Next mail day, when I arrived in Kitscoty, wherever I went, invariably I was greeted with, "Oh, you've got back from your honeymoon. I hope you'll both be 'appy."

I think Mrs. Bonnet had "breathed every wawd of it" and more, to every living soul in Kitscoty.

Part 4   Homesteading Marches On

About a month later, Alex came again to me grinning
and said, "I've a nice young lady passenger for you, Fred."

"Is she coloured?" I asked.

"Yes."

"No, No! No more Lucille's." I told him.

He said. "Well, go up and see her."

There was no anticipation in my steps as I mounted
the stairs this time. However, this, "young lady" was a much
older lady than Lucille, and much more warmly clothed. I asked
her, "How are you dressed? Warmly, I hope? Have you good
warm underwear on?"

I wasn't taking any more chances with a passenger
dressed in Oklahoma summer togs in our deep, cold winter
temperatures.

I guess she had heard about the cold from Lucille, for
she whipped up her skirts and showed me some good, heavy,
woollen pants, and good, warm overshoes, and fur wraps. This
was Lucille's mother who had come to take her back to
Oklahoma.

The weather had moderated so I felt there would be no
untoward episode making the delivery of this package to the
Brown's, which I did.

This was one of the experiences I had in carrying "His
Majesty's Mail" in those early days.

Part 5   For better, for worse

CHAPTER 14

For better, for worse

H arry's place was never a "Shack" - always a
"House" much to the amusement of all of us. It
was a log "House", built of the logs that he had got out of the
surrounding bush, and put on a cement foundation, which was
also one of the first cement foundations, if not the first, in the
district. It was very picturesquely situated in an open space
surrounded by poplar, willows and birches and really looked the
"Love Nest" Harry meant it to look and to be.

"That's the first shingle roof in the Marwayne
district." said Harry proudly, when he had finished building his
house, on his homestead.

Now he sent for his sweetheart, Alice Warren, whom
he had left behind in England, and about whom Ted and I had
teased him so often that first winter in that terribly cold little
shack. I can still see him sitting close up to the old, wood stove,
we had brought with us from Prince Albert, his writing pad on
his knee; trying to thaw out the ink, and chewing the end of his
pen while waiting to get another drop. We teased him, about the
"burning love in his heart" for her, and the "emptiness of his
soul" without her. Finally, he discarded the pen and ink in
favour of a little stub of a pencil, which was so short that he got
cramp in his hand trying to write with it.

"You'll have to buy a new pencil soon," Ted told him
one day.

"Why should I buy a new pencil?" Harry asked.

Part 5   For better, for worse

"Well, that stub won't last long at the rate you're burning it up with all those hot kisses." Ted told him.

Once when we were starting out for Lloydminster, Ted called after us. "Don't forget a new pencil. This stub is all charred."

"What charred it?" asked Harry, dashing back to look at it. Then seeing Ted's grinning face, he turned back smiling, as Ted called after him, "That last bunch of kisses was enough to burn up the North Pole".

"Wait till you get a girl." Harry told him once. "You'll see what will happen then."

"Well I had one once for a whole year and nothing happened, so I quit." Ted told him, laughingly.

However, in spite of all the teasing, Harry kept on faithfully sending kisses every week, and pouring out the ardour of his love, and telling Alice of the emptiness of his life without her, I assume. Now after, five years, his sweetheart was coming out to Marwayne and they were going to be married. Harry hoped that Alice would arrive in time to see Canada in its golden fall, so that she would get a good impression of the country before winter set in. But, it was nearing the end of November and there was snow on the ground, when she at last stepped off a construction train at Lloydminster. Harry, Fan, Molly, Mr., and Mrs. Bramley-Moore, who now lived in Lloydminster, were at the station to meet her. She stood in the doorway of the train as it pulled into the station, scanning the faces of the people on the platform. Twice she looked at Harry with no sign of recognition. "She doesn't know us." said Harry. When the train

235

Part 5   For better, for worse

came to a stop and he went up to her, she allowed her glance to rest on him for a brief moment before rushing to his arms.

"Oh, Harry! Harry!" she exclaimed, in evident relief, and tears gushed from her eyes.

Fan and Molly then went to her and Alice, after kissing them, said, "How changed you all are. I wouldn't have known any of you if I hadn't been expecting you."

"You nearly didn't as it was." Molly told her.

Harry then introduced her to Mr. and Mrs. Bramley-Moore, and they bade her welcome to Canada, and said they hoped to have her and Harry for their guests for a few days before they went out to their new home on the homestead.

Alice was petite, golden blonde, with a most lovely complexion and large merry blue eyes. We all thought how lovely she looked when she stepped off the train. She has always laughed easily and enjoyed a joke. She made them all laugh when she said, after Harry kissed her the second time, "Oh, Harry, I just can't believe that you're the man I used to kiss at Woollen's Brooke."

"Well, I am and you'd better believe it, or take my word for it." Harry told her, "For we are going to be married tomorrow."

"Tomorrow!" She exclaimed in surprise.

"Why, of course." said Harry, "Didn't I tell you so in my letters? Didn't I tell you that I would have all arrangements

236

For better, for worse

made for our wedding, so that we could be married as soon as you arrived?"

"Yes. I know Harry," said Alice, a little dubiously. "But it's so sudden."

"Sudden?" almost gasped Harry, "Why Alice we've been courting for almost six years."

"Oh, I know, Harry, but it's just sudden. I didn't realize—"

"Good God, Alice, you're not going to renege on me now?"

"No, No! Harry." and her arms were around his neck.
"Well, let's go home and have a cup of tea. Alice, you must be nearly dead with fatigue." Mrs. Bramley-Moore said, and this was a welcome suggestion to everyone.

Next day, Alice was her old, gay, merry self. Harry hired a rig and they drove out to Streamstown, accompanied by Fan and Molly. There they were married by the Reverend Smythe in St. Patrick's Anglican Church, and as Fan and Molly, afterwards recounting the incidents connected with Alice's arrival and the marriage, said, "They both seemed to be deliriously happy. But," said Molly, "If Harry had worn his black shirt and his bib overalls, I feel sure Alice would have turned and gone back home."

"Oh, no she wouldn't," said Mother. "Alice is made of sterner stuff than that. I think it was very brave of her to come out all alone and marry Harry at the end of her journey, after not having seen him for over five years. It stands to reason that they both have changed. Yes, I think she is very brave."

"Anyway," said Fan, "she couldn't have married a handsomer man. I thought Harry looked lovely, and so did Alice, God bless them."

"Amen!" we all intoned, not too reverently, I'm afraid.

Harry now seemed to be well on the way to a prosperous and settled life. He had always been a good worker and always very provident and careful with his money. At the time of his marriage, he was becoming well healed; he had a good line of horse-drawn farm implements, and a good team of heavy work mares. He also had a good stock of domestic animals and poultry, and when their first baby a boy, was born, Alice and he seemed a very happy and contented young couple, indeed.

His wheat crop the following summer was the talk of the district, and his brag. "If you want to see a good crop of wheat, come and have a look at mine." He would boast. He was awarded the first prize by the Lloydminster Agricultural Society for the best standing crop of wheat in the Lloydminster district, when it was just in bloom. Then came a frost and we all thought his wheat ripened very quickly soon after. When the threshers came to thresh it, they found that there wasn't a kernel of wheat in the whole crop. Harry felt this set-back very keenly; however, it was but the prelude to others. The following spring he lost both mares with swamp fever, and a short time after, one of the oxen he had bought to complete his seeding and spring work, bloated and died, just a few days after his purchase of them. He now felt that the fates were really against him. He tried to laugh it off to Alice. "It's the way of the prairie." He

Part 5   For better, for worse

would tell her. "We just have to take the good with the bad.
We'll get over it."

"But how can we? We have so little left."

"We have each other and our darling little boy."
picking his little son up in his arms, "and he's worth a whole lot
of horses and bulls. Aren't you, boy?"

But Alice was not to be pacified so easily. She wept,
"I have brought you bad luck. I know it's all because of me.
You were doing well until I came here."

Harry put the baby down. "Get your face washed and
clean up, and pack all the baby's clothes. I -"

"What are you going to do, Harry?" Alice asked in
surprise.

"I'm going to take you and the boy down to Dad's to
stay for a few days." He told her. "I'm going out to Vancouver
to get work."

"To Vancouver!" She exclaimed. "But you haven't
said anything about going to Vancouver before."

"I didn't know before. I've just made up my mind this
moment."

So he brought Alice and the baby down to Dad's home
and off he went.

"I'll be back in a couple of weeks, I think." and he was
gone.

Part 5   For better, for worse

A few days later, when I arrived in Kitscoty for the
mail he came out of the hotel. I didn't see him so I was startled
when he said, "Hello, Fred, have you room for a passenger out
to Marwayne?"

"Hello, Harry. Where have you dropped from?" I
asked him.

"From Vermilion. I've got a job, with Sherwin, the
building contractor, for the summer. I have sub-contracted the
bricklaying and plastering from him. How's Alice and the
boy?"

Harry stayed at home and called a sale, after which he
went back to Vermilion, taking Alice and the baby with him,
and they have resided there ever since. Harry soon began
contracting for himself, and has been very successful in his
business. Alice and he have raised a family of eight, four girls
and four boys, all of whom are now married, and Harry says,
"Up to the present we have twenty-four grandchildren."

Soon after Harry's wedding, Fan went back to
Edmonton, where she hoped to establish a
rooming house. She wrote home regularly, always entertaining
letters, with nearly always "dribbling some little bits of news
about boy friends", which Molly found quite exciting as a rule.
She also spoke of her struggles and efforts with the rooming
house, "But then, I'm trying to flit to the stars, but on, oh, such
earth bound wings," she commented. There was never, even a
hint of her settling down.

"She's more flirt than flit, I'm afraid," Mother
remarked. "I always thought she would be the first of the family

to get married, she has always had such taking ways with her."
She would bemoan.

I always think Mother worried more over Fan than she
did over any of her other children.

On mail days, when I reached home, I would hand the
mailbags in at the door and then put the team away in the barn
and feed them. One day, in the following spring, I came back to
the house after attending to this chore to find Mother, Dad and
Molly all in a state of great excitement. Mother was weeping,
Molly on the verge of tears and Dad fuming, ready to explode at
any moment.

"What's the matter with you all?" I enquired.

"Fan's married!" Molly said.

"Married!" I ejaculated. "Who to?"

"Billy Shaw."

"Well," was all I could say at that moment, I was so
astounded? Then I looked at the others and I burst out laughing.
They all looked so stricken.

"Billy Shaw! I'd never have thought of him. I've
never seen any signs of love-making between them." I said.

"No. That's the astounding part of it. It is so
unexpected." said Dad.

"Where is she now?" I asked.

241

Part 5   For better, for worse

"She wrote from Banff. They're there on their honeymoon." Mother said.

"When were they married?"

"The day before she wrote. That must have been a week ago yesterday." Molly volunteered.

"Well, it's nothing to cry over. It might be her funeral, the way you're all taking it." I told them.

Then Mother began to weep again, "Poor Gilbert". She said, and that was the thought at the back of the minds of all of us. We had all been hoping that some day she and Gilbert would span the breach that had come between them. We all still regretted that he was no longer one of us. We still missed him, but other than Mother's "Poor Gilbert" none of us voiced any comment, but I know Dad was feeling badly about it.

"We'll have to send them a wedding gift," said Molly the practical one.

"Wedding gift be damned!" roared Dad.

"Yes, Molly," said Mother. "Fan's made her choice. It's her right to do so."
"Oh, Billy's a decent old stick. Sure we'll send them a silver toast rack, or something useful." I suggested.

"Well, that's something they'd never use, but it'd look nice on a shelf if Fan kept it polished." Molly then said. "I wonder how a set of glasses would be."

Part 5   For better, for worse

"Glasses!" fairly snorted Dad in disgust. "Anything out of a glass would kill that fellow - a cup's his measure."

"Well, he's not a bad looking fellow." said Molly.

"No," said mother, "and the fact that he's steady and doesn't drink is all in his favour." with a scathing look at Dad.
"H-m-m," said Dad, but that "H-m-m" didn't exactly express agreement.

Bill then came in. "Fan's married!" We all told him.

"Fan's married! Who to?" He cried.

"Billy Shaw."

Then Bill threw his head back and guffawed, "So he's made it at last." He said.

"What d'ya mean 'made it at last'?" Asked Molly.

"Well, he's been sniffing around here ever since he first met her, hasn't he?" he said.

"No, none of us noticed it. He "sniffed around" as you put it, before we ever came out here." Molly told him.

Then Bill guffawed again, "Fan! The high falutin' poetic Fan! Billy Shaw! Aw well, he's a decent old stick, anyway."

"We want to get them a wedding present. What would you suggest?" Molly asked him.

Part 5   For better, for worse

"A 'Mickey' might be the best thing in the world for him."

"That's what I think." said Dad with a twinkle in his eye.

"We're not thinking of the gift that you two would enjoy most." Mother reminded them.

"Then how about a bottle of quinine wine?" asked Bill demurely.

"Why do you all call him 'old Fellow'? He's not much older than Fan, is he?" asked Mother.

"That 'old' is just a term of endearment." I told her. "We all love him, don't we?"

"Another 'Bill' in the family." said Molly, "We have Dad, who's William, and Rose's William or Billy, and little Billy – Rose's son, brother Bill, and now Fan's Billy."

I don't remember what the family gave them, or whether they ever gave them anything.

"Let 'em all come," said Bill. "So long's you don't call me Billy."

"What've you been doing today?" Dad asked him.

"I operated on one of the bulls this morning?" Bill told him.

"Is he bloated again?"

Part 5   For better, for worse

"Yes, the darned, old glutton! He was as round as a ball when I got them this morning."

"Where do you stick him?" I asked him.

"Just here, below the ribs", pointing to the place on his own back. Then, laughing, "You should have seen him before I let the gas out."

"Do you think he'll get better this time?" Molly wanted to know.

"It would be hard to say," he told her. "Anyway, he was going to die if I hadn't stuck him, and I wanted to have the satisfaction of killing him, the ornery, old bugger."

"The ups and downs of prairie life,'" sighed Mother.

"Ah," said Bill, rolling his eyes piously. "Prairie life's just like married life, 'For better, for worse', you know."

"What do you do with the wound?" I asked him, "Just leave it open?"

"I stuck the funnel out of the coal oil can in it. That worked all right last time." he said.

The bull got better and some weeks later Bill was out in the field one day, breaking with his team, when a man drove by in a buggy and with a very swanky driver. He stopped on the trail and waited till Bill came near to him. "That's a nice team of oxen you have there." He called over in a 'high falutin" voice, as Bill described it afterwards.

Part 5   For better, for worse

"Yes." Bill agreed. "They're a dandy pair of workers."

"I can see that," said High Falutin' looking at the team appraisingly. "Would you take four hundred dollars for them right now?"

"I might do," said Bill, trying to force hesitancy into his voice, while the alacrity in his heart almost made him too giddy to unhitch,

"Would they travel behind the buggy?" asked High Falutin'.

"Like lambs," said Bill, but added quickly. "Of course, they won't gambol. They are too well trained for that."

By this time, Bill had them unhitched and almost out of their harness.

"Will you sell those halters?"

"Oh, I'll make you a present of them." Bill told him. "They're not worth very much."

"Thank you, and now will you help me to tie them up to the buggy? I think perhaps, you know more about that than I do."

"I guess I do." Bill agreed.

Bill tied the oxen to the buggy as securely as he could. Then High Falutin' took his wallet out of his pocket and drew

For better, for worse

forth four bills, each for one hundred dollars and handed them to Bill, who took them, his head swimming with excitement.

"Goodbye and thank you," said High Falutin' as he drove slowly away.

"Goodbye and good luck." Bill called after him.

When he burst into the house sometime later, waving the bills, and exclaiming, "I've sold my bulls." I thought he was the luckiest man in the world. I told him so.

"I pity that poor beggar next spring when old Rufus bloats," he said. "I bet he won't think he's very lucky."

"Who?" I asked. "Rufus or the man who bought him?"

"The man, of course. Rufus would just glory in dying, that's why I never gave him the satisfaction of doing it." Bill said.

"What's his name?" asked Dad.

"He never told me." Bill said. "Now that I think of it."

"Does he know yours?" Dad asked.

"I don't know. I never told him and he never asked me." said Bill.

"Well, that's the 'rummest' business transaction I've ever heard of." Dad said, laughing.

Part 5

For better, for worse

"Maybe you'd better clear out of the country before he brings them back." Molly suggested. She seemed quite serious which made us all laugh.

Part 5   For better, for worse

CHAPTER 15

Exchanging vows

There were still dances every Friday night in the winter and these were still well patronized by all those outside the members of the Methodist church, who, at first, were shocked and scandalized by our abandonment and frivolity. These dances were generally held in the schools and were always advertised in advance, and everyone was invited, and "Please bring your own lunch and cup for your party"

'Some could articulate and some could not' wrote the Persian poet, speaking of a visit to a pottery shop. What stories those articulate among us could have told of the fun and frolic; of promises kept and broken; of heartthrobs and heartbreaks; even of plain cupidity.

Molly pretty well always brought home a cup inferior to the one she had taken. One evening when she was packing the lunch, she held up an old, iron-china cup without a handle, and with an extremely ugly crack down one side. "I can't very well be bested on this one." She said. Next morning when she unpacked the lunch basket, she held up a cup, laughing, and said "Sold again." The cup she had brought home was cracked and without a handle and had a mend-it in the bottom. We were not particular about the eggshell china at those affairs so long as we got a cup of coffee.

Several times throughout the year, we'd have masquerades at Stretton School. The first one I went to I got first prize for the most original costume. I went as "Black and White", white all down one side and black on the other, even to

Part 5   For better, for worse

a black boot and a white one. A Miss Mary Marlow, later Mrs.
W.G. Urquhart and I also got first prize that night for waltzing,
and that was surely a big surprise for both of us. I also got a
prize for a comic costume at another dance. I went as an old
woman apple seller – a pioneer Apple Annie, and though I
behaved most decorously, I got into trouble with some of the
younger girls for sitting among them on their side of the room
and endeavouring to get into the ladies' dressing room. Neither
would the men allow me to go into theirs. That night I was a
complete outcast of society.

"Hello, there, Fred. You're just the boy I want to see.
Jump in and have a ride."

It was at the Stretton picnic, and Duncan Currie was
there in a buggy, resplendent in its new and up-to-datedness. I
got in and we went for a three-mile ride.

"By gosh," he said, "I do get a kick out of these
picnics. That married women's race alone was worth driving
twelve miles to see. Did you see it?"

"No," I told him. "When was that?"

"About half an hour ago." He said.

"Oh, I was over throwing horse shoes then-." I told
him.

"I didn't see that. I follow the women's events. They
are always more fun than a monkey cage. I wouldn't have
missed that race for a dollar." Dunc said, laughing.

250

Part 5   For better, for worse

"It must have been fun all right." I said, with arch meaning. Dunc had the name of always being very hard-up and tight with his dollars.

"What happened at it?" I asked

"Oh, it's just that women are so funny, I guess." He said.

"How do you mean? How are they funny?" I inquired.

"They are such a bunch of contradictions, or opposing elements. They are so modest, or supposed to be and yet every woman, placed in the right circumstances - cajolery, opportunity, appeal, allure – or all of them, will forget modesty, throw respect to the winds, and become degenerately brazen." He said with finality.

"You speak from experience, I suppose?" I said.

"Oh, I know I have the name of being a devil with women, and I admit that I love the whole damned, deceitful caboodle of them, but I'm no worse than any other man would be in my place; I console myself that I'm not, anyway." He said with a flourish.

I laughed.

"Yes," he added ruminatively, "every damned one of them has her price."

"Well, let's go back to the beginning. What happened at the race?"

251

"Oh, that." he laughed. "You know that big tall Simpson woman with the very deep coarse voice? She's a breed I think. Well, she lined up alongside that wee school-girl looking Mrs. Falliss, just now pregnant to the brim. That girl can't be more than sixteen or seventeen. She's quite short, and speaks with a tiny, wee voice. Those two stood, each with a foot advanced, poised, ready for the start and conversing. Mrs. Simpson was looking down at Mrs. Fallis, and speaking with a growl like an angry bear, and she looking up, chirping like a little, full-blown, sparrow. Gosh it was funny."

"Who won the race?" I asked him.

"Oh, the pregnant one, by a good half length." He said.

"The offspring should be athletic." I laughed.

"I don't know just how that acts. How are you enjoying the ride?" he asked.

"Great. This beats riding in a wagon."

"I'll say. Do you notice how smoothly it rides?"

"Yes. I like these new low styles. Most of the buggies are so high. One almost needs a step ladder to get up into them." I said.

"Yeah. They are mostly vintage from Ontario. They have been transporting generations of kids to and from school back there, and should have been thrown on the junk heap in grandmother's time. Do you notice there are no rheumatic creaks, no jolting; the springs are so strong and supple. They-"

Part 5   For better, for worse

"You didn't come to the picnic to watch the women's events, only?"

"No," he laughed, "I believe in combining business with pleasure. I suppose you'll be in the market for a new buggy this year?"

"I'd like to think so, but I wouldn't bank too much on it if I were you." I told him.

"Dang it all, I thought you'd be a good prospect for this year." He said with disappointment.

"I hardly think so, but it's been a very nice ride. Have you sold many?" I was intrigued.

"Yes, I've done pretty well, but I'm disappointed that I haven't got your 'John Henry'

"I am too." I said

"Well, think about it. I can offer real good terms." He pressed.

But I had already thought, and I had made up my mind that I would own one before another year, but I wouldn't buy it on time, I'd pay cash.

I bought one the following fall.

Every year now brought its own quota of acquirements. Each year we got more acreage broken, and the natural increase in our herd was always most gratifying. We could now get a living off our own homesteads,

Part 5   For better, for worse

without going out to work, other than the mutual help among neighbours. I think it was about a year later that I quit driving the mail. A new Post Office had been established at Lea Park, at the mouth of the Vermilion River - the scene of our arrival, by scow, from Edmonton, in 1904. The mail driver was required to drive the mail from Kitscoty to Lea Park three times a week, stay overnight at Lea Park and return the next day to Kitscoty with the outgoing mail. This would have entailed my living at Kitscoty, and the salary would not have been adequate to cover the extra expense, so I gave up the contract.

"Why don't you get that crop of yours in? Are you waiting for the frost or something?" Dad asked Ted, whose crop of oats that year, 1908, was the only good crop of oats in the district.

"Well, it's not quite ready yet. I want to let it ripen thoroughly before I cut it."

"I wouldn't wait much longer. 'A bird in the hand is worth two in the bush', you know."

"Yes, I guess, you're right, Dad, but I'm hoping to make a haul out of it next spring, selling it for seed. Nearly everybody will have to buy seed oats then and the riper the better for seed, I'm told; but I plan on making a start on it tomorrow."

That very afternoon a most devastating hailstorm came up out of nowhere, and after it had passed over there wasn't a spear of crop left on Ted's oat field. It looked as if it had been summer fallowed.

254

Part 5   For better, for worse

Next morning he came down wearing his best suit and carrying his suitcase.

"Suitcase and all?" said Mollie, as he entered the house. "Where do you think you're going?"

"I'm quitting," he said and the disappointment and disgust in his voice brought tears to Mother's eyes.

"Where do you think you'll go, Ted?" she asked him, sadly.

"I think Vancouver's my best bet. According to 'The Bulletin', there's lots of work there, so I may get some. It may not be much, but at least I'll get some pay for my work." He told her.

He left after lunch to walk into Kitscoty, where he boarded the train for Edmonton that night. A little better than a week later, Mother had a letter from him from Vancouver. He had found work almost as soon as he arrived in the city.

"I saw men working on a new building. I went to one of them and asked 'Where's the boss?'

'Over there' he told me pointing to a little bit of a fellow, that reminded me of Gilbert, and somehow I took to him right away. So I went to him and asked, 'How's the chances of getting a job?'

'Can you drive a nail in straight?' he asked me.

'Oh, sure,' I told him, 'I've done quite a bit of carpentering.' I thought I'd be my own trumpeter for once just

255

to see how it worked. He fell for it. 'All right, son, you're hired,' he told me. "I began to work right away. So far he seems very pleased with the work I've done."

He worked and wrote regularly for about two years. In that time he traded his homestead for nine lots on Lynn Creek, across Burrard Inlet from the city. He sold them later for $350.00 each. At that time it was a tidy sum, but today a fashionable residential district exists in that same place. Each of those lots would be worth a considerable amount of money today. Sometime later, we got another letter.

"I'm now in the real estate business. The boss liked me so well that he's taken me into the business with him. He's just in a small way, but he thinks he and I together can make a go of it. I like him real well, and am doing all right working on a commission."

Some months later, we got a picture post card of Stanley Park, with a young man and a girl looking through a fence at a deer. On it Ted had written, "I often come here to feed this deer. She's very tame and loves to feed from my hand. I mean the one inside the fence!"

"As if any of us would ever think he would bother with a girl," said Molly. "Girls are just not in his line."

"I wouldn't be too sure of that." was Mother's comment.

Then early the next spring in 1911 he wrote:

"I've become quite interested in Spiritualism and go to the séances regularly every week. A Scotch girl here also is

For better, for worse

very interested. She and I usually go to the séances together. She is a professional violinist, and gives music lessons in Vancouver. She seems to be a nice, sensible girl."

"That's breaking it gently." said Molly. "The next we hear they'll have been married."

"Nonsense!" said Mother. "You were just saying a few months ago that girls are not in Ted's line."

"That was before I heard of them going to the spiritualist séances and holding hands in a darkened room." Molly said.

"Ted didn't say that." said Mother.

"No, but that's what they do at those séances. Fan says all the spooners join the spiritualists. They are regular spooning dens."

Just then, Bill came in.

"What do you know?" Molly greeted him. "Ted's got a girl."

"Now Molly, you're jumping to conclusions." Mother chided her. "Ted merely said that he goes to the séances with her. There's nothing in his letter, to indicate that they're sweethearts."

"Where's his letter?" asked Bill. "I'll believe he's got a girl when I see it."

Part 5   For better, for worse

"Well, I'll be darned." He said, putting the letter aside. "I bet she's a dilsie."

"What's a 'dilsie'?" asked Mother.

"The kind of girl that would get Ted to go to them 'say-ma-bob's with her every week," Bill said.

"She's possibly a very nice girl. I can't see Ted taking up with anyone who isn't nice." said Mother.

It was about three months later, that Ted's letter arrived.

"Miss Meldrum - May - and I were married last Tuesday. I hope you will all like her, but I'm sure you will. She's a very nice girl; she's a wonderful violinist. When Paderewski (I don't know how to spell that name, and May's out just now) anyhow May was on the stage with him and played before him, and she's very proud of that honour. She finished her violin education in Vienna, so you can see she's a real tip-topper. I don't know why she ever bothered with me. She gets after me, and tells me I don't make enough of myself, that I'm lacking in confidence. Oh, I can't begin to tell you all about her, but we hope to come home to see you all some day. May says in the not too distant future. She told me to give you all her love, and, Mother, she hopes you'll like her, for, she says, she already loves you from what I've told her about you."

Mother had read the letter aloud, pausing now and then to wipe the team away from her eyes.

Part 5   For better, for worse

"Bless Ted! Oh, I am glad and happy for him. I must write him right away and welcome May into the family." She said.

"Great old Ted! I can't see him with a High Falutin' dame like that. I bet she's a high stepper," said Bill. Then, laughing, "So Ted didn't go to them say-me-bobs, for nothing."

"Bill! Learn to say 'séances'. I don't know what May will think of all of us. I'm afraid she will think we are a very uneducated lot of people." said Mother.

"She's only married Ted." Bill reminded her.

"Well, we'd better send them a wedding gift." suggested Molly, who just loved marriages, weddings and all the trimmings.

"Yes," agreed Mother, "We must send them something really nice. Now let us all think. We must take it something serviceable, but nice and good."

"How about a silver toast rack?" I suggested.

"When you die the word 'toast rack' will be writ on your heart," said Molly.

"How about sending them that dress suit of Dad's, 'Swaller tiles', silk hat and all?" asked Bill seriously enough.

"Don't be so provoking, Bill." chided Molly, in real anger. "You are never helpful."

For better, for worse

"Oh, but I am. If Ted's going to be on the stage with that old Paddy whiskey, he'll need tails and a silk hat. He has to make the best of him self, you know." He said, twisting his face comically.

"And don't forget to put in the piece of black velvet to polish the hat." I warned them.

"Yes." said Bill, keeping up the joke, "Dad will never use either the suit or hat on his homestead. They just aren't suitable either for walking after the plough or feeding the pigs."

"No." I said, "The darned pigs would chew the tiles off."

Then Molly burst out laughing, "Just fancy Dad wearing his silk hat and his tails floating behind him, walking after the plough on a windy day." Even Mother joined in the laughter that followed Molly's remark. We sent them a carving set, if I remember rightly.

For about a year now, our district had been formed into a Local Improvement District, governed by a council consisting of four councillors and a secretary-treasurer, who was Billie Ashworth. This council now collected our taxes, instead of our having to send them to the Provincial Government in Edmonton, as had been the case hitherto. If a homesteader wished, he could work out his taxes on the road. We were getting our road allowances graded up into roads, which ran North and South every mile, and East and West every two miles, and now we were using the new roads instead of the former trails as in most cases these were blocked by fencing. This often entailed a greater distance between points as the old trails had always 'cut across'.

Part 5   For better, for worse

"Ah, you'll have a little farther to travel now on your trips." Dad almost jeered at me, and I sensed an acrid satisfaction in his remark. He had never forgiven the Springfords and the Aston's for 'inveigling' (his word) some of our congregation to the Methodist Church.

I ignored the bitterness.

"Yes," I said, amiably. "We'll all have a little farther to go now."

I knew he was referring to my friendship with the Aston's and the Springford's, whose homes I visited quite frequently, in the long idle winter evenings. One evening when I went to Aston's I met a Mrs. Green - Nan - a widow who had recently lost her husband, a sister of Ada. It soon became apparent that Nan was deeply interested in her religion, the Methodist religion, and shortly after her arrival at the Aston home, she began to organize a choir in the Fair Haven church. I met her one evening, walking; she was on her way to a choir practice. I stopped and offered to drive her and she accepted the offer very gratefully as it was quite a cold evening. Then we entered the church. I was astounded at the number of men assembled for the practice. Looking them over it seemed to me that the whole bachelor population, including all the toughs of the countryside, had gravitated to the choir practice that evening. Mr. Magwood, the pastor of the church, was there, conducting, and the contortions that man went through in his endeavour to achieve harmony among all those conflicting voices, were quite amazing. I tried to join in the singing. Not being either a sure or a strong singer, I soon shrieked off into the prevailing discordance. What a medley of noises we made!

Part 5   For better, for worse

"When I stoop down, so, you sing very softly - "Sotto"; when I rise up, so, you gradually sing louder - "Crescendo". Now you understand. Let's try again, Mrs. Green please," he said.

Nan was playing the old, wheezy harmonium. So we tried again.

"Crescendo - crescen ------- sotto, there Mr. Rogers."

"Rogers has swallowed a swig of his own brew," whispered one.

"Sounds as if he was gargling with it." whispered another.

This evoked boisterous laughter among that group.

"What the hell does 'crescendo' mean?" someone asked half aloud.

"Damned if I know, I think it's when he touches his toes without bending his knees." Winking and surreptitiously slipping a huge quid into his mouth.

"No, you ask him. You know him better than I do, I only joined last Thursday."

"Why did you join? Do you think you can sing?"

"I know damned well I can sing as well as you can." truculently.

"I know I can't sing." Laughter.

262

Part 5   For better, for worse

"Then why did you join?"

"Oh just for the devil of it. It's lots of fun."

"Gentlemen, please. I must ask you all not to talk during the practice. You distract those who want to try." appealed Mr. Magwood. "Again, please."

"Cres-cen-do, cres-cen -" Almost tying himself into a knot.

"You don't seem to have any difficulty in getting male voices." I remarked to Mrs Green on the way home. "Wouldn't some women's voices be a welcome addition to the choir?"

"Yes", she said, "but the women don't seem to want to come out in the winter months."

"Do all those men who were there this evening sing at the Service?"

"Well, they do their best, I guess. I wish you'd join our choir, Fred." I burst out laughing. "I'm afraid the timbre of my voice isn't suitable for choir singing. I would just be another gurgler like Sam Rogers."

"Oh, no, you wouldn't. I think you could be a very good singer. I wish you'd come, and help us out."

One day the following week, I met Fred Bennett in Kitscoty.

"I hear you've joined the Methodist Church choir." There was levity in his voice.

Part 5   For better, for worse

"You've heard wrong." I told him. "Who told you?"

"Oh, Mrs. Green just said she thought you might join."

"Yes, she asked me last Thursday, but I haven't made up my mind yet." I told him.

"You may as well join. I promised her today that I would." said Fred

So he and I both joined the Methodist Church choir, but whereas I wasn't much of an acquisition, Bennett was a really good singer, with a strong, well-trained voice. Mr. Magwood was delighted to have us both, but more particularly Bennett. I have seen women weep when he sang "The Holy City", as he did frequently afterwards in the Fair Haven church on Sunday evenings.

Now Mrs. Green and I were thrown more together, and I soon began to be attracted by her, and wondered if the attraction were mutual. She was, when one became better acquainted with her, a girl of great charm and possessed, of very endearing ways. Soon I found myself looking forward to meeting her. This went on for some months before I began to pay court to her. I now found my new buggy very handy, as Nan and I often went for rides in the summer evenings. I came to love her very dearly and I know she returned my love. After courting her for several months, we were married very quietly, in the Methodist Church, by the Reverend Magwood.

During the courtship days, I had built a little shack of lumber on my own homestead. It was to this shack I brought my bride. I now, also, built barns and a chicken house of logs from

264

Part 5   For better, for worse

the surrounding bluffs, and began to settle down to a happy,
married life and serious farming.

Part 5   For better, for worse

CHAPTER 16

Nor all thy tears wipe out one word of it.

I t was Pete McCann talking to Dad in the Post
Office.

"Have you met any of these newcomers yet, Mr.
Marfleet?"

"No," said Dad, "Who are they? More
Homesteaders?"

"Homesteaders nothing! That would be offering them
tea in a tin, to call them 'Homesteaders'. These people are
'farmers', and don't you forget it."

"Oh, as bad as that, eh? Who are they?"

"There are several families of them - one named
Walsh, another named Cousins, and still another named
Creaney. They are all related or intermarried or kithy in some
way."

"And none of them homesteading?"

"No. Between them, they have bought several
sections of C.P.R. land and Hudson's Bay land. They are
hauling a lot of lumber out from Kitscoty to erect buildings.
They seem to be a very high brow lot of people."

"Where do they come from?" Dad asked.

266

Part 5

For better, for worse

"From Ontario, I believe."

In the year 1910 an influx of settlers from the East came and bought land and erected 'frame' buildings and even painted them and introduced the status 'Farmer' among us. Was there then a little sense of the infra dig., or even opprobrium's attached to our log buildings and unpainted homes, and the term Homesteader? If so, be it said to our credit that we raised superior to it. We realized the coming of these people meant 'progress' and set up a goal for emulation among us, so when some of these 'Farmers' began to raise a cry for a Municipality to supplant the outmoded Local Improvement District, most of us were with them. However, there seemed to emerge from among us an element of resistance. Those responsible for the controversy were the ones who wanted to take advantage of the homestead offer and make a killing out of the new country, then return back home to their native land and enjoy their gains, ill gotten or otherwise. Every project that would mean a cent or two out of their pockets was decried vehemently. Luckily they were in the minority.

After a lot of Controversy over it, and much acrid spleen emitted on both sides, we ultimately petitioned the Provincial Government to establish a municipality. This it did.

The municipality was divided into six divisions for each of which a councillor had to be elected. That was a time of great excitement. Then brotherly love and former true friendships were shattered by a difference of selection of a nominee for councillor. The anticipation of benefits accruing from the successful election of the nominee, such as roadwork contracts, or a road opened to one's residence, or many other favours it would now be in the power of the Councillor to bestow largely influenced our vote.

Part 5   For better, for worse

So when one met the burning question, "Who are you voting for?" It was always wise to find out for whom one's interrogator intended to vote, before committing oneself.

One of the first projects that the new municipal council embarked upon was the construction of a road running north from Kitscoty to the Saskatchewan River. This road, when completed, was and still is named the 'Government Road' because the council had received a substantial grant from the Government for the purpose of building it. Now improvements came more quickly and our taxes became higher in consequence. Soon other roads running East and West, and North and South were opened up. New frame buildings painted - the homes, conforming to the vogue set by the Easterners, white with green trimmings, and the outbuildings, red - became increasingly evident, and, as Pete McCann put it, "The terms 'Homestead' and 'Homesteader?- have ceased - - deceased - - now we are all 'Farmers' operating 'Farms'."

Yes! The raw, untamed, 'untrodden' wilderness of 1903 was now assuming the staid, decorous appearance of a settled, civilized country. All this was very gratifying to the early settlers, and to each member of our family, for I believe there was not one of us who had not wondered, perhaps many times, if it had not been a great mistake, our coming out to this country. Nearly every Sunday the whole Marfleet family met at one of the homes, and we would speak of our struggles, or our new ventures, many of which were pathetic, but more were amusing, or the vision of the days of plenty that lay ahead of us. We were all still young enough, and romantic enough, to see everything through rose colour glasses. Then our neighbours and their vagaries, sometimes annoying, more often amusing, were discussed and there was always an undercurrent of fun and humour at our gatherings.

268

Part 5   For better, for worse

"Have you seen Bennett this week, or lately?" Bill asked.

"No, why?" someone answered.

Bill laughed, "He's gone completely native."

"Is he any worse than he was last winter?" Molly asked.

"The other day at the ranch he was sitting on the table, and we we're all talking and laughing. Mrs. Beatty, the new housekeeper, looked over at him and said. 'Close your legs, there, Bennett. You're indecent.' His seat was just as bare as a bubblin's." Bill told us.

"He's surely an enigma," said Dad. "Anyone can see he has had a good up bringing. His people must be –"

"Hush," warned Molly. "Speak of an angel and ye shall hear the flapping of its wings. Come in, Fred," she called in answer to his knock.

He entered, asking, with his usual easy grace, "May I join the family circle?"

We showed our pleasure at having him join us, and he was soon sitting among us taking an affable and witty part in the conversation.

Fred was about my own age when he first came to live on his homestead, just East of Dad's. He soon made himself known to us, and we all liked him from the very first, and he seemed to like us, but his natural graciousness and

Part 5   For better, for worse

happy disposition made everyone think he liked them, and when
I think of him I believe he did. We never got to know anything
about him until long after he had left Marwayne to seek other
horizons. Anyone seeking to probe into his past soon felt
disarmed by his ready wit and clever evasions. That he came
from a very good family was manifest in his every action - his
accent, his education, his knowledge of music and of church
music more particularly, his singing, his dancing - all
proclaimed a cultured and affluent upbringing. He never
mentioned his background. He never wrote or received letters.
Who was he? What was the mystery surrounding him?

He always came to our parties, which he seemed to
enjoy thoroughly. He liked to dress up in my naval uniform and
pillbox, and sing, "I'm a little tin soldier in a little cocked hat,
and I ride a tin gee-gee". Or, he would whip a large tapestry
tablecloth, that I had brought from Gibraltar, off the table, wrap
it around him, tie a sash round his waist, twist a piece of paper
into a hat, and run around singing, "China man no money makee
allee life long. Washee, washee once he takee, washee, washee
long." from "The Geisha", I believe.

His Sunday clothes bore the marks of costliness and
high class tailoring, yet on weekdays he was often shamelessly
sparsely clothed. He called into our house one morning, about
seven o'clock, on his way to get firewood north of the river, a
distance of about twenty miles. It was a bitterly cold morning
and he sat down and held his feet up to the stove to warm them
and the soles were quite bare. He had neither sock nor sole to
his rubber. Neither had he any warm overcoat on, he just wore a
thin sweater. Molly wanted to offer him a warm pair of rubbers,
or moccasins, but did not for fear of offending him. He called
again on his way home and stopped for supper with us and he
had as big a load of firewood as I have ever seen.

270

Part 5   For better, for worse

He pulled out of the country about the year 1911 and no one knew where he went. We never heard of him again till World War I. We all missed him when he left.

"How about giving me a hand at building my barn?" Bill said to me one day.

"Fine" I told him, "After I get my crop in."

"By-the-way." he said. "Molly had a letter from Ted yesterday. They are coming to Marwayne for an indefinite stay, he says."

Ted and May arrived a few days later. Ted said, laughingly, "I've come to lay my bones among you."

"It's not as bad as all that, surely." Dad said.

"It's pretty bad. There's a terrible slump now in Vancouver. Everything's just at a standstill."

The morning after their arrival, Ted came up to my shack and after some conversation, he asked me. "How would you like to come in with me in raising hogs and chickens on a large scale?"

"Well, I'm pretty well committed for the summer." I told him. "I have just got a contract for a roadwork job that will take all of three weeks, and I want to break another ten acres after I get my crop in, and I've promised Bill that I'll help him build his new barn."

"So you really are tied up for the summer." He laughed.

Part 5   For better, for worse

"Yes, I have a pretty full program. Do you think there's money in raising chickens?"

"I'm sure of it. If people out in B.C. can make money on a chicken ranch, where they have to buy all the feed, it should be a much more profitable venture on the prairies where one could raise all the feed they require. I believe there's a fortune in raising both hogs and chickens on the prairie."

His argument sounded very reasonable.

"Had you any plans?" I asked him.

"Yes, I thought I would get some real good buildings put up this year, and then next Spring I would buy several chicken incubators and brooders and really get going."

He eventually made an arrangement with Fan and Billie to start on their farm. He bought a shack for May and him to live in and began his buildings with all his usual earnestness and enthusiasm. That was a good summer. My sister, Annie's, eldest girl Dorothy came to us for a prolonged visit prior to entering a hospital for training in nursing. She was a very bright girl with most engaging ways. I hadn't sold my buggy at my sale, so I often took Molly and her out driving in my spare time. I also had two young colts, which I now broke-in for driving and for saddle riding and we three did quite a bit of riding. Dorothy was an excellent horsewoman, and I have always enjoyed horseback riding.

On Sundays, we all met at either Fan's or Rose's or Molly's, as we all now spoke of Dad's home. May always brought her violin along and we all enjoyed her playing. She had completed her studies as a professional violinist in Vienna.

Part 5   For better, for worse

The she returned to her native Edinburgh, but found no lucrative demand for her musical skills. She was advised to come out to Vancouver as that was fast becoming a center of culture in Canada. Her Vienna qualifications would be highly prized and in demand there. She came out to Vancouver about a year before meeting Ted and had immediate success. Once, as she finished a selection, Fan said, wistfully,

"I know that piece so well. Mr. Nicholson often played it. What's the name of it, May?"

"That, I think, is my favourite of all Bach's comp—"

She had used the full guttural pronunciation of 'Bach'.

Bill took the pipe out of his mouth and, with twinkling amusement, said. "Say it again, May, please."

May proceeded to repeat it.

"How do you know when to stop getting it out of your throat?" he asked her with so much amusement that we all laughed with him.

"How do you spell it?" Dorothy asked May.

"B-A-C-H." May told her.

"So that's how to pronounce B-A-C-H." Bill mused.

"How would you pronounce it?" May asked him.

"Batch, of course." He said, slyly.

273

Part 5   For better, for worse

"Doesn't that sound crude?" said Molly, "after hearing May say it?"

"It does, doesn't it?" agreed Fan, and we all thought 'batch' sounded crude or said so.

"Yes." Bill agreed, "I guess it does when the Bank Manager asks me, "What is your marital status, Mr. Marfleet? If I want to impress him and not seem crude, I'll say in future, 'I'm a baughlor'," and this sally amused us all. May laughed just as heartily as the rest of us.

"By the way –" began Fan.

"Borrower's thrilling words," Ted said. I looked sharply at him and he, May and I all laughed.

"Where did you get that?" I asked him.

"Made it up." He told me.

"Now, Ted." Admonished May, who obviously knew more about the truth.

"No," he laughed. "You remember those 'Head and Tail' puzzles in 'Answers', or 'Tit-bits' where you chose a word or words and made up another word or other words connected with them and beginning with the same initial letters. That was a prize winner once."

"I remember," Molly said. "You used to sit up half the night working on them."

Part 5   For better, for worse

"Yes, and spent many a 'last sixpence in the world' on them and never even got honourable mention."

"Oh, yes, you had to send in a sixpence with every answer, I remember." said Bill. "You sent in quite a few of my 'last sixpences in the world' too, and they've never got mention since, honourable or otherwise."

"No, but think what you would have got if I had won." Ted asked him.

"Yaa! I might have got honourable mention in that case." Bill said wryly.

This type of life was entirely new to May; she was out of her element. She loved to play the violin and soon became famous in the district. She was in demand at all the church socials and dances, but she felt her audiences did not appreciate the type of music she loved to play. Ted knew she was unhappy.

Ted and May left abruptly. May received a letter from a distant relative in Calgary asking Ted to go there to work with him. He sold his operation to Billy Shaw and started out for Vancouver. They stopped off in Calgary to visit May's relative, and here Ted got into the real estate business with an acquaintance of May's relative named Beatty. This relative was in the real estate business and at that time, there was a boom in the town of Redcliff, which turned out to be what Ted afterwards termed, "'Another 'South Sea Bubble', while it lasted."

Ted afterwards wrote us. "When we arrived there, the whole town was in a ferment of speculation. Everyone that came into the office wanted to invest in something. It didn't seem to matter what. I had heard of 'mass hysteria', and I saw it then." Ted told me later, "We would scoop the money off the top of the counter into pails, which we kept underneath for the purpose, but in a short time, the top would be littered with bills of all denominations, again. We both got scared so I was glad when Beatty shut down, and not too soon. I have heard that when the bubble finally burst, that the life-long savings of many of the residents were lost. However, they could only blame themselves. You just couldn't reason with them."

Ted and May went back to Vancouver from Calgary and Dorothy, who had gone to Calgary with them, continued on her way to Medicine Hat, where she was due to enter a hospital to start her nursing training. Ted and May settled in Vancouver where May again picked up her classes and Ted began carpentering.

I was now putting all I had into making a success of my farming. Had I not every inducement to do so? Nan was a very loving wife; a clean, thrifty housekeeper, and a very good cook, and when she told me we were going to have a baby our happiness was indeed complete. We both looked forward to the event with joy and gladness. Those months of waiting, how long they seemed. Especially must they seem long to the mother. Ada, Nan's sister, was so kind and helpful at this time; she visited us often, as did my own sisters. We all put much thought and care into the preparation for this "Blessed event",

Our baby, a little girl, was born March 21st, 1911, on her Mother's birthday. This coincidence, we all thought, was a happy omen. We named her Edythe Meta. We both hoped for a son, but were proud and happy to have a little daughter to bless

276

For better, for worse

our home. She was so good and healthy; we never had a
disturbed night with her for those early months of her life.

That was a dry, sultry summer - one of the most
oppressively hot summers I have known. The suns burning rays
beat down unremittingly throughout the day, even at night the
air was close and hot, and without its usual cool and alleviating
freshness.

At that time, it was my custom to hitch up after supper
and take Nan and the baby down to Dad's to get our mail and to
visit with my people. One evening as we drove back home, Nan
said, "Why that crop looks quite ripe. It will soon be harvesting
time again."

"Yes." I said, "We are going to start to cut Dad's
wheat tomorrow."

Dad, Bill and I worked together at that time in all our
farming operations.

"So soon!" she said, then, after a pause. "How
quickly the summer has gone and I seem to have got nothing
done. All this sweltering heat has taken it out of everyone, I
think. I just feel limp and all in, all the time."

"It can't last much longer." I told her. "We'll soon be
in September."

"Fan was saying that there's a lot of sickness around
Lloydminster and Streamstown."

I hadn't gone into the house with Nan. I had stayed
outside with Dad and Bill planning the harvesting operations,

and had just called for a minute to say 'Hello', and get Nan and the baby.

"Was Fan there?"

"Yes," she told me, "She was just ready to go when I went in. She says Doctor Hill's on the go night and day; there's so much sickness."

"What kind of sickness is it?"

"She says it's a stomach up-set; some people call it 'Summer Complaint'. I have known the disease called summer complaint in Manitoba."

"Is it dangerous?"

"Oh, no. Not if it's caught in time, I think. It affects children mostly, I believe."

That was the first we heard of the sickness of that fall. It soon became epidemic; if one member of a family got it all the others seemed to get it. Molly was the first victim in our family and then the others got it one after the other. Mother was the last to succumb to it, and she soon became very ill, and didn't respond to the home remedies that had been effective with the others. She had suffered from the heat during the summer, some days being completely prostrated by it, and no doubt, this had rendered her more susceptible to the full virulence of the disease. Bill had gone to give a neighbour a hand with his harvesting, and I was working with Dad at the time. One day I called at the house at noon, on my way home, to enquire about Mother and to get my mail. Molly came to me and she was so pent up with emotion she could scarcely speak.

Part 5   For better, for worse

"Oh, Freddie," she sobbed, "I'm scared about Mother. She seems so awfully weak, and this morning she has had delirious spells. I wish you'd go to Lloydminster, and bring back the doctor."

"I'll go as soon as I can get ready." I told her.

It was a five-hour drive from Marwayne to Lloydminster, and I did not arrive there till around seven o'clock. I drove straight to Doctor Hill's house, but was told by his housekeeper that he was out of town (at Onion Lake) and was not expected back till the next day at the earliest, so I put my team in the livery barn and went to Ada's. Claude and she were now living in Lloydminster. Claude was working in a drug store.

Next day I went again to the doctor's, but he had not yet got back, so I went to the drug store and Claude gave me a bottle of medicine which he said the doctor was prescribing for the malady. I had left my name with the housekeeper and had asked her to tell the doctor to come out at his earliest convenience, that Mother was very seriously ill. This was all I could do.

It was late in the afternoon when I arrived back at Dad's. Molly was weeping. She told me Mother was very low. Fan was there with Molly. She too had been weeping.

"Is the doctor coming?" they asked me as soon as I entered.

"He wasn't at home." I told them. "He was at Onion Lake. I left word with his housekeeper that he was to come out as soon as he could." I then gave them the medicine and told them that Claude had said it was the medicine the doctor was prescribing for the complaint.

"We'd better give her a dose right away," Fan said and prepared to give it to her.

I went in to see Mother, but she seemed to be asleep. I then went to the barn to see Dad. He held out his hand to me but he could not speak. Never had I seen such utter misery in his eyes, or in anyone's. He looked so sad and grief stricken. I stood wishing I could say something to comfort him. I told him that I had brought the medicine, and that the doctor would be out tomorrow, I thought. I soon left him and went home.

When I entered the kitchen, Nan came out of the bedroom. Her face was streaked with tears and ghastly pale.

"What's -?" I began, completely shocked by her appearance.

She threw herself into my arms, "Oh, Freddie, Freddie," she sobbed, "The baby's got it!"

"The baby!" I exclaimed incredulously, and putting her gently aside, I went into the bedroom.

Little Meta was lying on the bed, limp and white. It was incredible that any sickness could have wrought the change in her in so short a time. I bent over her and spoke her name. She opened her eyes and smiled a wan, spiritless, little smile, and began to cry, a pitiful weak little cry that struck a fearful chill to my heart. I asked Nan, "When did she begin with this diarrhoea?"

Part 5   For better, for worse

"I changed her napkin just as soon as you drove out of the yard and it had begun then, and has never stopped since. I've had to change her every two or three minutes, and she hasn't touched her bottle since yesterday afternoon", she told me.

"I've brought some medicine out for Mother. Claude says it's what the doctor's prescribing in most cases. I'll go down right away and get some." and I went out leaving Nan weeping.

When I told Fan and Molly that our baby had the complaint, they both looked alarmed. Fan warned me, "Don't give her anything, Fred, without making sure it's been boiled."

When I returned, Nan lay on the bed asleep from sheer exhaustion. I picked Meta up and changed her napkin, and tried to give her some of the medicine. She struggled against it with all her frail little strength. I forced a little into her mouth, but I couldn't be sure that she'd swallowed any.

It was three days before the doctor got out to Marwayne, and by that time both Mother and our darling baby were beyond any help he could give them. Mother died two days later and the next day little Meta, too, passed away.

The loss of these two loved ones was a grievous sorrow in all our lives. They were both missed so much. It had always given me so much pleasure, when I came in for dinner and supper, to hurry-up with the unhitching, unharnessing and feeding the horses, and go into the house to be greeted by the smiles of both Nan and Meta. Now Nan smiled, but such a sorrowful, mirthless smile, and went about looking like a ghost. I thought one evening that her sorrowing attitude might just be a

Part 5   For better, for worse

reflection of my own, so I determined to assume a more cheerful
demeanour in her presence and noted, in a day or two, that
indeed she did seem to liven up. She also enjoyed her meals
better - at first, she had scarcely eaten at all. I now talked to her
seriously; I told her.

"We have lost our darling little baby, and that is an act
of God. We did all in our power to save her, but it just was not
to be. It was God's will. We must pray that this next one will
be spared to us." Nan was then five months pregnant. From
that day we both took heart and determined "to look to the sun,
and leave the shadows behind," though we knew the memory of
little Meta would forever be green in our hearts.

It had been Nan's custom to walk down home on mail
days and bring back the mail. In fine weather, she always took
the baby along in her carriage, and had tea with Mother and
Molly. She had loved Mother very much and I believe Mother
had loved her in return. Now she didn't want to go. "It made
her feel too sad," she said, but when I pretended that it took too
much of my time to fetch the mail, she again began to go. At
first she seemed very much overcome with grief at Mother's
absent place in the home, but she missed, most heart-breaking,
the company of little Meta, in her carriage, on the way to and
from the post office. However, she soon began to feel better; the
outing became a diversion for her - something to look forward
to, and she seemed to derive great benefit from the exercise and
fresh air. The color came back into her cheeks, and soon she
seemed so immeasurably improved in health that her sister, Ada,
and the relatives on both sides said they had never seen her look
so well.

Part 5   For better, for worse

Our second baby was born, again on her birthday,
March 21, 1912, again it was a girl, but Nan died from
haemorrhage giving her birth.

I was distraught with grief. Nan had always been a
delicate woman, but even so, there seemed no reason why she
should lose her life over the birth of a second baby, especially as
she had been quite healthy and well throughout the months of
her pregnancy.

Fan then came to me. "Have you made any plans,
Fred?" she asked,

"No," I told her. "I just want to get away. I shall sell
out and go, and I don't care if I never come back to Marwayne."

"Oh, don't say it, Fred," She told me through her tears.
"A complete change will do you good. Time and change are the
surest and best healers."

However, as I listened to her, I felt no desire to be
healed.

"What are you going to do with your baby?" She then
asked.

"I'm hoping Ada will look after her. That's all I can
do with her at the present."

Then Fan pleaded, "Oh, give her to me, Fred. Please,
let me keep her till you can make better arrangements for her. I
have none of my own, and I shall give her every care and love
her, just as if she were indeed, my very own. Will, too, would

like you to leave her with us." and the tears were blinding her
eyes.

　　　I had never thought of Fan taking the baby, but I
hadn't given the matter much thought. I had just taken it for
granted that Nan's sister would be the one to entrust with my
baby's care. Now, I knew that Fan must have her. Ada had
then, four children. That was the first time that I fully realized
just how starved poor Fan's heart was for children of her own. I
decided to let her keep the baby for the time being.

　　　Then Ted and May wrote asking me to go out to them
and stay until I "got adjusted", so I went to Vancouver and
stayed with them for eight months and met May's friends.

　　　These were the most Bohemian lot of people I have
　　　ever met. They were all professionals in the
world of music - pianists, violinists, singers and dancers, but
such a gay, mutually helpful lot of People! It was an education
for me to meet them. They were all so unusual, a different class
of people from any with whom I had ever before associated.
The change in Ted amazed me. He was a different man
altogether, from the Ted I had known. He had always been a
gentleman, but had been reserved, and had never seemed to
enjoy mischief nor fun nor banter with women. Now he was full
of gaiety, badinage, and quick repartee and I still think he was,
then, one of the nicest looking men I have ever known. No one
could have called him handsome; he was just good-looking.

　　　When I arrived at the C.P.R. station, Ted and May
were there to meet me, and after collecting my grip we went to
their home. May soon had a meal on the table and we had just
sat down when two girls about May's age came in. They both
spoke with a modulated Oxford accent. May introduced me

284

Part 5   For better, for worse

with, "This is Ted's, brother, Fred, and these are two of my friends, Daisy and Frankie." May spoke with a Scottish accent.

"Known to the police as Daisy Dumpkins and Fanny Frankfurter." Ted interjected.

"Pleased to meet you." I said, bowing soberly to each in acknowledgement of the introduction.

"Zounds! He's straight laced." One of them said, sotto voce, as they both went to the cupboard and helped themselves each to a knife, fork, and plate.

"Haven't you any more cups, May?" one of them asked.

"No," May said. "Here, you can have our saucers. Ted, give Daisy your saucer."

"She's just trying to save on the wash-up. We've lots of cups and saucers. Here, Dumpkins." Ted said, as he handed Daisy his saucer.

"Tell another while your mouth's warm." she said as she took it.

"By Jove, something wants warming around here." said Frankie, as after tasting her coffee, she jumped up and put the coffee pot on the stove, "Don't you people know the three musts for a good cup of coffee?" she asked.

"No, smart Alec" said May. "You tell us."

Part 5   For better, for worse

"It should be hot as love, sweet as sin, and black as hell."

"Hmmm--," mused Ted. "Hot as love. That's pretty hot isn't it, Dumpkins?"

"Oh, no! I got it mixed up." Cried Frankie "Now how does it go? It should be 'black as sin, sweet as love, and hot as hell. That's more like it." At which we all laughed.

"Well, it's as hot as hell right now." Cried Daisy, jumping up. "Zounds, look at this blighty stove."

The coffee had boiled all over it.

"This should be hot enough for anyone's love," said May, as she refilled the cups and saucers.

"By-the-way –" began Daisy.

"Borrower's thrilling words", interrupted Ted, rolling his eyes.

"You never made that one up." said Frankie.

"Yes, I did." lied Ted. "I make it up every time I pass a bank."

"Why when you pass a bank, pray?" Frankie asked.

"Just so I won't be tongue-tied when I go in."

"I don't get you." she told him.

Part 5   For better, for worse

"You would if you'd ever been in a bank to borrow money." Ted said.

"Precocious child," jeered Daisy, and added, "I was going to ask you to lend me a dollar."

"Nothing doing. You still owe me the last three you borrowed from me." He told her.

"I do not. I paid you back the last one."

"No, you didn't."

"Yes, I did. Didn't I May?"

"Don't involve me," said May. "I've no aptitude for high finance."

"Well, I know I did. But anyway, even if I didn't you've taken its worth out of my hide a dozen times over." She told him.

"Hush," warned Ted, holding up an admonitory finger, and pretending to look, sheepishly at May. Then, "Here's two." drawing them quickly out of his pocket and holding them towards her, but as Daisy reached for them he thrust them back into his pocket. He did it so quickly that everyone burst into laughter.

"Pig dog!" she called him, as the laughter subsided and she and Frankie got up to go.

I had sat quite nonplussed during the whole visit. How much of the banter and badinage had been serious and how

Part 5   For better, for worse

much just flippancy, I couldn't say. I had noticed May looking at me, with some concern, a few times, and now she asked me, "Do you think we are all fair daft, Fred?"

"Oh, I suppose you all understand each other," I said.

"You'll soon get into our ways. It was all strange to me too, at first, but now I rather, enjoy it." She assured me.

"Why don't you get some more cups, May?" Ted asked her later.

"I'm waiting for the sales. There should be one coming up in a week or so." She told him, and they both laughed.

"Can the leopard ever change his spots?" Ted asked laughingly.

"If you mean, 'Can a Scotch woman ever pass up a sale?' the answer is NO-O-O." She told him.

At this time I also met a woman they called 'Dirty Dora', who was introduced to me as Mrs. Jordan.

"You remember Dr. Jordan, don't you Fred?" Ted said, with a smirk. May told me later that this Dora had been wed to Dr. Jordan, and they had a son.

"Dora still has the boy." She said. Dr. Jordan had left the scene mysteriously leaving no contact behind. She had heard how he had been very successful operating a dog hospital, but that was before she had come to Vancouver and met Dora. She had very little knowledge about him.

Part 5   For better, for worse

I worked with Ted all that summer in 1912 and certainly enjoyed working with him. I helped him build a house on Point Grey. He was a real good worker. There never was a lazy bone in his body or an idle thought in his mind yet he was not exacting, and always seemed pleased with the work, I did. When the fall came, and the outdoor work, in Vancouver, more or less shut down for the winter, Ted had not enough work for both of us. I left and got a job on a dairy farm in Agassiz. That was a good place to make a fellow forget his troubles; there was never an idle moment. I never even got time to read the paper. Sundays and weekdays were alike. The pay was good, so I stayed with it all through the winter, but when April came, I told them to get another man, that I was quitting at the end of the month. I was going back to Vancouver!

Back to Vancouver? Was I? I had said to Fan. "I never wanted to come back." and I thought then I never would go back. Now? The prairie and everything about it called to me; the rhythm of the gently swishing native grass in the Spring, the minty fragrance of the new mown hay, the heart-some song of the meadow lark, the wide open views, away, away to the distant, hazy horizons in the Fall - all now had a charm, and a lure for me. My heart was filled with an aching longing to go back that I could not resist.

Part 5   For better, for worse

CHAPTER 17

Rumours and mysteries

I arrived in Marwayne at the end of April. Snow was still on the ground, but there was that exhilarating feeling of a long awaited, long hoped for spring in the air. I went to Fan's, and my little baby whom we had named Winifred Marie was now thirteen months old. Marie, after her mother, at first wouldn't come near me. She was a darling, little baby - strong and healthy looking - and I could see that both Billie and Fan just doted on her, and I knew now that I must never take her away from them.

While I was staying with Fan and Billie, I heard that a neighbor was selling out. I had left a large boar with him when I left, and I decided to see if he still had it. It was still there, even bigger and fatter it seemed. Charlie told me I could take it. He also had some other stock for sale, so I bought a new team. On the way home, the boar slipped off the lead and disappeared into the bush. I couldn't chase after it, and decided to come back to search for it later.

I stayed at Fan's a couple of days and then went to my own shack, and began batching. A morning or two later Bill sauntered in, smoking his pipe, as usual.

"So you came back?" he grinned.

"Yes" I said, "I guess the prairie's got me."

"I see you bought back your boar." he said.

Part 5   For better, for worse

"Yes. How did you know?"

"He's lying asleep in the pig-pen."

"Well, I'll be darned." I said. "When I was coming away from the sale yesterday evening, I told them to cut him loose and I would drive him, but he rushed into the bush and I couldn't find him. I was just going back now to look for him."

"It's a good thing I happened to look in the pen as I passed. Fancy him remembering to come home after being at Charlie's for over a year. You know it's marvellous the instinct that animals have. Did you buy anything else?"

"Yes, I bought Charlie's big, black team."

"Planning on getting lots of road work this summer?" he asked me.

"Yes, I want to keep busy. I intend to do quite a bit of breaking after I get my crop in."

Now harvesting was at hand. That was a year of good crops. I did well that summer; got my breaking done, and cleared of roots. I also got my roadwork completed in good time for which I received a welcome cheque. My stock had also done well. So taking it high and by it had been a rewarding season.

Not long after I returned to Marwayne in 1913, we heard from Ted that he and May had bought a farm at Oyen, in Alberta. When they got settled at Oyen, May used to visit a few of the surrounding towns such as Olds and Innisfail to give violin lessons. Ted began farming his section of land. We never saw either Ted or Dorothy again.

One day in the fall of 1922, when he was harvesting his wheat, the horses suddenly took fright and bolted, overturning the binder. One of the operating handles pierced his lung. He died in hospital a few days later. May was heart-broken. I saw her about a month after the funeral and was shocked at her appearance. I was not surprised when she wrote a short time later and told me she had been advised by her physician to leave Oyen and go away to strange and new surroundings. The doctor had suggested Los Angeles, so she went there.

She kept in touch and soon after reaching Los Angeles, she resumed her professional career. About eight years later, she married again, a druggist named Huhn. She stopped writing and we did not hear from her again for a long time. Recently, our eldest son, Creasy, received a letter from her. She had heard of him through a friend who had attended one of his lectures. She was on holiday on the isle of Capri and living in comparative ease. She had returned to live at her childhood home in Edinburgh, Scotland.

Many who came to the area at that were outstanding for some reason or other. Something about them distinguished them from the usual homesteader. I suppose each of us can lay claim to some individuality, but the occasional outstanding personality would appear with a background different in every respect from the rest of us. Two of these stand out in my memory.

One of them was Fred Bennett. He came to live on a homestead just east of Dad's, and was a frequent visitor. I have

292

For better, for worse

mentioned his ability at dancing and singing, and the obvious
signs of a cultured upbringing; however I have never seen him
properly clothed on a weekday. His Sunday clothes were
impeccable. He wore a beautiful English tailored expensive
suit, but on weekdays he went more native than the natives
themselves. I was working with him once, haymaking at
Lindsay's during a summer. He came to the table one day
without a vestige of covering on his seat. Mrs. Bresneau, the
housekeeper said, "Fred, close your legs! You're indecent." He
looked down and closed his legs, but in a few minutes was back
in the exposed position, just for pure mischief. Then she made
us all get out.

He was shameless, never embarrassed, always poised.
Nothing perturbed him, or caused him a moment of concern. He
was a real good worker, though when he first came among us his
hands were unblemished and delicate like a lady's. They always
looked fresh and clean when he was playing piano, or
gesticulating in conversation. Neither women nor liquor seemed
to have any place in his life. The mystery surrounding him
fascinated everyone. Some assumed that he had been kicked out
by his family, cut off without the proverbial shilling. But, why?
Nothing seemed to fit. I am sure he was often hungry during the
winter, but whenever he came for a meal, he was the perfect
gentleman. If he were hungry he never showed it.

He called a sale after being with us for a little over two
years, and left. It was rumoured, after he left, that he had gone
north to work with the Eskimos. That rumour was more or less
verified later. The next we heard of him was during the second
year of World War I, when we saw his picture on the front page
of "The Daily Mirror". He was with the Royal Air Force in
England, and had been decorated for some daring exploit. Later
we again saw his name in the old Country pictorials. He was

wearing Eskimo clothing. There was quite an article about him, giving the name and status of his parents. The article stated that he was going back to Canada, "much as his family would like him to stay with them, but he was going to be back with his beloved Eskimos." That was the last we ever heard of him.

The other individual was a sinister character. Dr. Jordan came in the early days with his wife and daughter. He brought with him a large herd of pure Hereford cattle. He had a homestead near Stinking Lake, and bought a section of the surrounding C.P.R. land. Compared to the rest of us he was a man of substantial means, and soon acquired a very promising location for ranching. He had everything he required for his purpose, a good supply of water in the lake, and a bountiful supply of feed on the prairie. He stayed for several years.

Harry met him one cold winter day at the lake spearing muskrat. He said to Harry,

"Don't you think this is extreme folly for both of us, you an experienced bricklayer and I a qualified medical doctor, to sit here on this cold day spearing muskrat for a living?"

His daughter worked like a man, in fact, working with the hired man doing practically the same work. His wife was supposedly an invalid seldom seen by any outsiders.

He was not in the district very long before sinister rumours began to circulate about him, emanating mainly from the hired man. The rumours accused him of cruelty to his wife and daughter, and of bodily abusing his wife, and of having strong bluebeard tendencies. Whether these rumours reached his ears I do not know. He called a sale one day, sold all his cattle and household effects, and departed with his wife and daughter as suddenly as he had come.

Several years later I again heard of him in Vancouver when I went there to stay with Ted and May. He had operated a sick dog home there and made quite a bit of money. His first wife had died soon after they reached Vancouver and he had married again, and left suddenly, with no contacts. No one knew where he had gone.

About 1929 or 1930 he came back to his homestead at Marwayne, bringing with him a housekeeper and her son, a young lad about twelve years of age. He had driven from Blaine, Washington, in a Chevrolet car. He set up farming again at his homestead in the Silver Willow School District. This time he brought in no stock.

One day he came into the municipal office. I was then secretary of the municipal district, and I would not have known him. When he came out to Marwayne in the early homesteading days, he was a tall fine looking man with Prince Albert whiskers and moustache, and a commanding appearance. I remember how impressed I was the first time I met him. When he came into the office in 1930 he was a little stooped clean-shaven old man. He came for his mail and had not met me before so we had quite a lengthy conversation, mainly about the progress in the district. I remember he suggested, "Now, you people are in a splendid position here to sell moonshine. Get a store going and mark the moonshine down as tea." However, that kind of business was contrary to the code by which the Marfleets had always lived.

He was amazed that we now had the C.P.R. through the town, and the country was so well settled. His homestead

was in the Silver Willow School district; there had been no
school when he was there before, and he was astounded at how
much of the prairie had been cleared and broken. He spoke of
how the taxes had increased. When he was there before we had
no local government; the taxes were then levied and collected by
the Alberta Provincial Government. I said, "You must have
been receiving your tax notices, and seen that we had at first a
Local Improvement governing body, and then about sixteen or
seventeen years ago this was supplanted by a Municipal District
by popular vote of the rate-payers."

"Oh, yes, yes, Mr. Marfleet" he said, "You are quite
right. I was just speaking of how the country has advanced. It
gives me great pleasure to see the improvements that have taken
place."

He now farmed his land very successfully, and seemed
to be living down the rumours from those early days. He always
seemed to have money, and came into town often in the summer
in his car. His housekeeper and her son often accompanied him
when he came to town, and there seemed to be a very genial
friendly relationship between all three of them.

One very busy day he came into the office, and began
remarking on the unusual high number of cars on the street to
which I agreed and said,

"You know, Mr. Marfleet, I can walk up and down the
streets, and when I come back I can tell you the number on the
licence plate of every car now in town."

I declined to put him to the test, although I believe he
could have made good his statement. He then took from his vest
pocket a fire escape he had invented. It consisted of three small

296

wheels around which a quantity of strong silk tape was wrapped.
He tried to explain how it worked and according to him it was a
very simple invention. He told me he had, himself,
demonstrated this fire escape by leaping from the highest
building on Hastings Street in Vancouver. He had just come
back from Vancouver. I read in the Lloydminster times, a few
days later, that he had indeed made the jump.

He went on that day, to tell me of another invention he
had made when he was eighteen living in New York. It was an
improvement on a grain binder. If he told me what part, I have
forgotten. It was a busy day. He put his invention in the hands
of a patent attorney to have it registered, but the attorney double-
crossed him and proceeded to take the patent out in his own
name. He said, "I went to his office and shot him dead." Then
he explained that at his trial for the shooting the judge
exonerated him and said, "I would have done the same myself."

He was sick once and sent for Dr Hill. When the
doctor entered his room, he lay in bed with a loaded colt
revolver on his pillow. Dr. Hill reported it to the RCMP at
Lloydminster. I had the constable out the next day to tell me
that Dr. Jordan had a permit to have a revolver in his house for
protection.

One fall, when making hay, he fell off a haystack and
broke his hip. He was taken to the University of Alberta
hospital in Edmonton. While he was there his housekeeper went
up to the hospital and they were married in the ward.

After he recovered and came back to Marwayne, he
came into the office with his former housekeeper to introduce
her to me as his wife. He proceeded to explain that it was for
her protection that he had married her. Then turning to her he

said, "Yes my dear, if I had ever thought I would come out of that hospital alive, I would never have married you." She retorted, "And if I ever thought you would come back alive, I would never have married you." They both laughed, and seemed quite friendly over this little interchange of felicities, and we conversed quite affably for a while afterwards.

He was supposed to have been a Colonel in the British Army in the South African war, and Billie Ashworth said he knew him as an officer in the Army, but he could not say if he were a Colonel.

Once he told me that when he was a young lad he had been captured at the Custer Massacre by a band of Indian warriors, and they kept him prisoner traveling all over the western states and Canada. When they came in their wanderings, far north of Marwayne, they found a famine among the Indians. So acute was this state of hunger among them that when one of them dropped dead or fell from weakness the others pounced on him and ate him raw.

"Yes, Mr. Marfleet, I have eaten raw Indian flesh," he said.

When he was about sixteen, he escaped from the Indians and went down to the Eastern States. From then on he made his own way in life. He never said how or when he got his medical degree. However, Dr. Hill spoke to me of the wonderful medical books Dr. Jordan owned, also of the marvellous collection of surgical instruments he possessed. I believe Dr. Hill bought both the books and the instruments at a sale held a few years later by Dr. Jordan.

298

Part 5   For better, for worse

Less than two years after his marriage to his
housekeeper wife, she died suddenly and rather mysteriously.
No one saw him after she died. When some of the neighbours
went to the house to offer their help, he ordered them off the
premises with threats. She was buried at Marwayne Cemetery,
and Dr Jordan paid a Mr. Ray, then a resident of Marwayne, to
have flowers put on her grave regularly for many months
afterward.

Shortly after that he called a sale. That was the most
wonderful sale that had ever taken place at or near Marwayne.
It lasted two whole days. There were hundreds of cars at it and
people came from far and near. He had so much real good
merchandise of all descriptions, and other effects to sell. One
surprising thing that was on the sales bill were a number of bales
of pure silk and velvet materials that had never been opened.

After the sale was over and before Dr. Jordan left the
district, I received a letter one day from a lady I met in
Vancouver in 1912, 'Dirty Dora', as her friends called her. She
claimed she was the lawful wife of Dr. Jordan, and that her boy
was Dr. Jordan's lawful son and heir. She had heard that his
"wife" was dead and wondered if there were "any other
romances looming up". She would be "glad of any information
regarding his property etc., or other help I could give her
concerning Dr. Jordan's plans. 'What happened to the lad who
came in with them in 1929 or 1930?'" she asked.

The young lad, I assumed the son of Dr. Jordan's late
housekeeper wife, had wandered about the district for a few
weeks, picking up a little work and a meal here and there. He
did not speak of Dr. Jordan, he seemed afraid of him. He had
not gone back to live with him after his mother's death. We
heard later that he left the district to make his way to Calgary. I

wrote to her and gave her all the information I had about Dr. Jordan, telling her what was hearsay, and what I knew to be fact. I mentioned receiving this letter to one or two people, and very soon Dr. Jordan came to the office. He had heard that I had received a letter from his former wife. He confirmed that he had married her and that he was the father of her son.

"Do you know Mr. Marfleet, that woman did me the dirtiest trick that a woman could ever do to a man. After our son was born, she told me she had craved to have a son all her life, and that she had only married me so as to have a strong, upright, handsome man to father her son legitimately."

I couldn't help but think, 'Well, you are far from strong, upright, and handsome now.'

But I had known him when he was all three.

"She said she was now through with me and for me to get out to hell away from her. I left her." He continued, "But I bought her a fine, beautiful home and I gave her $4,000 to bring the boy up right and educate him. She then divorced me in Canada on the grounds of unfaithfulness and desertion. I had divorced her in Blaine, Washington, but this did not satisfy her. She wanted a Canadian divorce. I have the clippings from the papers to prove what I say."

He produced the clippings which were quite authentic.

Sometime later he left Marwayne, and went to Edmonton. We soon heard that he had married a certain Madam L., who was then a pioneer hairdresser and beauty specialist in that city.

300

Part 5   For better, for worse

A neighbour's daughter was at the time of the wedding, taking a beauty course at Madam L.'s salon and I heard her say that Dr. Jordan was a most gallant lover, and that he rarely came home without either flowers or chocolates for his bride, and that they were out to some entertainment several evenings a week.

During the summer after their wedding, he came back to Marwayne accompanied by his bride. He brought her into the Municipal Office for her to meet me. They were billing and cooing like turtledoves. He was so chivalrous and attentive to her every wish. When he left the office to go into the Post Office next door, she said.

"He's a darling, Mr. Marfleet, such a wonderful man, so kind and considerate. He anticipates my every wish. Nothing is too good for me. These furs -" She was wearing beautiful mink furs – "are just one of his wedding presents to me."

Some months later a neighbour from Marwayne, who knew her, met her in Edmonton and she told her. "He's a devil! Do you know he has invented a pistol that will shoot a poisoned needle through an oak door and no one can see where it went through it? I'm terrified of him. I'm living apart form him in the hotel. I wish I had never seen him."

We heard nothing more of either of them until we saw an announcement of his death in the papers in 1951. At the time of his death, he was over ninety years of age.

Why have I reached so far ahead in my story, or rather history, to record these details about one man? He was an enigma! I have never heard him speak discreditably of a

For better, for worse

neighbour or anyone, or of his being other than honest in his
dealings with them. He never interfered with them, just kept
aloof. I always found him to be both honest and
straightforward. Yet rumour, and rumour that persists can be a
very potent factor in understanding a man's reputation in a
community, had it that he was sinister, almost diabolical. I have
heard one of his former hired men say that he will swear on any
Bible, Jordan's first wife did not die a natural death. The
mystery that surrounded the death of his housekeeper wife is
still spoken of among those that knew him, or of him. However,
he has now gone beyond the reach of rumours, sinister or
otherwise.

That fall some Icelanders from Island Lake,
situated about one hundred and fifty miles
North-east of Marwayne, had contracted to sell a large quantity
of fish to a firm in Chicago. They came to our district to hire
freighters, who would haul the fish from the Lake to Kitscoty,
the point from which the fish were to be shipped. Ten men from
around Marwayne took the contract, my brother Bill and me
being two of them. When we reached the Lake the thermometer
registered sixty-three degrees below zero. The ice was cracking,
the woods were crackling, and everything was just brittle with
the frost. It was certainly cold.

The morning after we arrived at the Lake, I got up at
4:00 a.m. and walked across it to a log shed, where we had put
our teams for the night, to feed all the horses. I remember I had
to chop a piece out of the logs above the door of this shack to
get my team, Sam and Dick, in, as they were so very tall. As I
walked across the Lake I heard the timber wolves howling all
around, the cold brittle air resonant with their weird, inhuman
calls. I felt no fear until, about five hours later; an Indian came
along with a large black one he had just shot. Such a terrible

302

Part 5   For better, for worse

looking beast - it measured over eight feet from the point of its nose to the tip of its tail. It was hideously cruel looking. I said, "I wonder if you were one of those that were howling all around, when I went to feed the horses this morning." The Icelanders stopped in their work of packing the fish and looked at me.

"Did you go alone across the Lake to feed the horses?" they asked.

I said, "Why sure, why not?" but that 'why not' was not so brave sounding as it would have been before I saw the dead wolf. They all warned me solemnly never to do it again. I did not.

As we were travelling over a lake on the way home, we overtook an Indian walking. I stopped to give him a lift. He seemed a very, old man and looked very frail. When he tried to climb up on the wagon, he did so, so feebly that I reached down with all my strength to help him, and my arm sprang back holding him away up. He just felt as light as an even volume of feathers would. He was a medicine man, he told me. We stayed in an Indian log shack that night. It was the only place to stay, as there were no white settlers around that district. There was a sick girl in the next room - there were only two rooms - and the Medicine Man, - whom I had picked up, was in the room with her beating on the tom toms and making the oddest kind of music to scare away the evil spirits, which caused her sickness. A young Indian was there who seemed to have had a very good education.

He said to me, "That is their way. They'll never change or become civilized. My poor people."

Part 5   For better, for worse

He seemed to be very distressed. He went on after a few moments, "I came here from Cold Lake to try to induce them to send this girl to the hospital, but they only have faith in the Medicine Man and his tom toms. I could not persuade them to do anything for her." He continued, "You can tell I've had some education. I've had a real good education that I got in Toronto absolutely free. Any one of these people could have done the same, but they just will not. Oh, my poor, poor people!" He bowed his head, and whether he prayed or wept, I could not tell.

Indians are so very odd in their ways. When we entered their shack, they - not one of them - even looked at us, but just ignored our entrance. We sat down on the floor, there were no seats of any kind, and after a time I pulled out the makings, made a cigarette and offered it to one of the braves. He took it with a grunt and then began to ask us questions as to what we were doing on the trails. We had brought in our grub boxes and now ate our food, which we had brought with us, and which was frozen sixty degrees solid.

We white men were very amused at the Indians' ways with their children. There was a child - a little boy - about three years old, I would think, who tried to entertain us all. He kept shuffling his feet along the dirt floor and swaying from side to side and his parents thought he was just so clever. They sat laughing at him and singing, "Yah, yah! Yah, yah!" with mimicry play on the tom toms, and then laughing again hilariously; all the while that poor girl was dying in the next room. This went on for some time, and then the brave got up from the floor, reached to a shelf for a box from which he took with his fingers some powder that looked like powdered herbs. This he put in a cup and mixed it with water, using his finger to stir the mixture. He then took a large mouthful and - drawing

the child to him - put his mouth to that of the child and blew
hard. The child sputtered and coughed, but the brave kept his
mouth firmly on the child's till he had swallowed the medicine.

"Feeding him pigeon fashion" said someone.

Then it came to "retiring" for the night, we all rolled
up in our blankets and lay down on the dirt floor braves, squaws,
children and men all mixed up. We tried to make a row of our
own, but some late-coming Indians lay down some on each end
of our row.

One of our men, Johnnie Norton, was a very religious
man. He was always praying and that night he prayed aloud
after lying down, until he fell asleep. After the Indians lay down
beside him, a squaw came, threading her way through and over
the sleepers on the floor and pushed in between Johnnie and the
brave next to him, and composed herself to sleep. Bill, who was
always out for devilment, waited for some little time, and then
reached across Johnnie and began prodding her on the behind.
She raised her head and looked at Johnnie, but he was fast
asleep so she lay down again. Again, Bill reached over and gave
her a few prods and again, she raised her head and looked at
Johnnie, who lay with his arms crossed on his chest sleeping
innocently and soundly. This kept on for some little time and
then she finally turned round to Johnnie, shook him violently,
and when he woke up she motioned him to go to the end of the
row. Johnnie rose, looking very bewildered and stumbled to the
end of the row, where he lay down and began to pray in a loud
voice. Now Bill was next to her and the mystified look of
chagrin on his face was most amusing. He tried to move away
from her, but we all pushed him to her, and the noises of our
suppressed laughter made a most unusual harmony with the
ordinary sounds made by a number of people sleeping in one

small room. Next day, when we teased both Johnnie and Bill, Johnnie bowed his head on his chest and prayed, "Forgive me, Oh, God, for it was my sinful nature, over which I did not have control while in the sleep that Thou didst vouchsafe to bless me with." or some such prayer. Bill just grinned and said, 'She made plenty good jiggy-jig." Mischief and fun occurred, even in the midst of hardships.

Bill and I made two more trips, and were paid Thirty dollars per trip. Each trip took us ten days. We travelled mostly over lake, river and slough, as offering the easiest road. The trails, where there were any through the dense bush, were so winding and devious that it would have taken much longer to travel by them. Though often when crossing the lakes, with which that country was dotted, some large, some small, we often wished we were on dry land for the terrific cracking of the ice in the extreme cold makes one think that the whole frozen surface is breaking up.

That was the most extreme cold I have ever experienced. So intense was it, that one had the feeling of being in an unreal world - a world of cold, inimical silence – "plumb-full of hush" - as Service has fitly described it.

When we reached home, after delivering our last load at Kitscoty - each load had weighed three thousand pounds and we had each made Ninety dollars - I said to Bill, "I'll be good and hungry the next time I contract to haul fish."

"Yes," he agreed, "let the other fellow haul them. They make damned good eating, but I don't like the smell of those Indian bugs."

Part 5   For better, for worse

There had come out to this country, about a year prior to this time, an elderly couple - a Mr. and Mrs. Morgan. They had taken up homestead rights on the quarter section west of me - the one that had originally been filed on by Gilbert Nicolson. I had helped them all I could from their coming, and Mrs. Morgan and Nan had become good friends. Mrs. Morgan had often come up to our home to help Nan when there had been extra work to do. She was a very lovable old-soul with a heart of kindness and goodness. When I began batching in 1913, she had very kindly offered to do my baking and laundry, and I had accepted her offer gratefully.

One evening in early May of the following year, I walked down to fetch my laundry. When I entered the yard, Mrs. Morgan and her brother, Charlie Woodward, who had recently arrived from England and who was almost stone deaf, were in the garden planting potatoes. I went over to them and began talking gardening. Soon Mr. Morgan came out of the house "Ah," he said. "I thought I heard your voice, Fred."

"I'm just getting some pointers on planting potatoes." I told him.

"Gracious, mercy, how quick that girl walks." exclaimed Mrs. Morgan, looking towards the Government Road. "She only left Lowes' just as you came into the yard, Fred, and here she is."

I glanced disinterestedly towards the approaching figure.

"I must be going." I said. "I'll take my washing if it's ready, Mrs. Morgan."

307

Part 5   For better, for worse

"Won't you stay and meet the new school marm?"
Mr. Morgan asked.

"No. I have to get home." I told him. "Bill said he
may be up this evening to give me a hand. We are going to
brand some calves." Mrs. Morgan and I went into the house to
get my laundry.

Soon I heard a musical, lilting voice say, "Good
evening, Mr. Morgan. Isn't this a lovely, prairie spring
evening?"

"Now you've said that just right, Miss Lee. This is
just what you called it - a prairie spring evening."

"I thought you would say that." With a rippling laugh,
that was very attractive.

"This is my brother-in-law, just come from England."
said Mr. Morgan, introducing Charlie. "He's from
Birmingham."

"Oh, you're from Brummidgeham. That's not far
from Nottingham, though I've never been there." she said very
amiably as she shook hands with Charlie.

By this time, I was at the door, looking and listening,
and quite ignoring what Mrs. Morgan was saying.

Charlie seemed to have heard her every word though
she hadn't raised her voice.

"Ah," he said, "I coom from Brummidgeham. You
coom from Notingum?"

308

Part 5   For better, for worse

"Well, I taught school there for several years. Do you know it?"

"Ay, I worked at Beeston for nigh on eight year." he told her.

"I know Beeston well. I often cycled out there and rowed up the Trent to Thrumpton." She told him.

"That are a nice place, are Thrumpton." Charlie began but Mr. Morgan interrupted him.

"You'll be crying like a homesick kid, Charlie, if I let Miss Lee talk to you any more."

Miss Lee then said. "I've brought you some work, Mr. Morgan. You're required, by the Department of Education, to complete these forms, and have me sign them." with a little bubbling laugh. "I wonder if they think I'll be difficult."

Mr. Morgan took the papers and looked through them. "The clerk must have made a mistake." He told her. "I've got the forms that were meant for you, but let's go inside and fill them out, and no harm done."

When they entered, I was introduced to Miss Lee. She acknowledged the introduction with a graceful bow.

We all sat down while Mr. Morgan completed the forms Miss Lee had brought.

She said, "You've been having quite an exciting time here lately, I understand." as if to make conversation.

Part 5   For better, for worse

"What was that?" Mrs. Morgan asked.

"Haven't you all been voting on the free range issue?"

"Yes," I said, "how did you hear about it?"

"It's about all I have heard about these past few days in school."

"Now just fancy that." said Mrs. Morgan. "The children have been telling you."

"Oh, yes, the children are all very excited and very vocal about it. By-the-bye, Mr. Morgan, I hear some of the trustees want to pay me only seventy dollars per month."

"Yes," Mr. Morgan said, looking a little uncomfortable, I thought. "I don't know what Jennings thinks, but two of them think seventy dollars is a very good salary."

"Well, I would like them to be informed that seventy dollars is not good enough for me. I stipulated seventy-five dollars, and I shall not teach here for less."

Mr. Morgan, still looking uncomfortable, said, "I'll have to call a meeting. I wonder if Springford's home."

"He'll surely be home Saturday night, won't he Fred?" Mrs. Morgan said.

"He usually is." I told her.

"Well, I'll get them together for Saturday evening and let you know on Sunday." He told Miss Lee.

310

Part 5   For better, for worse

"It might be a good idea for Miss Lee to be present at the meeting, and then everyone will know where everyone else stands." I suggested.

Without the least hesitation Miss Lee said, "That's an excellent idea, and I shall be pleased to go if the trustees want me to be present." and she stood up to take her leave.

Throughout the conversation, I had been trying to determine just what was the attraction about Miss Lee. That everything about her had appealed strongly to me, I was pleasantly aware. Her dark intelligent eyes, where humour or amusement seemed to twinkle in and out continuously, her slim lithe figure, which gave one the impression that she was taller than she really was, her accent and laugh, all combined to make her a very charming girl, I thought. As she rose to go, I also rose. On the spur of the moment, I asked her, "May I have the pleasure of walking home with you, Miss Lee?"

Her eyes gleamed with amusement but she lowered them quickly and accepted my offer graciously. That was my undoing; since then I have been in thrall to her; her bondsman and slave, but I will now let Miss Lee tell you all about that in the remaining chapters of this story.

For better, for worse

CHAPTER 18

Arch O' Mine Eyebrows

Marwayne, May 4th 1914.

A re you lonely?

Am I? Ye gods of Rome! I'm permeated, saturated, and every other conceivable - ated with the darndest pangs of lonesomeness that could possibly lay siege to a lone, misguided female spinstering her way around a cruel, mocking world. Can't you just feel the yearning of my soul to be back again among you all, at the Machray, dancing, prancing, gabbing and drinking tea at the noon hour? Oh, how I love you all, ensemble and á seulement (excuse the gridiron, but how does one say individually in French?) I wish now that I had made more of my chances to learn the 'lingo' from the Future Conditional!' He really did know his French, but then, of course, he should.

I arrived at Kitscoty, (and that's the name, all right) at 1.10 Friday morning. There was no one to meet me though Mr. Morgan had said, definitely, that I would be met. When I got off the train I stood looking around, but the only person on the platform, besides myself, was the postal clerk getting the post, pardon 'mail' off the train. As the train began to shriek its departure, and the 'mail' creature slung the mailbags over his shoulder and began descending the steps that lead from the platform, I approached him and asked, "Do you know if there's anyone from Marwayne to meet a new teacher?"

312

Part 5   For better, for worse

"Nope" He said over his shoulder without even glancing my way, or slackening his step. I felt as droopy as a hen in the rain.

Off the platform the mud was everywhere knee deep. I stood wondering what I should do. The thought of descending the steps into that sea of mud filled me with a cold fear. I looked around the station to see if I could find a nook or cranny into which I could crawl for the night, but nothing offered. Then I bethought me of the waiting room but when I found it, it was locked. As I stood feeling terribly and awfully sorry for myself, a young man came running on to the platform and hastened towards me.

"Are you Miss Lee?" he panted at me.

I told him "Yes".

"There's a room reserved for you in the Hotel." He told me. I hugged him with my eyes. I had never even thought of there being a hotel in that mud enshrouded outpost.

The young man then seized my suitcases and we made our way over a slimy, mud-covered walk to the hotel, and all the while he was most volubly explaining that he had "just dozed off and never heard the train come in".

I thought he must be the 'Boots' from the way he talked.

Inside the hotel, there was quite a nice rotunda where several men sat playing cards. When we entered they stopped playing and talking and watched my every action with a great show of interest.

313

Part 5   For better, for worse

'Boots' said, "Will you sign the register, please?"

"Certainly," I said.

When I did so I noticed that the name above mine was, "Pat Rafferty and wife". That seemed odd but in keeping with the "Nope," I thought.

'Boots' then led the way upstairs, and half way up I looked down into the rotunda, and every one of those card players was at the register, admiring my signature, I hoped.

When we reached my room, 'Boots' said "Goodnight" and departed.

I took off my shoes and put them outside my door. They were very muddy and I thought I must give him a little extra tip in the morning if he makes a good job of them. I was soon in bed and asleep. After some time I woke up, and wondered at the odour in the room and then realized, that I had forgotten to blow the lamp out.

Next morning when I reached out for my shoes they were not there. I found them one at each end of the passage and uncleaned! I had wondered what all the giggling was about after I got into bed.

After breakfast, which was served in the dining room the proprietor, Alec Gilmore, whom everyone addressed as Alex, came to me and told me that, Mr. Morgan would be in to 'Get' me about noon, and I could wait in the parlour till he came. The 'Mr.' gave me the impression that Mr. Morgan must be a very imposing personage; everyone else seemed to be "Tom", "Dick", or "Harry". I got out 'At the Foot of the

314

Part 5   For better, for worse

Rainbow', which you so kindly put in my suitcase, and for
which, thank you, darling, and began to read, stopping now and
then to watch the activities of the street below. About eleven
o'clock a little man drove past, seated in the most ramshackle
vehicle I had ever seen, drawn by two very skinny horses. His
headgear was as strange as his equipage was sorry looking. He
wore a flat round hat with a curtain of white cotton material
which hung from under the brim and which reached completely
round his head except for a space in front of his face. After he
passed, I returned to my reading but was soon interrupted by the
door of the parlour being thrown wide open, and Alex
announcing, "Mr. Morgan", and Mr. Morgan entered! He was in
face, figure, nose, and belly a perfect replica of Santa Claus. He
wore glasses upside down and with only one glass, but the eye
that looked through that glass gave one the uncomfortable
feeling of being seen through, both literally and figuratively. All
the time I knew Mr. Morgan, I could never tell him a lie, or if I
did, I knew that the eye knew. (And this, after you all 'stuffing'
me that the Secretary would be a dashing young bachelor!)

He said, "I've come to get you, Miss Lee. Are you
ready?"

I told him, "Yes, quite ready". I put on my hat and
suit coat, paid my bill and followed him out to the street. There
stood the ramshackle vehicle I had seen pass some minutes
earlier and the skinny horses. When Mr. Morgan donned the hat
with the curtain, and climbed up into the crazy seat, I gathered
that I was supposed to climb up beside him, which I did and we
drove out of town, and surprisingly, no one seemed to want to
even look at us!

"Was he at the station to meet you?" he asked me,
referring of course to 'boots'.

315

Part 5   For better, for worse

"Well, he was a little late. He just dozed off and never heard the train come in, he told me."

"Ah, he was playing poker." Mr. Morgan said. "Now I'll just complain to Alex about that."

"Oh, don't, please," I begged him. "He was only a minute or so late."

I felt the eye look right into my soul.

Mr. Morgan beguiled the time on the way home (about four hours) by giving me a sketch of his life. He had been in the British Army, and spent many years in India and Ceylon, and his last years in "the Service" were spent on "The Rock," (Gibraltar) "and I've been on the rocks ever since." he laughed.

His horses wore no blinders, and I was amused at the coy look they would each throw over the right shoulder at him when he told them "Giddy up". We just jogged along, and I really enjoyed it and I believe the horses and Mr. Morgan enjoyed it, too.

Mrs. Morgan is a very lovely person. She made me very welcome and asked me to have dinner with them for which I was very grateful. I was just starving! There were several men there, who had been fighting a prairie fire, and Mr. Morgan told them that I'm Irish. If he had told them that, 'I'm a Hottentots' they could not have expressed more wonder. Yet there are several Irish families around, but they're all via the States and have gathered the moss or patina of American civilization on the way, I suppose. Whereas I am the raw, uncut, un-ground, or un-something article I suppose. Woe is me! Or is it?

316

Part 5   For better, for worse

Wednesday

I should have mailed (got it that time) this letter on
Monday, but wanted to chat a little longer with you before
parting with it, as I know when it's gone I shall feel more
lonesome than ever. Zooks, Jess, I miss you – I miss everyone
of you – tremendously! This is really the first time in my life
that I'm without the company of lots of people of my own age.
At home there were eleven of us girls, varying in age from the
mewling and puking infant to my eldest sister who was a young
lady of about sixteen when I was sent to a boarding school in
England and I've always had lots of congenial companions ever
since.

I'm boarding in the home of George and Annie Lowe.
There are three children two of whom attend school. The
youngest, the spoiled brat, is going on five. Mr. Lowe seems to
be a negligible quantity – apart from the children, of course.
He's never at home except on Saturday night, she says. She's a
very (how I miss the Old Country usage of the word, "Homely,"
here. I was told on the boat coming to Canada that I must never
use that word of a lady of any age in this country) anyhow she is
– oh, pleasant to live with.

I asked Mrs. Lowe this evening, "Are there any young
people around here at all?" She smiled and said with conviction,
"Oh, yes. They'll soon be around."

"Do you think any of them will be interested in
playing tennis?" I asked her then.

She said, "I don't know about tennis," then archly,
"But they'll want to play."

317

Part 5   For better, for worse

Her eyes go on a twinkling spree when she's amused
and without knowing she is funny. She said to me the other day,
"If I could only get two 'clookygens' I wouldn't call the queen
me hant!" I thought she said "Clooky gems," and wondered
what kind of gems she meant: the Koh – in – or, or the Hope
perhaps two out of the Rajah of Mysore's turban but later
discovered that what she wanted to ensure blissful immunity
from all future poverty for the Lowe family was just two humble
and lowly clucking hens. How little some people ask of this
world's riches! Two clucking hens and she wouldn't call the
queen her aunt!

The school is terrific! There are twelve pupils ranging
in age from eight to fourteen. The age fourteen proposes to
write her grade eight exam in June. She's smart but awfully
backward. I shall give her a lot of extra time 'til she writes. The
others know next to nothing about learning, and don't seem to
be particularly anxious to find out. One of them asked me
yesterday, "What's the use of us learning? We're only going to
be farmers."

When I tried to explain to them some of the
advantages of an education, they sat smiling and looking at me
so pityingly that I began to feel sorry for myself, but what they
don't know about the sex affairs of the animals on the farm you
could 'put into the corner of your eye' as my dear old granny
would say. One of the grade one's told me the other day what a
'gelding' is. He seemed to be tickled pink to be able to impart
this information and did so so innocently and forthrightly that I
couldn't inhibit him.

I have met the word 'geld' in Burn's poems, but just
didn't tumble when this boy told me that a horse that was

318

Part 5   For better, for worse

passing by was a gelding. I asked without thinking, "Is that a driving horse?"

I'm going to the Post Office now to post this letter. It's about three miles to it, but a nice walk. I'd love it if it were not for these dastardly mosquitoes. The bally pests have just about ruined my beauty. I bet I've killed millions of them already!

Tell all the girls I love them and how I miss them. I even love gobble – gobble and chou chou and miss the fights I so often had with them. I just loved those fights. I hope they miss them too.

Give 'Bloom o' my lips' a big, big hug. Will you ever forget that evening, Jess? I never shall. That was the evening of the Geisha, wasn't it? Oh, it was a grand, grand evening to remember.

And now I send you all and each, a weepy, snozzly kiss. Bye – bye, Jess, darling. Do write soon.

Paddy

Such was the letter I wrote to Jess Greenwood a few days after my arrival in Marwayne. I was feeling lonesome and undecided and scared. "Have I acted wisely in leaving the Machray School and all the nice friends I made in Winnipeg?" I kept asking myself. And "had I better go back and forget this crazy idea of travelling round the world that has enmeshed me?" But, "No, I would go on. I can't turn back now. They would make too much fun of me, at home." So, my thoughts harassed me.

Part 5   For better, for worse

On the Monday, when recess time came, I went out
and tried to get the pupils interested in playing the ordinary
school games. We began with 'Nuts-in-May', usually the
melting pot of all reserve between a new teacher and her pupils.

A few of the younger ones wanted to play but the
older ones stood aloof and uncooperative. Then I tried the
'Hindmost of Three', but again the older ones stood remote, so I
sat down on the steps and left them to their own resources. They
stood for a while talking in whispers till suddenly one girl cried
out, 'Last round the school stinks to beat the band!' Oh and how
those pupils ran! Just as if their very lives depended on not
being the last, and when the poor unfortunate 'Last', came home
the others held their noses, and fled from him and otherwise
ostracized him. After they had played this exciting game a few
times I said, 'I don't think that's a very nice game. Can't we just
talk?' This seemed to have more appeal for them. They
gathered round and were soon telling me about 'Herd Law', and
'Free Range'.

"And you say you voted on it?" I asked them.

"Not us. Just our fathers."

"And now everybody's cattle can roam all over the
prairie, and no one can impound them." Another told me.

"And they can eat all the grass off of the C.P.R. land."
Another added.

"Which is the C.P.R. land?" I asked them.

"They own all the odd sections of land." They said.

320

Part 5   For better, for worse

"Do the farmers own the even sections?" I asked.

"No. some of them are owned by people that live in the East and in the States and..."

"My daddy says they are just sittin' on their asses waiting for the farmers to break up all the land and then they will sell their sections and make a big haul of money out of them." One of the younger ones ventured. Some of the older ones snickered a little at this piece of information.

"They are called speculators." The grade eight pupil informed us all, learnedly.

All the pupils seemed to be highly delighted at the success of the 'Free Range' vote.

When I gave them an exercise to do on the blackboard, each pupil surrounded his work with a number of lines. The more lines and the wavier the more artistic he or she seemed to think it was.

"What's the idea of all these lines?" I asked them when they first drew them, but no one answered. Then I told them. "Well, I want you to stop drawing them. They are just a waste of time, and are not at all pretty." Still, they continued to draw the encircling lines. Finally, in an effort to make them understand that I did not want the lines, I raised my voice and said, "Now, I want you all to get this. There's to be no more herd law on the blackboard. You must give all your work free range." From then on I had no more difficulty with them wasting time fencing in their exercises with lines.

Part 5   For better, for worse

That first afternoon I had a visitor just as the pupils were marching out of school to go home. He was a Mr. Child the catechist, who took the services at Tring Anglican Church. He introduced himself and then said, "I guessed you'd be feeling lonely, so I just called to have a chat and drive you home. You have quite a walk to and from school every day."

"I don't mind it." I told him. "In fact I'd enjoy it if it weren't for these blood thirsty mosquitoes. Aren't they despicable creatures?"

"Yes, and they seem to be quite partial to Old Country blood." He said. "Our Dean at College always has a great joke out of the boys from the British Isles every year. He tells them, "Oh. Don't mind them. They will soon cease to be troublesome.' Then, when they ask, 'Why?' he says 'Because you Old Country boys kill so many of them the first year you're out here.' And, then he laughs hilariously."

"Don't they bother you?" I asked him.

"Well, I don't just enjoy them, but I guess we Canadians are just a little tougher or not so sweet tasting or something. They don't seem to punish us as they do you Old Country people."

"And the moral of that is; hurry up, Miss Lee, and get tough and sour." I laughed.

"Now I didn't suggest that." He said, also laughing.

When we reached Lowe's, he tied his horse up and came into the house with me, and sat talking to Mrs. Lowe and me till she got supper on the table. When she invited him to

322

Part 5   For better, for worse

have supper he accepted gladly. We had just finished when a
Mr. Rogers knocked on the door and Mrs. Lowe invited him in.
This seemed to be the cue for Mr. Child to take his departure.
He rose immediately, thanked Mrs. Lowe for the supper and
took his leave. Mrs. Lowe then introduced Mr. Rogers - Sam,
she called him, to me.

After conversing a few minutes he said he was going
for his mail, and rose to go.

"Are you coming back this way?" Mrs. Lowe asked
him.

"Yes," he told her. "Did you want me to bring your
mail?"

"Well. If it's not too much trouble, I wish you
would," she said.

"Not at all. How would you like to come for a ride,
Miss Lee, and see a bit of the country?" he asked me, but before
I could answer Mrs. Lowe spoke up.

"Yes, go, Miss Lee, and then you'll know where the
Post Office is." Mrs. Lowe suggested. I got my coat and hat
and went with him.

"What do you think of the school?" he asked me as
soon as we started.

"It's all right. The pupils are quite backward though."
I told him.

Part 5   For better, for worse

"You can't wonder at that. The school is only open for a few weeks in the summer." He said, and added. "I think that's a great pity."

"Yes, I think so, too. Why don't they open it in the winter?"

"Oh, it's too cold. Some of them have to come over three miles."

"I know," I said. "When does it close for the winter?"

"That depends on the weather, but usually about the middle of November, I think. Why? You're not anxious for it to close already, are you?"

"No. I was just wondering."

"Have you signed your agreement yet?" He then asked me

"No."

"You asked for $75.00 a month, didn't you?"

"Yes."

"They're talking of offering you $70.00, but if I were you I wouldn't take it."

"Thank you for the hint. I shall certainly hold out for $75.00" I told him.

Part 5

For better, for worse

"That's all right and no one need know you've been put wise. I'll just run in and pick up the mail." He said as he got out of the buggy and went into the Post Office.

There was only an official letter for me from the Department of Education, which I read when he handed it to me.

"I think this was meant for Mr. Morgan." I told him.

"Do you want to call in with it as we pass?" he asked me.

"No. Perhaps I'd better take it home and read it more carefully."

"As you say." he said. Then after a few moments he said, "I think you'll be very comfortable with Mrs. Lowe. She's a real good sort, and a mighty fine cook. She boarded a lot of us boys one winter when George Lowe and we were working in the mines in Edmonton, and she sure was good to us."

"Yes, I can imagine she would be." I told him. "I think she's fine. I like her very much."

When we arrived back at Lowe's, Mrs. Lowe asked him. "Won't you come and have a bite of lunch with us, Sam?"

"No, thanks, I have an early start in the morning." he told her. Later when she and I were having a "Bite", she remarked. "I think Sam has been having a drink or two."

"Has he?" I exclaimed in surprise. "I never noticed it. Was he in town to-day?"

Part 5   For better, for worse

She smiled and the eye went on a spree, "He don't have to go to town. He makes it right at home."

I was shocked for a moment. Then I laughed.

"What's amusing you?" she asked me.

"I'm just imagining the shock they'll all get at home when I write and tell them that I go out driving with a "Poteener", and a drunken one at that. My brother will cable me to come home right away. How do you know he's been drinking?" I said.

"He'd never 'ave refused the lunch if he 'adn't." She said.

Two days later when I got home from school Mrs. Lowe was entertaining two visitors - a Mrs. McGill and her daughter, a girl about seventeen years old. After supper I excused myself, went into my room, donned my hat and coat and when I appeared in the kitchen, Mrs. Lowe asked in surprise, "Are you going out, Miss Lee?"

"Yes." I told her. "I'm taking, this letter to Mr. Morgan." Both of the visitors exclaimed, "But won't you be tired? You've just walked home from school."

"That's nothing," I told them. "We had no horse or vehicle of our own in Ireland, so we just had to walk wherever we wanted to go."

I was on my way to the door when Mrs. McGill arrested me.

326

Part 5   For better, for worse

"Excuse me asking, Miss Lee, but did you buy that suit in this country?"

"No," I told her. "I bought it in Belfast."

"Isn't it lovely, Mrs. Lowe? Such a beautiful fit! You've had it altered to fit you, I guess."

"No." I told her. "I chose the material and had it tailored."

"Isn't that lovely goods?" she asked Mrs. Lowe,

"Yes, I've admired it every time Miss Lee has worn it." Mrs. Lowe told her. "I sure like these new narrow skirts, don't you?"

"On Miss Lee, yes, but," laughing, "I'm afraid our curves wouldn't look very good in one. That style's for tall slight figures."

"Gosh, Ma. I like it. Couldn't I get one? There's a dandy in Eaton's spring catalogue." The McGill girl said.

"Maybe, if we get a good crop this Fall; but I'm making no promises mind you."

"I like Miss Lee's hat. Hilda and me have looked all through the catalogues and we can't see anything like it. Was that bought in this country, Miss Lee?" Winnie Lowe, her eldest daughter, asked.

"No, Winnie." I told her. "I bought it in Belfast also."

For better, for worse

"The styles over there must be away ahead of this country." Mrs. Lowe suggested.

"No. I don't think so," I told her. "I thought the styles in Winnipeg were very smart."

"I don't like black as a rule, but I sure like that suit. It looks so good. Do you ever wear colours, Miss Lee?" Mrs. McGill asked.

"Almost always," I told her. "I got this black when my Mother died in 1911."

"Is your Father living?" she asked me then.

"No. He died in 1912, or I wouldn't be out in this country." I told them, with a break in my voice. For, I still could not bear to speak of the death of my parents, casually.

They looked at me sorrowfully as I went out.

Mr. Morgan and a brother-in-law, whom I later came to call Charlie, were in the garden planting potatoes, when I arrived there. I went over to them, and after some conversation, I gave Mr. Morgan the letter from the Department of Education. He adjusted his glasses, upside down, on his cherry coloured nose and after perusing it, said, gleefully, "So they're not infallible up there either. The clerk must have made a mistake; I've got the forms meant for you, but let's go inside and fill them out."

When we entered the kitchen, Mrs. Morgan greeted me very amiably and then introduced a young man who was

Part 5   For better, for worse

sitting in a dark corner of the room. He rose and bowed
graciously.

When the forms were completed, Mr. Morgan asked
me. "Well, how's school going?"

"Fine," I told him. "The pupils are beginning to settle
down. They were certainly excited Monday over this Free
Range issue. I could hear about nothing else."

"Now just fancy that." said Mrs. Morgan in her kind
way. "Who would have thought that the children would have
known anything about it?"

"Oh, they seemed to know all about it; as a matter of
fact their knowledge of all farm affairs is quite profound, and
by-the-way, Mr. Morgan I hear that the Trustees are considering
giving me only $70.00 a month."

"Ah," He said. "Two or three of them think $70.00 is
a good salary." He seemed a trifle disconcerted, I thought.

"Well, it's not good enough for me." I told him
laughingly. Then more soberly, "I shall not teach here for less
than $75.00."

He then said he would have to call a meeting of the
trustees and Mr. Marfleet, the young man in the corner,
suggested that I be present at the meeting. I said I thought that
was a good idea. Though I didn't know whether it would be
such a good idea, but it was the first time he had spoken and I
thought maybe he needed a little encouragement! The
encouragement soon bore fruit, for when, a few minutes later, I

329

Part 5   For better, for worse

rose to go, he also rose and asked, quite debonairly, "May I have the pleasure of walking home with you, Miss Lee?"

Part 5   For better, for worse

CHAPTER 19

Of ancestors, bed tester, puce gowns, and Paisley shawls

M y parents duly reported my arrival to the
       Registrar at Armagh; that I was female, that my
name was Sarah Agnes Lee, - Sarah after granny, and Agnes
after St. Agnes. I hope I have not let her down too often. I was
born to Henry Lee and Catherine Lee (nee McCool) on the 28th
of August and was being registered on the 28th of September the
same year, 1884. Henceforth my address would be Ballywilly,
Loughall, in County Armagh, Ireland.

"It's another girl, Henry."

No response.

"Oh well, there's luck in odd numbers, says Brian
O'Lynn." Granny said.

Henry didn't give a damn for what Brian O'Lynn says,
or said, or was about to say. He wanted a boy, another boy.
Two girls were enough in any family. But, I was here to stay,
strong and lusty. My Dad, Henry, heard the news and went off
to clean his guns with Monkey Brand.

The registrar, no doubt to parade his profound
knowledge of the meaning of words, said the repetition of the
28th was a tautology. He said it to the wrong man for my Dad
knew the dictionary, from A to Zxyomma.

We had at home one mahogany cabinet containing one
dozen solid silver fish knives and forks with mother of pearl

handles, also the carvers and servers to match, all duly hall-marked. Also one Jubilee sovereign, and a Bradbury sewing machine; trophies he had won in contests for his knowledge of the meaning, derivation, and pronunciation of words.

If all this doesn't prove that Dad knew his dictionary, then I can't prove it.

Dad contradicted the worthy registrar, and a near fist fight ensued in which the registrar called Dad 'You dhirty, low, papish taycher.', and Dad retaliated worthily by calling him 'a dhirty ignorant old orange omadhaun'.

Encore again begorra, the Battle of the Boyne duetto.

My father and mother both taught school, and I was the fifth child and third daughter of their union. Their first two issues were males, and the next eleven were 'of the female persuasion' as my eldest brother used to maintain.

How Dad's guns must have shone and what bricks of Monkey Brand he must have used by the time the eleventh arrived!

Eleven wee bunches of petticoats! Always one of those petticoats just had to be of red flannel. A red flannel petticoat in those days was the very 'height of illigance', and no lady, or lady in potential, could afford not to flaunt one. At the beginning of winter, Mother used to purchase bales of red flannel and then cut and sew up on the Bradbury, till each one of us had a good 'saucy' red flannel petticoat, always scalloped and embroidered in black wool by Granny.

Granny, dear darling old granny!

Part 5   For better, for worse

She was petite with a bust and waist that even in advanced years, when I remember her, winked invitingly even through her puce gown and paisley shawl. She had a foot and ankle that would have lured Prince Charming from his allegiance to Cinderella, if we can believe all that we have been told about that gentleman's 'wakeness' for a 'nate foot', so slight and neat were Granny's. She had the gayest and most blithesome laugh in the entire world.

Our family lived with her and Granddad, Thomas Lee, on his farm at Ballywilly. Dad was their only son, and as Dad and Mother both taught school, it was left largely to Granny to bring us up. Granddad often took a hand in 'operation rarin of girls'.

How we loved them both!

Granddad believed in austerity, - sometimes. His was an amazing complex of the most incompatible traits of character that ever entered into the make-up of a human being. He was loud in his denunciation of 'the dhrink', but when he was well under the influence of drink, he would hold up his glass and say, "Bushmill's is as mellow as crame."

He was a great reader of the Bible and often quoted it, usually in reverse as it were. He said, "The Lord says a just man falls seven times a day." So, he argued that a man, to be just in the sight of God, must fall seven times a day. He certainly lived up to this interpretation because he not only fell often, he catapulted.

He was a tall, handsome man of charming manner, a 'bhoy wid a way wid him'. The women all fell for him and this he exploited to the full. As a matter of fact, he was an old roué,

Part 5   For better, for worse

but the most likeable old soul in the world. Though a strong and
ardent catholic, he never went to church. Thus, as I say, his
nature was a strange conflict of theory with practice. His
grandfather had been what was called a turncoat. He had
become a Catholic when he married Granddad's grandmother, -
one Mary O'Neill. Perhaps it was the name O'Neill that
suggested to Granddad when he was 'in his cups' as Granny
politely put it, that he had blue blood in his veins; that he was
directly descended from Owen Roe O'Neill, King of Ulster, and
one time favourite of Queen Elizabeth. However when he was
sober we never heard a word about it; so there must have been a
crooked branch in the family tree somewhere.

Granny was the opposite, always full of life and fun.
She loved to go to 'town', - Portadown, four plus miles away.
So often on Saturdays she would don her puce gown, paisley
shawl and bonnet and trip down the loanin', a driveway, a light
of anticipation shining in her blue eyes, and a look of
determination to meet up with 'all and every' in each step of her
dainty feet.

She would come back around five o'clock in the
afternoon, her bonnet often slightly awry, but light-hearted and
gay. Full of adventures she had met up with or the people she
had 'fell in' with, and the gossip she had heard, which she
always seemed to have filed away in its proper category in her
memory. We youngsters listened avidly, taking it all in, though
it was assumed by our elders that we were too young to
understand it all.

It usually went something like this.

"Well, ould Carragher over took me in the Cash
Hollow."

334

Part 5   For better, for worse

"Good morrow, Mrs. Lee," says he, 'and will ye be takin' a lift?'

"I will indeed and thankee." Says I.

"Och," says he, "sure and you do be walking like a young girl this mornin'."

"I wasn't letting on I noticed his blarney." Granny said.

"How is your tic douloureux, Mr. Carragher?" says I.

"Och," says he, "Sure an it nearly dhrove me crazy last week. I went into ould Duggan in Richhill an' not a damn thing, savin' yer presence, could he do for it. He says to me, says he, 'You'll just have to cut down on your atin', as if atin' or not atin' has anything to do with neuralgia."

"Then he says to me," Granny continued. "Have ye heard anything about me pig?"

"What pig?" says I.

"Didn't ye hear about me pig that was stole out of me shed a week gone last Thursday?" says he.

"No," says I. "How could anybody steal a pig out of your shed? Wouldn't its squealing wake you up?"

"Och, no." says he. "The pig was dead."

"An' what the divil for, savin' yer presence," says I, "would anybody steal a dead pig?"

335

Part 5   For better, for worse

"Ye don't be undherstandin'," says he. "Jep Haggan killed six pigs for me for market," says he, "an'hung them up in the shed an' next mornin' when I wint to load them there was but five."

"Oh, I beg yer pardin'" says I, "but if one o' your pigs was stole 'tis hopin', I am, that some poor hungry cratchur got a good bit of it. There's too many hungry wimmen and childher around, Mr. Carragher. The men spend too much money altogether on the dhrink." Says I.

"But that ould devil is so hard-hearted and hard faced you just can't shame him. He'll sell his rotten whisky on his way to hell, savin' yer presence, Catherine." Says granny. "He dhropped me off at Hagen's Nell and then I fell in with Barney McNulty. Poor Barney, he can't help it if the good Lord saw fit to afflict him with reel feet, and the way the women thrate him is a dirty shame. We met Mrs. Tommy Dale, - she's yon way, - must be seven months gone anyway, and they've only been married a matter of four months. And what does she do, but turns around and bends over, tears a bit off the tail of her shift an' throws it afther him when we passed her. I could feel me face burning. As if God, in his goodness, would cast her unborn chile with reel feet, just because she happens to meet Barney when she's yon way. An' Barney the poor unfortunate harmless cratchur, he knows why she done it." She paused.

"What do you think he told me?" She continued. "ha, ha, ha!"

"He says, 'Have ye heard that Paddy McGinty is coortin' Lizzie McCartney?' he says, an' laughs."

336

Part 5   For better, for worse

"Well, truth an' I laughed too. An' I says, Paddy McGinty and Lizzie McCartney! Ah, get away wid ye, says I. Why she's over thirty if she's a day. She's been wearin' a bonnet these last seven or eight years."

"They must both be nipping the ass off forty, savin' yer presence" says he. "An' who do you think is blackfootin' them?" says Barney, and he laughed again.

"Och, I wouldn't be knowin'." says I.

"Well, truth and sowl," says he, "an' ye'll laugh. Why who else but Ned Rafferty."

"Ned Rafferty! Well in truth, Catherine, I laughed till I nearly --," she stopped and looked shamefacedly at us youngsters, "fell over"

"Ah, you nearly said it, Granny." Said Molly.

"Well, I didn't then and I didn't mane it either." said Granny. Then Mother made us all go into the kitchen and shut the door. But Nan could always latch it so that it soon came ajar, and when we listened again Granny was saying.

"That omadhaun! Why I bate a sixpence when he goes to bed at night he pulls the clothes over his head so he won't see witches and warlocks. Then I met Mrs. Peter McCann and stopped to bid hir the time o' day, an' she tells me that Pat McGeough's wife has another chile, a girl again."

"It will soon be time Pat showed his ability." Says she,"that's the third girl."

337

Part 5   For better, for worse

"Sure an' I think he's showin' his ability well enough." says I. "They've only been married near five years."

"Then I fell in with Mr. McPhail an' nothin' would do but I go an' have a half-a-one with him, an' we went to Grew's Hotel, an' who would be sittin' there havin' a half-a-one too, but Betty Cullen an' Felix Morgan. Felix used to be afther her before she married upon ould Cullen, ye know. She might a done betther to have had Felix, but as they say 'as God made them, He matched them'. So who am I to blame the Good God's match-makin'?"

And so on and on, - just bubbling with all the news and gossip she had heard.

My first day at school! I was three years old.

My first reading lesson was 'An ox – my ox'. When I came home I told Granny I could read. She said she would like to hear me, so I repeated from memory 'An ox – me's ox'. I do not remember the incident, but she has often told me about it.

I do not remember anything of those first years at school. I remember children of three years coming to school when I was older, and how those little tots would chirp up, when the roll was called, with "Prisint sor".

One of the first incidents that I can recall happened when I was about six years old. One day, I asked permission to go out. Mother asked me, "Are you going to the 'necessary'?" The 'necessary' was the toilet. The boys used to fling their hands up, and call out loudly, "Please sor, may I go to the necessary?" We girls were more modest and asked Mother's permission sotto voce.

Part 5   For better, for worse

There were two 'necessaries' side by side, one for boys and one for girls. They were separated by a single board partition full of knotholes. The doors did not reach to the top of the doorway; there was a space about eight inches at the top of each. When we sat on the seat we kept a finger in the knothole through which a peeping tom might peek, or we put a paper in it.

These 'necessaries' were divided from the school playground by a high stone wall around a small yard, at the end of which were the two 'necessaries'.

Mother warned me, "Do not sit on the seat. It is wet. Just sit down in the yard."

Accordingly, when I went into the yard the doors of both necessaries were ajar. And thinking both were vacant I pulled up my clothes and opened my drawers, and was just going to sit down when I heard a giggle. I looked instinctively at the boy's door and there was the face of Ned McKee above it, laughing at me. He was quite a youth at the time, and was with a number of other youths being privately tutored by Dad for the intermediate or higher education exams.

I fled into the school weeping so bitterly that Mother had to send me home. Our home was a between ten and fifteen minutes walk from the school. I wept all the way and was still weeping when I arrived there.

"What is wrong?" Granny asked.

I said, "Ned McKee saw me sitting down to pee."

"Oh never mind," she said, "Ned McKee has to pee too."

Part 5   For better, for worse

"But, he saw me bare!" I wailed. "I was standing toward him with my drawers open and he saw me bare and laughed at me."

"If he denies the thrade let him lay down his tools." She said, half jokingly.

I was still disconsolate and continued to weep.

"Oh, he saw me bare Granny. He was looking over the top of the door and laughing at me." I cried.

The Granny lost her temper with me. She shouted at me.

"Och, my God chile! If he seen anything his mother hasn't got, let him throw his hat on it."

I fled upstairs and threw myself on a bed and cried myself to sleep. During the night I woke up crying, and Granny called to me to come into her bed. She was so consoling and kind to me that I soon went to sleep again.

Granny's bed was funny but we children thought it was lovely and just loved to get in with her and Granddad when anything was wrong with us. The bedstead was of mahogany with four very massive high posts, one at each corner. On top of these posts rested a tester and all around the tester were iron rods strung with rings to which were attached curtains of dimity in a large check pattern in blue on white. When Granddad and Granny got into bed at night they drew the curtains close all around. It must have been very unhealthy to sleep so closed up, but to Granny that bed and those curtains were priceless.

340

Part 5   For better, for worse

CHAPTER 20

Operation: 'rarin' daughters

A s all teachers were in late nineteenth century
Ireland, Mother and Dad were paid quarterly.

How affluent we girls would feel when we heard the
salary warrants had arrived! There were always some of us
needing footwear, and it was up to those 'footwear needy' to
scout around in school, alert to hear of any neighbour who
planned on going into town on Saturday, so we might get a ride
with them. Very often we walked. We had no horse or vehicle
of our own. Often when we set out there would not be one
penny among the lot of us.

On arriving in town, Dad would go to the Bank of
Ireland to get the warrants cashed, and soon after would emerge,
looking like a king, with Granny's blue eyes shining happily out
of his face. He would walk down those granite steps as if he
were walking on springs. Then first to Hoey's to get us
footwear, and then to Grew's Hotel for dinner.

How opulent! How prodigal! How delightfully
extravagant! It only happened four times a year, so why not?
Next Dad and Mother went round the stores, purchasing the
necessities for the next three months, and distributing their
combined salaries among their creditors. They never knew what
it was to be out of debt.

Then home on Paddy Mulligan's jaunting car for hire.
This, above all, was the acme of 'illigance', the zenith of
grandeur, the indisputable proof of our prosperity. If only all the

Part 5   For better, for worse

boys and girls at school could see us now. The drive was always too short; we reached home too soon.

Paddy Mulligan's jaunting car for hire was that most decrepit of vehicles, the one horse shay of the town. How that old knacker hauled us all still remains a mystery! His old bones should have been in the button factory years before. Paddy would whip him up into a trot when entering or leaving the town; the rest of the way the horse would amble painfully along at his own sweet will.

When we reached home there would be great excitement and turmoil among all the children. All would help to carry in the parcels which were piled up, in and on top of the well of the car, and each one of us had a large one on his or her knees. Each one tried to avoid the parcel containing the old boots, which were always brought home to 'wear out around the doors'. To carry in the old footwear was considered menial and always evoked the derision of the others.

After the car was unloaded, Paddy would be asked in for a 'thrate' in which Mom, Dad, Granny and Granddad would join. This would take place in the parlour, and we children would be 'chivied' into the kitchen, but Nan would leave the doors slightly ajar and we would take it in turns to peek.

Ah, those toasts!

They were wonderful, magnificent!

All five would stand around the parlour table and Dad would pour and pass the drinks – Mom, Granny, Paddy, Granddad and himself. Then he would raise his glass and say, "Our friends!"

For better, for worse

Then Paddy would raise his and say "Here's health."

Granddad would say, "Where it goes!"

And Granny always last and always the best, we thought, "Here's to the next time!"

Then she would take a sip and a beatific glow would suffuse her face.

Nectar! How she loved a "wee drop of the crathur" and always took hers "nate".

Granddad would watch her covertly, a half smile on his face that said, "I love you Sally, but I don't approve." Who recked? Not Granny.

On these occasions Mother always brought a gift home for Granny and it was always very, very, much appreciated.

Once, Mother brought her a bonnet. Granny had made one of her little jaunts into town a few weeks prior to this and had come home with her bonnet not only slightly awry, but also looking as if it had met with foul play.

Some time later I went up to her room one day and surprised her looking very dolefully at the wrecked head gear and trying to pull it back into shape. When she saw me she said, "Don't tell your mother that I was looking at me bonnet." If she had not admonished me, I probably would never have thought of telling Mother, but now I just had to.

Part 5   For better, for worse

When Mother gave her the gift, Granny's blue eyes lit up with admiration and she said, "It's a 'napper tandy', Catherine. A rale 'napper tandy" Then tears came to her eyes.

Napper Tandy was a nickname for Napoleon. I don't know where Granny got hold of the expression, but when she wished to say anything was the ultimate in perfection, it was always 'Napper Tandy'.

Mother said, "Put it on, Granny and see how it fits."

Granny did so and it fitted perfectly, and that was it. No mirror required.

In those simple, far-off, happy-go-lucky days, the selection of a bonnet or hat was not the highly specialized art it is today. The 'fit' was the one important requisite.

None of this going into a salon and trying on dozens of hats in front of a mirror, standing up, sitting down, front view, back view, side views, off the face, over the face, etc., etc.; until the smile on the poor clerk's face becomes fixed and rigid and her nerves worn to a frazzle, and then walking out without making a purchase. I always feel I should give her a small tip by way of rewarding her for her patience, only I'm afraid of insulting her. Besides, many of them deserve it. They unblushingly tell me that the most outlandish and atrocious models were 'just designed' for me. When this happens, my 'ego' slips to the vanishing point and my feet assume a contortion of corns, bunions and spread that are not apparent at any other time. When she says, "Look at the back view." I can see only my awful feet. Why should this be? I can never tell, but it takes a mighty "chic chapeau" to get those ugly feet out of my mind.

344

Part 5   For better, for worse

W hen Nan was about sixteen and I was about
        twelve, we hated each other most cordially. We
could both get along with Molly, red-haired, retrousse and fiery
tempered, but Nan and I mutually loathed each other, and lost no
opportunity for getting each other in trouble.

        She seemed to step all at once from the lanky, spindle-
shanked, gauche stage of girlhood into the staid decorum of a
young lady, and when she turned up her hair, -

            "Whose glossy black to shame might bring,
            The plumage of a raven's wing --"   Scott

        Like Scott's Ellen, I was madly jealous of her.

        The first Sunday morning she wore her long pink
dress with voluminous skirts right down to her heels, and new
black patent leather shoes, she certainly gave herself airs. It was
my turn to stay at home from church and help with the baby and
other chores. One of these jobs was to tether a goat in the
grazin' or pasture, which was directly across from the gates
leading from the loanin' to the highway. The goat was quite
temperamental, particularly when hit on her neck. I waited in
ambush till Nan and the girls were about half way down the
loanin' and then gave the goat a sharp cut across the neck with a
switch, which started her off after them. She must have had a
strong aversion to pink, for she made Nan the central target of
her venom and spite for the cut I had given her. Nan was
terrified of her.

        She gathered up her skirts nearly to her waist, and
those spindle-shanks of hers fairly flew through the gates and
down the road, the other girls racing to keep abreast of her, the
goat close on their heels, and I bringing up the rear scarcely able

                           345

For better, for worse

to stay on my feet for laughing. Past the corner where two roads
branched off and along what was called the Moss Road we all
went and "devil take the hindmost". Nan's shoes seemed to be
torturing her and her beautiful pink skirt was all crushed and
rumpled. Gone now were all the airs and graces of a few
minutes earlier. When we reached the rampart, I felt satisfied
that I had punished her enough, so I hauled on the goat's tether
and got her headed for home.

        Horrors! There were the MacDonnell's on their way
to church. They were the snoots of the neighbourhood!

        They had witnessed the whole chase. Must I meet
them? Oh no! I thought of jumping over the hedge into the
meadow below. But the hedge was thick and it was a drop of
eight feet, besides the poor goat would never make it. So, I just
had to run the gauntlet of the MacDonnell party, about eight of
them. They all seemed highly amused at the incident, and in
spite of my embarrassment and confusion at meeting them, I
thought, 'This is the first time and only time I have ever seen
these snobbish hussies so natural and human'.

        Dick MacDonnell was the only one of them that spoke
to me, though they all knew me. His eyes gleamed with
amusement as he raised his hat and said, "Good morning Miss
Lee."

        What marathons we used to have with that goat! We
would tease her to get her really mad, then up the loanin' we
would run, really scared with the goat after us, till we reached
the shed, where we would turn and, if our courage did not fail
us, grab her by horns and hold her till she got over her temper.
If we missed she really hurt when she got her bunt home. Poor
Molly once got it in her rear and later said tearfully, "She nearly

knocked the seven senses out of me, Granddad." He said, "Odd place you carry your seven senses, Molly!"

Dad often taught sciences in the evenings in the schools of the neighbouring town, sometimes as often as four times a week. We children loved it when he was away, because then Granddad would teach us, or try to teach us, to dance. I remember him telling us how he used to dance with his shadow in the moonlight on his way home from the 'flagary', as he called the dance at the Cross Roads. We had a very large kitchen and he would clear a space in the center of it and whistle and dance with us, always quadrilles and jigs till he would be out of breath. We surely enjoyed those dance evenings and always had such fun.

Granny, although so light on her feet and such a good walker, could not dance, but would try to jig with Granddad and we would almost raise the roof with our gales of laughter and merriment.

When Dad was home we did homework with him. We would all sit around the parlour table and Dad would give us spelling, arithmetic, grammar, and French. It sounds awfully dull, I know; particularly, would it sound dull to most young people of today, but we did not find it so.

Dad could always imbue his pupils with a spirit of emulation. It was the striving and contriving to beat the other, with a word of encouragement here and a word of praise there that lent an appealing interest to those evenings. He was a master in the art of getting the utmost effort out of his students. No wonder that former students always returned to visit him when on a holiday to their homes. He never lost interest in any one of them, and always followed the career of each one with pride and satisfaction.

Not one of us hated school. We all really enjoyed learning and studying. When my sister Evaleen allowed her youngest boy to leave school at age fourteen, though both our parents had been dead many years, I thought she had let them down. I wrote upbraiding her. I said, "It is a far cry from the Lee tradition, that a boy or girl shall leave school at such an early age. He will be hampered all his life by his lack of scholarship." But, I was talking to the wind. Both she and the boy came to regret it.

When Molly and I were about twelve and ten respectively, we began to go 'kaleidghing', if that is the proper spelling. It is pronounced 'kaleying', and means 'visiting', to John Atkinson's. John who was about sixty at the time was our nearest neighbour. He lived with a cousin housekeeper named Lizzie, who was blind in one eye.

We had both often been to their home, and they in ours, but we now began to visit them regularly every evening. Mother objected to our going, but we would sneak off when we saw a chance.

John had a deformed thumb on his left hand. He had had a 'whitley', whitlow in it at one time and the first joint had been removed. "Pulled out" he said. His thumb looked like it. The flesh of the upper part sat on the joint or knuckle of the lower part, making the thumb look just like a miniature cottage loaf. We would ask him, "Show us your thumb, John.", and he would hold it up and we would laugh, - all three of us. He would try to wiggle it and this would cause fresh outbursts of laughter, till the old beams of the kitchen fairly rang with our

348

mirth. Then we would ask him, "Can you spell your name, John?" and he would spell it, 'jaw- aw- hn'. This would evoke more laughter from all three. I say three, - Lizzie was there, always reading the bible, but never joined in with the foolishness of us 'three youngsters'.

Also every evening, I never knew him to miss; Warren McReady came to kaleidgh with John. He really came to get a smoke, as his wife would not allow him to smoke at home. We could always set our clocks by the time of his coming and going, seven to nine each evening, winter and summer.

He would sit on one side of the big open fireplace in the kitchen, John on the other and Molly and I on low stools between them. In winter a lovely big peat fire burned on the hearth. As soon as Warren arrived, John would get out his pipe and tobacco; fill the pipe and smoke or a little while. Then he would wipe the mouthpiece with his finger and thumb and pass the pipe over to Warren, who would take it and smoke with an expression of pure joy and contentment on his face. When the pipe required re-filling, he would wipe the mouthpiece with his finger and thumb and pass it back to John, who would fill it again, smoke for a while, wipe the mouthpiece again and pass it back to Warren. This procedure continued throughout the two hours and never varied.

They never conversed about anything, - perhaps they did not get a chance to do so as Molly and I kept them entertained. We would tell them what boy had kissed what girl in school, and who had written a love note which had been intercepted by Dad, who had been caught stealing plums out of Preston's orchard, etc., etc. They always seemed interested.

One evening I told on Molly.

349

Part 5   For better, for worse

"Peter McCann kissed Molly during the geography lesson." I said.

Molly denied it saying, "May god forgive you, Aggie Lee, for telling lies."

John burst out with, "Dammit sowl, Molly, don't swear. By God, I'll tell your mother on you." Thus he would brook no departure from decorum in us and he never yet told Mother on us."

One evening at a loss for some form of entertainment, I repeated from memory my latest reading lesson. It was the story of the lost camel, and went like this.

> "A Dervish was traveling alone in the desert when two merchants suddenly met him.
>
> "Have you lost a camel?" he asked the merchants.
>
> "Indeed we have." They replied.
>
> "Was he blind in the right eye, and lame in the left leg?" asked the Dervish.
>
> "He truly was." They answered. The Dervish went on to ask had the camel lost a front tooth, and was he laden with honey on theright side and corn on the left.
>
> All of which the merchants affirmed,and then requested that the Dervish lead them to the lost animal.

The Dervish, however, denied having seen the
animal, and explained that he had observed that
the herbage on the left side of the road only, had
been cropped, - and that had told him the camel
was blind in the right eye. He noticed a small
tuft of herbage left at regular intervals, signifying
the space left by a lost tooth. Also he noticed bees
buzzing busily on the right side of the road, getting
the honey which had dropped from the container -
likewise, birds of the desert were fighting over the
kernels of corn which had fallen on the left side of the
road. He remarked that the footprints on the sand
showed a lighter imprint from the left hind leg, which
told him the animal was lame."

John and Warren were so interested that they asked
me to repeat it, which I did. Then Molly took over and began a
quiz.

"How did the Dervish know that the animal had lost a
front tooth?" she asked John.

To which he answered mischievously, "Because he
was lame in his left hind leg." We all shrieked with laughter.
This answer was the cue for all the other silly answers that
followed. Molly got a willow rod and John was holding out his
hand, 'for the cane', and we were all bursting with laughter
when Dad walked in!

He had come to find out what attraction John
possessed that we two found so alluring.

John said the story of the "Lost Camel" was 'a quare
good story'. He thought it was in the Bible. Warren said he did

351

not think it was in the Bible, but 'it bate' anything he had ever heard in the 'London Budget'. Neither John nor Warren could read or write.

The London Budget was a weekly publication that was very popular with every family in the district. All the divorce cases, rape and assault cases, and other items of interest, particularly from the seamy side of life, were recorded verbatim in it. Also there were always serials of Buffalo Bill stories and detective stories of Nick Carter, which Molly and I read avidly each week.

Next evening and for many evenings thereafter, we two were back at John's with our reading books.

John was a bachelor of long and obdurate standing, but every once in a while he would fall from grace, as it were, and go on a spree. At such times his fancy would "turn to thoughts of love", even to visions of conjugal felicity. Sometimes Nan would be the object of his connubial designs. He would come to our house accompanied and always fortified with a bottle of 'Old Bushmills' and tell Dad and Mother of his deep and abiding love for her. Nan would go to bed and cry and make me promise not to tell the girls at school. I would promise faithfully, but the next day at school I would find the temptation to make them all laugh too great, and so I would mimic John. How he held up his glass, and swivelled round on his chair and sang how "Young Jock, he followed afther and hid in the bush." I would regale them with his ardent promises of 'silks and laces and a carriage and a pair' for Nan. Then how he would weep about Lizzie, - the "poor afflicted cratchur", varied sometimes with "the cornoptious cratchur". "Cornoptious" was coined by John, a twist on cantankerous, and has become an abiding word in the Lee vocabulary. Indeed, we girls have introduced the use

352

Part 5   For better, for worse

of it wherever we have been in loving memory, maybe, of John on a spree.

Poor Dad and Mother! What a job they had to "rare" all eleven girls! Always tormented by the question, - what shall we do with them? Teaching in Ireland was out. There were far too many in the profession already. The nursing profession, too, was overcrowded.

Just at this time they met a friend who suggested sending some of us to a Convent High School in England, where fees were reasonable, and through which we might qualify for the teaching profession in English schools. I was now twelve years old and what Molly could not think up in mischief, I could, and usually, got blamed for it all. They decided that I should be sent. Granny and Granddad fought hard against it. They both said it was 'Transportation'.

I was all agog to go. I thought it was elegance in the super, to be going to an English Boarding School. I could just see how smart I would be at it, - the cynosure and envy of all the eyes there and certainly, also, when I came home for a holiday.

It was just the night before I left that I really realized just what was about to happen, but all the preparations were now completed, so "Fare thee well Killevy". I went.

Part 5   For better, for worse

CHAPTER 21

To the land of the 'Sassenach'

Mother had got a list of the requirements in clothing that I was to take with me to the school; four petticoats, six pairs of drawers, six chemises, three pair of boots, six pairs of stockings in black, two hats in black, four dresses in black, one mackintosh, one winter coat in black, one pair of slippers, and a work-box with two knives for table and desert, two forks for table and desert, two spoons teaspoon and desert, towels, and soap were just some of the items. I was appalled at the quantity. There were more clothes than I had had hitherto in all my life. I also had to have a traveling trunk, all my own.

How good Dad was to me! He bought me far more than he could afford. Mother also, sewed and sewed in the evenings after school, and Nan was always ready to help. Granny and Granddad were quiet and did not offer to do much in the way of helping. It had taken several weeks to make all these preparations. It also had been arranged that I was to meet, at Portadown station on January 6th, three girls who were returning to the convent after their Christmas holidays, and I was to travel back with them. This arrangement saved the expense of some adult member of the family traveling to England with me.

It came to the evening before I was to leave. I was in the parlour with Mom and Nan, who were both sewing, putting the finishing touches to my wardrobe, and I was sewing on buttons and helping where I could. Granny came to the door and beckoned me out. She put two shillings in my hand, and

gave me a bag of liquorice candy to which I was very partial,
and said,

"There's a shilling each from your granddad and me.
Your Granddad bought the sweets for you last Saturday when he
was in town. Eat them when you get over there in that foreign
country." And she sobbed.

The other children were all in bed and Dad, Tom, and
Jim were at night school. I sat down at the kitchen fire with
Granny and Granddad and we talked.

Granddad used to go quite often to Hagan's in the
evenings to kaleidgh when Jep was home. This evening he had
just come from there. He said to me, "Ellen was hoping you
would go to say 'goodbye' to her. She is feeling badly this
evening about Minnie."

A bout eight years prior to this time Jep and Ellen
had adopted a little girl named Minnie Ross.
Minnie was two years younger than I. She always came to
school with me and I liked her very, very much. She was fair
with beautiful blonde hair and Ellen always kept her
scrupulously clean. She was a very lovable little girl and both
Jep and Ellen doted on her. They had just had her about five
years when she became very ill. I also had been ailing for some
time and had not been allowed to go to school or to see Minnie.
The Hagan's called Dr. Griffith, our family doctor, and he
diagnosed Minnie's illness as diphtheria. Everyone was scared.
The schools were closed and no one was allowed to go near the
Hagan's home. I fretted about Minnie and begged to be allowed
to see her, but, of course, that was impossible.

For better, for worse

One afternoon Mother was told that the doctor was at Hagan's and she took me down to consult him. Hagan's poor, little, mud-walled house was only a few yards from where we met him. While Mother was telling him the symptoms of my illness, I looked over to Hagan's house and there stood Minnie looking at me, clean as always, with her blond hair caught up in a knot in front and tied with a blue ribbon, as always, and her finger in her mouth. I waved to her and she just shook her head ever so slightly and did not remove her finger from her mouth. I was just going to call her when Dr. Griffith said to me, "Put out your tongue." I turned to do so, and when I looked back again, Minnie was gone.

When we reached home I said, "Minnie Ross can't be so very sick. She was standing outside the house when we were talking to Dr. Griffith." Mother said, "Oh, you must be mistaken, Aggie. She could not have been." And turning to granny she said, "Dr. Griffith says she is very low."

The next morning we heard that Minnie had died.

I saw her. I know to this day, I saw her.

Minnie's death left quite a blank in my life. I missed her. She had been so loving and lovable, and I loved to mother her. I wept and fretted about her so much that Mother became really concerned. True, I had wept over the death of a dog which had been poisoned; and a kid that had hanged itself around a dock leaf; and a pigeon, a great pet of our whole family, that had disappeared; and a canary that we found dead one morning in its cage. In fact, Mother often said I would "cry over the ducks going barefoot". These were all dumb animals and their death could not be helped, but Minnie could talk and say nice things and play with me and, unreasonable as I knew it

Part 5   For better, for worse

to be, I blamed Ellen. I thought, without having any grounds for such an unworthy thought, that Ellen had been negligent or lacking in some care, but I never spoke of my suspicions to anyone. I knew it would be useless to do so.

Minnie's death had occurred about three years prior to this, - the eve of my departure for England. I had not thought of going to say 'goodbye' to Ellen, but somehow I felt now that I must go.

It was about nine o'clock and drizzling rain, and very dark. I said, "If Mom will let me, I'll go now, Granddad. I'll ask Nan to come with me."

"Oh, it's too late chile, and it's a miserable night." objected granny. "You'll get your feet wet, and catch your death of cold."

I said, "It won't hurt, Granny. We can take umbrellas."

Granddad said, "Get your coat on, and I'll go with you."

He took his walking stick and we went out. It was a miserable evening, - dirty and wet underfoot and still drizzling. Hagan's poor little cabin was about seven minutes walk from the highway on a dirt road called the "Headrigs" which separated our land from that of a neighbour. When we reached it, there was just a candle burning in a tin candlestick for light, and a small peat fire burning on the hearth. Jep sat on a homemade chair in a corner near the large leather bag in which he kept his butchering knives. The room was wonderfully clean, the walls and ceiling were whitewashed and the board top of the

357

homemade kitchen table glowed white as snow in the semi-darkness. The dishes on the shelves shone in the faint light cast by the candle.

When we entered the house both Ellen and Jep seemed surprised to see us, but Ellen said, "I'm rale glad ye cum Aggie, bawn."

I felt awkward and ill-at-ease. I dreaded, somehow, to talk with Ellen about Minnie, though I no longer attached any blame to her for Minnie's death.

Jep and Granddad began to talk about the rain and the winter wheat and where Jep had been butchering lately, and Ellen showed me some crocheting she had been doing. She had quite a lot of it. When she had shown it all, she produced a pair of black woollen gloves she had knitted and gave them to me, saying, "I hope they'll keep yor hans warrum in that cowld haythen country." I felt some misgivings about accepting them as the list of clothing, we had received, stipulated definitely 'three pairs of black kid gloves', but I could not refuse them, so I thanked her and put them on and showed them to Granddad and Jep, who both admired them. Ellen said, "You will think of me when you wear them, and" she raised her eyes to the ceiling, "she will be praying for both of us."

That was the only reference she made to Minnie throughout the visit. I was glad and relieved, but I felt very sad. I wanted so much to say something comforting to Ellen, but could not think of anything suitable to say.

Granddad rose and said, "Well, we'll be going. Aggie wanted to come and say goodbye to you but," cheerfully, "she'll be home again in July, so it really isn't 'goodbye'."

Part 5   For better, for worse

I said goodbye to Ellen and Jep and we left. I felt
mean and a cheat insofar as I had not even thought of going to
say goodbye to the Hagan's until Granddad suggested it.

What a poor little travesty of life theirs was, - so
humble, so poverty stricken, so lacking in everything but the
bare essentials to keep body and soul together. Neither one of
them could read or write. They had never had any children of
their own, and this little adopted girl that they had built their
hopes on for company and comfort in their old age, - that they
had grown to love and enjoy, - she too must be taken away from
them.

There were ten of us girls, - one more was born after I
went to school in England, all healthy and strong. It seemed so
unfair. I said to Granddad, "How cruel God is! Why should He
take Minnie away from Ellen and Jep?"

He just said, "It is one of those things we just do not
understand."

And there were many more badly off than Ellen and
Jep. There were men with families, who worked in the
limestone quarries, hewing out limestone to be burnt in the kilns.
These men worked from 7:00 o'clock in the morning until 6:00
o'clock in the evening for ten pence a day, with half an hour at
noon to go home and eat dinner. Dinner was usually potatoes
and buttermilk, and sometimes they did not even have the
buttermilk!

The owner of the quarries also kept a little store
"licensed to sell tea and tobacco" and the workmen had to buy
their groceries at this store. The owner's wife looked after the
business and I was present one evening in the store when she

359

For better, for worse

was docking the wages of some of them because they had taken shelter for half an hour when it had rained heavily.

What exploitation! Cruelty worse than slave driving. No wonder labourers, the "pisantry" as they were snobbishly and hatefully referred to by the would-be patricians, landlords, etc., were ready to join any revolt that seemed to offer relief or amelioration from such dreadful bondage.

When we reached home again, Granny had gone to bed. Mom and Nan were still sewing and I went into the parlour to show them the gloves Ellen had given me. Tears were streaming down both their faces! This was the last straw. I sat down and bawled.

It came to me then, for the first time that I was leaving home forever! That henceforth, except for short holidays, I must spend my life among strangers! As I felt the full impact of this realization, I was overcome with grief and sadness. I was seized with a new tenderness and love for Mother and Nan, whom I thought I hated, and whom I had thought hated me. Memories of the many, many times she had saved me from punishment came to torture me. There was a time, when I was quite young, that old Keegan caught a lot of us stealing pears from under the pear tree near the school. We had to climb under a barbed wire fence as we ran to seek sanctuary in the school. My dress caught in the barbs. Nan saw it and came back and got me free, just in the nick of time for both of us.

Also the time when we were both following the hunt over soft, wet, ploughed field and my boot came off. My petticoat came down and I stood mired. Nan again saw my predicament and came back and freed me, wiped my runny nose

For better, for worse

and tear stained face and took me home. Another time I was
reaching for lilies and fell into a drain in the bogs, and was
drowning. Nan risked her own life to come and save mine. She
had helped Mother make my summer dresses, that everyone
admired so much, and each week ironed them for me, and took
just as much pain and care with them as if they were her own.
All these memories filled me with remorse and a feeling of guilt
for all the times I had been jealous of her and broken my
promises to her.

Dear, dear Nan! She has always been so good to all of
us.

Next day, Dad, Mother, Jim and I went to town in
John Atkinson's car. John had recently bought a new Jaunting
Car and he drove us to Portadown Station and stayed with Dad
and Mom to see me off. Mother was then just thirty-nine years
old and I remember how lovely she looked that day. "A lovely
gracious lady" said everyone who knew her. Sometime after we
were back at school the three girls, whom we met at Portadown
Station, told me that before we mutually recognized each other,
they had noticed Mother and had remarked to each other how
lovely she was, - particularly had they admired her hair. She
had a wealth of the most gorgeous auburn hair that I have ever
seen. The station, a busy junction at all times, was very
crowded that day and we were quite some time before we
recognized the girls.

When John said good-bye to me, he put a half-a-crown
into my hand and said, "Buy yourself some wee thing to mind
me by." I told him, tearfully, I would always remember him and
thought I would keep the half-crown forever. But alas, during
the following Easter holiday four of us stole away from the
vigilance of the nuns, one day, and went to a café in Lime Street,

where each of us had an individual meat pie and piccalilli. I
paid for the treat with John's half-crown! To this day I love
meat pie with piccalilli and I always think of John when I eat it.

The good-byes to Mom and Dad were distressing.
Mom kept her tears back bravely, but could not speak. Dad held
my hand tightly and so fondly as if he thought the moment he let
it go I was lost to him, and I felt so too. I clung to him and cried
most unashamedly. Jim came on the train with us, the three girls
and myself, to Belfast and saw us on the boat. When he said
goodbye to me at the last moment, he told me afterward, he
quite thought I would run down the gangway after him.

However, it never occurred to me not to go through
with it. I just felt that I must go.

The first three months at school I suffered terribly
with homesickness, especially Sunday afternoons. I would see
our big kitchen with the tiled floor and glowing peat fire on the
hearth and the blue willow plates on the shelves, shining in the
light from the western sky. I missed Molly's companionship.
Oh, I missed everything!

I remember how horrified Sister Jeanne was when I
asked her if they took the "London Budget". I wanted to read
the Buffalo Bill and Nick Carter serials.

Sunday was letter-writing day. All correspondence
both incoming and outgoing was read by the first Mistress. I
wrote to Molly and asked her how John and Warren were
getting on with their reading, and Sister Jeanne, the first
Mistress, thought they were boyfriends and asked me about
them. I explained who they were and she said, "Well, that is
certainly a most astonishing friendship. Do your parents

approve of it?" I answered naively, "Well not exactly, but there's no harm in it. John is sixty and Warren is older and married."

Another time I wrote and asked Mother to send me the gizzard of the Sunday chicken. The gizzard had always been a favoured tidbit for me. I enjoyed it even though it had often belonged to a tough old Pater or Mater familial of many fowl generations.

The food at the convent was plain but very good. Many of the girls grumbled at it, but it suited me all right. It would have suited them, the grumblers, all right too if they belonged to a family of seventeen, including Granddad and Granny, on a teacher's pay. Much of the grumbling was an attitude assumed by the would-be sophisticates to impress the rest of us with their superiority. There are some in every school or college or other institution.

Each form had its own mistress, who was responsible to the Principal for the discipline, progress and general deportment of her pupils. On Friday evenings, after supper, for a period of two hours, there was an entertainment put on by the form whose turn it was. The Principal and the whole teaching staff and the other pupils were the audience. There was good-natured emulation among the mistresses as to whose class could produce the best entertainment. It did not matter what the pupil did, but each one was required to do something – read, recite, sing or tell a story. The idea, of course, was to give us poise and confidence, like Caedmon of old, I could not sing, it only remained for me to recite. I had quite a brogue at the time; as a matter of fact I have never lost it and never wanted to, - apart from what was compatible with teaching in English schools. I have always memorized poetry very easily and I knew several long poems but I just could not decide which one. I knew the whole of Byron's Prisoner of Chillon, Scott's Chase from The Lady of the Lake, Tennyson's Lord of Burleigh and, of course, The May Queen. I say, of course for this reason.

Dad loved dogs and guns. He had many friends who were keen on sport, especially snipe shooting in the Ballywilly bogs, and Dad always kept at least two dogs, an Irish Retriever and an Irish Setter among them. These he would buy as pups and train. My sisters and I loved to train the young dogs to play "Gin's Land". Behind our house rose a high hill, with an excavation into which the house had been built, leaving a bank of from two to eight feet high surrounding it. "Gin's Land" was on the top of the bank, and had to be kept free from marauders by Gin. Anyone whom he caught on his land had promptly to become Gin. The marauders would run up the slopes of the bank and Gin had to catch them, the dog would catch our skirts in his mouth.

Dad had strictly forbidden us to play "Gin's Land" with the dogs, but we, as soon as we would see him go off with his gun and the older dogs, would get a young one out to play the game. When it was really exciting and at its best, Molly would say, "Do you know we are being wicked?" We all did. "Then let us go in and read 'The May Queen'," so in we would go and up stairs and get out an old reader and read part II of 'The May Queen' and cry ourselves sick with misery over it. Then out we would go and have another game of 'Gin's Land'. In this way we all became expert at reading 'The May Queen' part II. Indeed, we hardly ever required the book, we had all memorized it.

It came the turn of my class to give the entertainment. I had thought all day I would recite the Prisoner of Chillon, and

Part 5   For better, for worse

was quite prepared to do so. However, I had had a tough day. I could not get my algebra and at tea time there was a letter for me from Molly. Dad, Mother, Jim and she had been to town on John's car, so I was sick for the excitement of the arrival of the salary warrants, the dinner at Grew's Hotel and the parcels when they reached home. I was feeling blue and sick for home.

When my name was called to recite 'The Prisoner of Chillon', I came forward and began 'The May Queen' part II. There was a very audible snicker in the audience, but I cared not a whit. I proceeded.

Whether it was the nostalgic misery that was consuming my soul, or the brogue that lends itself so easily to pathos or humour, or just that I had read it so often at home with the intent of making others cry, I do not know, but soon all the girls were sobbing and many of the nuns sat far from dry eyed. I became, after this my debut, very popular as a recite-r and spent many hours that should have been devoted to more sober subjects, memorizing new pieces for some entertainment.

I have mentioned my difficulty with algebra. I had felt the need for Dad's helpful teaching before, but never so much as now with algebra. It was nonsensical. $A + B + C$!!!

It just could not and did not mean anything. I loathed it, and was the despair of my teacher over it, until one day we began simple equations and I was introduced to 'X'.

'X' was wonderful. He could represent or equal anything; the number of apples in a basket, or the number of miles a man walked, or the age of a person, or anything whatsoever; and whatever he was sent out to equal he always fulfilled his mission with éclat. He would travel incognito through a maze of intricacies in a problem, up and down, back

365

For better, for worse

and forth, across and back again, and would emerge ultimately with an identity as solid and irrefutable as that of the Rock of Gibraltar. I just loved him and later, when quadratics introduced his two girl friends 'Y' and 'Z', why he was romantic; he was glamorous, if I had known the word then. As John Atkinson would have said, "He bate anything in the London Budget."

After this I really got to like algebra and usually did quite well at it.

We went home for holidays twice a year, Christmas for three weeks and midsummer for six weeks. We had a week at Easter and another at Whitsuntide, but these were too short to admit the Irish girls going home.

How we always cried after we came back. Some of the girls went round with red swollen eyes and noses for two or three weeks after our return. The nuns were always so sympathetic and good to us and tried to get us into the routine as quickly as possible.

Every Sunday morning, after breakfast, it was an old tradition in the school, that we sing our hallelujah song. Starting with after Christmas it went –

> This day twenty-six weeks where shall I be?
> Out of the Convent of S.N.D. (Sisters of Notre Dame)
> No more Latin, no more French,
> No more sitting on a hard old bench,
> No more eating bread like bricks,
> No more chewing cheese like sticks.
> When my trunk is in the hall
> Waiting for the cab man's call,
> When the cabby rings the bell,

Part 5   For better, for worse

Then the Nun's may go to Hell – elujah."

And, oh the joy, the glory of it, when it came to 'This day week where shall I be?' How the recreation Salle resounded with that 'Hell-elujah!" The nuns used to laugh at us. Many had sung it in their own convent school days.

We played rounders, cricket, and tennis. Tennis then did not appeal to me. It was vapid and puerile, suitable only for exercise for curates and old maids. When Susanne Lenglen, a few years later put virility into the game, I really loved it. But at boarding school the more vigorous rounders and cricket appealed very strongly to me. When I got to college I loved cricket. Many and many a morning, in the summer, I have gotten up at four a.m. to play the game. Our usual getting up time was 5:45 a.m. We used to take long, long walks, always with a picnic at the end. The teaching nuns usually took part in the games and the walks. In the winter we danced after supper in the lovely big recreation Salle with its beautiful polished floors. Square dancing, only was allowed, but we did not call it 'square' dancing. There was the Washington Post, the Barn Dance, the Mazurka, - a lovely dance, Roger de Coverley and others. Positively no waltzing, but we did waltz on the Q.T. with someone keeping 'Cave' or 'Nicks' at the door to give us warning of the approach of a 'hostile', a nun who would not approve.

Oh, they were happy carefree days, those far off days in the convent. True, we irked at the restraints and inhibitions and lived for the day when we would be finished and ready to go to College. I always feel deeply grateful to the nuns for the sound education and affectionate care I received while I was under the convent roof.

Part 5   For better, for worse

Two years after I went, Rosa came, and after her, Winnie. In all, eight of us Lee girls received our education there, following each other up at regular intervals. How my parents must have scraped and saved to send us all. I have always been and still am, deeply sensible of the sacrifices they must have made to achieve this. For them with their restricted resources, it was a stupendous undertaking.

I was seventeen when I entered the Training College for Teachers at Mount Pleasant, Liverpool.

Here the two-year course passed uneventfully and quickly. In some ways we had better times, in others not as good as the Convent. We were given more liberty and treated more as adults. We had to study harder, and somehow imperceptibly, we were made to feel that we were the "Masters of our own Fates", that we were on our own feet, as it were, that we and we alone were now responsible for our actions. When I passed out of the Training College, I still lacked two months of being nineteen, but I felt old! Oh! So very, very old!

Part 5   For better, for worse

CHAPTER 22

Meet the world, Miss Lee

I got an appointment to a school in Nottingham.
Nottingham on Trent, - The 'Laceham on the Floss'
of George Elliott's 'Mill on the Floss'. There was a relic of the
old mill and George Elliott's house still standing in
Nottinghamshire, a few miles from the city, when I left there.

En route to Nottingham, I enquired, when necessary,
for the train to Nott-ing-ham and each time I noticed the porter
look oddly at me. When I reached Beeston, a little town about
four or five miles from Nottingham, a big fat woman with a
bundle of dirty looking lace which she carried hoisted on her
big, ample bulge of a stomach, entered the compartment I was in
and flopped down on the seat opposite me. She almost swiped
my face with the bundle of lace and certainly pushed my hat
right off my head. Not at all abashed or apologetic, she enquired
of a porter through an open window, "Am I right for Not-in-
goom?" I thought, 'Oh, I've got it wrong. It should be
Notingoom.' But still I had my doubts, too. I soon learned that
the pronunciation is Not-in-gam, with the emphasis on the 'Not'.

So armed with a pallid sense of humour, some new
clothes, a brand new Humber bicycle, which Jim had bought for
me, and a whole heap of ambition I set out to be the very best
teacher in the city. But, dis-armed by a persistent and annoying
tendency to blush, a timidity where I should have been
aggressive, and a ponderable lack of all worldliness, I arrived at
Nottingham.

369

Part 5   For better, for worse

Why do poets, painters, etc. all laud and eulogize the innocent young woman abroad in the world? I often wonder. I was innocent, or 'just plain daft' one and the same thing. Such a rare avis is extinct these days, happily.

However, by the time I had been the rounds of a few boarding houses, and had fallen into intimate and revealing conversation with the boarding-house ladies; who opened my eyes to, and filled my mind with, some of 'The Sweet Mysteries of Life', I was ready to crawl back into the convent and never look out of the window on the world again. Perhaps that is how nuns are made.

I had thought adult life was romance, and married life ecstatic happiness. Now it seemed that the romance was both dubious and precarious. Without either active volition or purpose on her part, a woman's life was just and only what a man condescended it should be. A wife was a non-entity, a mere chattel and babies were the result of man's selfish and inordinate lust. Man's selfishness ruled the world. A woman's life, after marriage, consisted in 1) feeding the brute, - this was of primary importance; 2) trying to keep him clean, - emphasis heavily on 'trying'; 3) rearing babies, - seemingly always unwelcome and not always avoidable, but withal necessary to keep the old world wagging.

One of my boarding-house ladies was a Mrs. Hitchcock, a name she abominated. She was a few years older than I, and my opposite in every way. She was blonde and very pretty. I was a brunette and not even my best friend could say I was pretty, but for some reason she admired me and we liked each other really well. Her husband used to tease us about 'our mutual admiration society', consisting of two members. He said we were such poor drawing cards no one else would want to join us, and so forth.

When Mrs Hitchcock went shopping, she always wanted me to go with her so that, if she wished her purchases to be sent, I could give her name to the shop assistant or clerk, because she, positively, could not pronounce the 'H'. I used to get her to practice saying 'Hitchcock', until she seemed to say it quite easily when we were alone, but from nervousness or confusion, when asked in the store for her name, she would always say 'Itchcock'. On one occasion, when I told her that I definitely would not say the name for her, and the clerk enquired, "What name, Madam?", the colour rose up her throat, neck and face and she blurted out "'Itchcock, Mrs. 'Itchcock, Haitch-i-t-c-h."

I have heard her beg of her husband to have the name changed, but he always refused. "What? Change a good old Saxon name like that! Not on a bet." One evening, after we had been trying vainly for some time to get him to consent to change the name, I had thought to subdue him with one mortal blow. I said, "Your name without the 'H' just suits you." His laughter rang to high heaven! "The demure Miss Lee! How do you know? Naughty! Naughty!"

I felt horrible, and Nellie, Mrs. Hitchcock, was laughing with him! This added to my confusion and mortification. She and I went out soon after and joined the Women's Suffrage Movement. After this we were the 'sweet suffragettes', and he would bring home all the "Women's Suffrage" publications he could find.

I soon got to know other teachers and joined a swimming club. I also got invited to join a clique for dances and

371

Part 5   For better, for worse

whist drives. In winter, I joined a few of them in a French class
at la Roche School of Languages, and I kept up my 'suffragette'
commitments. I also cycled quite a lot. In fact, by the end of
my first year in Nottingham, I was so immersed in a flow of
social activities that I began to think life was good, - there was
romance in it. Who now wanted to be a recluse?

One evening I was getting ready to go to a dance when
a girl friend, who lived next door, and who belonged to our
clique, called round to Mrs. Hitchcock's. She was quite excited
about a Mr. Logan, who was to be at the dance. It seemed he
was a very eligible bachelor, - one of those lucky individuals
who did not need to be embarrassed if "his bank slip were
showing". Also, but not least he was an Irishman from
Tipperary.

When he entered the dance hall, I was definitely
disappointed. He was a man of thirty-four or thirty-five,
thinning hair, tall but stodgy and un-athletic in appearance, but
spoke with a very attractive Irish accent and dressed very well.

"Now, that's the type of man I admire." said my
friend, "a man with a few years on his shoulders."

"Some, few, many," I answered, quoting the last three
words of a rhyme of indefinite adjectives, I had learned in
Ballywilly School.

He came up to us just then and was introduced.

My friend whispered, "Oh isn't he aristocratic?" I was
impressed only with his 'money-cratic' and condescending
aplomb, which I somehow resented. Coming from the north of
Ireland with my name 'Lee' seemed to intrigue him. Later,

372

Part 5

For better, for worse

when we were dancing together, he asked me, "How far back can you trace your ancestry, Miss Lee?"

I thought, 'What consummate impudence. Who the dickens does he think he is?' I answered, icily, "I have never tried to trace it backwards, but my Grandfather, at times, used to brag he could trace his back to Owen Roe O'Neill."

He seemed rebuffed, as I had meant him to be, but laughed about the Irish bull I had made. He enquired, "Do you trace your ancestry forwards and your posterity backwards?"

I answered, "I shall leave it to my posterity to trace their or its ancestry whatever way it likes.

Our dance soon ended.

Later he sought me out to explain that he had meant no impertinence, but that his mother's maiden name had been Lee, and that an uncle or granduncle of his had gone from Tipperary some generations back, and had settled near Lurgan, where he engaged in the linen trade. He wondered if I were a descendent of this avuncular relative of his.

I told him, "Hardly! My great, great grandfather bought the home and farm where I was brought up, and it is at Ballywilly, - a long way from Lurgan." Lurgan was actually less than twenty miles from Ballywilly. In fact there was a long and continuing rivalry between football teams from Lurgan and Portadown that was quite an annual event when the boys from Lurgan visited our town. They were considered a rough and uncouth bunch, and many a fight broke out in the public house after the game when members of the two teams sat down for a pint together.

373

Part 5   For better, for worse

A story was told to me by one of my brothers about an evening in the pub, when a Lurgan patron was called by nature and had to leave a nearly full glass at the bar. He wrote a note in large bold letters on a napkin. 'Don't drink this, I spit in it.' When he returned to his place at the bar, someone had written at the bottom of the note, 'So did I'. Of course, he demanded to know who had done it, and refused to pay for the pint he ordered to replace it. A fight ensued.

Later when I went home for holidays, it was determined that that very James Lee was indeed my progenitor, a great uncle, who had originally bought granddad's home and farm.

Patrick and I became great friends afterwards, and until I left Nottingham we cycled, played tennis, and boated on the Trent together. He taught me to scull and feather the oars. I loved it, and became really expert at it. He also helped me with my tennis, which I now liked very much, but at which I was not so expert.

We were both 'rattling good' walkers, an expression of his, and we went regularly for long walks in the winter. We also went to the theatre, where we saw many of the best operas and musical comedies. I could always depend on him for an escort. In times of grief and trouble he was always there, ready with sympathy and help. Our friends used to think we were sweethearts, but neither one of us ever regarded the other in the light of any other relationship than that of a friend. We explained to our friends that our relationship was purely platonic, and among them we became derisively nicknamed 'the pure plats'.

374

Part 5   For better, for worse

I have dwelt on my friendship with Patrick, a friendship sincere and true, which I prized and still prize to this day, for through him I made many nice friends in Nottingham, visited many places of interest in and around the Dukeries, saw many operas and plays, played tennis and boated on the Trent. In short, I enjoyed a cultural life to which my own social status would never have given me access. He married about two years after I came to Canada and died about three years later. When his wife wrote and told me of his death, I felt as if a part, - a fond and cherished part, of my world had gone.

The second summer I was home for the holidays from Nottingham, I had my first proposal of marriage. It was true to the type 'So sudden you know' and came about in this way:

There was, and still is, I believe, in Ireland a custom peculiar to that country, the custom of 'blackfooting'. A 'blackfoot' is a male friend who accompanies a suitor when he goes a-courting. The 'blackfoot' had always to be ready to support the suitor's cause or to give his morale a boost, if need be, or to fill in an awkward pause with a tactful remark, or to supply eloquence if the suitor's tongue were jammed. In short, by the aid of his wits, to help win the lady, and then the most exacting of all his duties, when success for the suitor seemed nigh, to broach the subject, tactfully and delicately, with the lady's parents of 'How much fortune (dowry) goes with her?"

Although a very difficult diplomatic task, some men were born to the faculty, as it were, nature having endowed them with the wits to "act well the part". One such was Larry McShane. He was suave, clean-shaven, smartly dressed and apt of tongue and very popular as a 'blackfoot'.

Part 5   For better, for worse

Why some of the 'wooee's' did not ask "Why don't you speak for yourself?" can only be explained by the fact that it was a popular belief that Larry was immune to the charm or wiles of women, that maybe for him "the light that lies in a woman's eyes, lies and lies and lies".

At this time, the summer of my first proposal of marriage, there were a great many eligible young bachelors in our parish, and one Sunday Father McIlroy, who had been trying without much success to get them connubial minded, really lashed out at them during his sermon.

After speaking of the family potentiality that existed in the parish among these bachelors and maidens, he scathingly attacked the men's love of single status and their selfishness and unnaturalness. "Why doesn't each one of you cut loose from your mother's apron strings and fix your attention on some young woman in the Parish and take Larry McShane or some other Blackfoot along and pay your court to the lady?" he asked.

"It is most distressful to see the poor girls on their knees in front of the statue of St. Anthony praying to him to find husbands for them. I forbid any more single young woman to pray before the statue of St. Anthony. I will not have you make a Blackfoot of him. He's the patron saint of lost articles, but your husbands are not lost. They are right over there," He said, pointing to the men's side of the church, "but too bashful and weak-kneed to make the first advance. Then each of you girls single out the man you fancy for a husband, forget your prim prudery and cast a good rolling sheep's eye on him, give him the 'comethering' (come hithering) look and maybe he will be shamed into proposing. Go right after him and may God bless your efforts."

376

Part 5   For better, for worse

The single young men sat uneasy and red-faced and looked furtively, it seemed, across at the girls, as if each were apprehensive of having a beam from an unwelcome eye directed on him.

We Lee girls sat amused and aloof. We were only on a holiday, and of course Father McIlroy's words could not possibly have any implication for us.

When we came out of the chapel, the rain was coming down in torrents. We had a walk of three miles to get home. We started out and soon the McShane's came along in their new jaunting car. Larry was in the 'dickie' or driver's seat up in front. He stopped and asked Evaleen and me if we would like a lift. We accepted gladly and I got up between Pat and a younger brother on one side, and Evaleen went around and got up between Larry's sister and niece on the other. Pat stuttered quite badly and as a rule was very quiet and silent, but now, perhaps fired with zeal by Father McIlroy's sermon, he began making the most ardent love to me. I tried to pretend I could not understand him and talked at random. The rug which was supposed to keep our knees dry kept slipping off and I seized upon this pretext to try to divert the attention of the others from Pat's stuttering avowals of love. His leg sought mine lecherously, and I kept edging away getting closer to his younger brother, who sat convulsed with laughter at the episode. I was at bay.

I asked him politely to remove his wooing leg, but he took not the least notice. He continued to stutter sultry love into my face while the rain poured off the umbrella, which he insisted on holding over his own head, sending water down my back. Never was I so glad to see our gates and to know that the proposal of marriage was at an end.

Part 5   For better, for worse

I had often envisioned my first marriage proposal. Beautiful moonlight reflecting on the placid surface of the water, lovely soft accents, whispered in some secluded spot with just the two of us. Perhaps it would be in a boat gliding gently down a stream with the current, blissfully unaware of the weir ahead.

Well, this was it! Stuttering Pat McShane! The moth of my star came at last, and in the drenching rain. And Oh! The teasing and taunting that I knew was in store for me when we got home. Evaleen told them all with hilarious mimicry of stuttering Pat's proposal.

Winnie and Mother had gotten a lift with Peter Dooley. Win sat next to Peter and got into an argument with him over the sermon. She was "in complete accord with Father McIlroy" she said. Still on the supposition that we were out of the picture as we were just here on holidays, she said. "The young men are too bashful. There should be more marriages, etc."

That evening just before tea time 'me bowld Pether' arrived with Larry McShane, the Blackfoot!

Winnie was in the kitchen when they arrived and realized all at once what she had let herself in for. She was always a great hand at shifting or trying to shift the onus for her faux pas onto me. So she came, grinning, into the parlour and said, "Here's Pether Dooley afther Aggie." But, Mother came to my aid. She said, "Oh, no! He's afther Winnie. I saw you casting sheep's eyes at him on the way home." We girls stayed in the parlour and Mother gave Peter and Larry tea in the kitchen and got rid of them tactfully, without giving either of them a chance to speak of the purpose of their visit.

378

Part 5   For better, for worse

I got a scare the following Tuesday, the night before I was to leave to return to Nottingham. We were churning butter and Evaleen said, "Here's Pat McShane and some stranger coming up the loanin'." I mounted the stairs like a deer and had reached the topmost step when the laughter burst forth. It was one of Evaleen's jokes.

We always had great fun churning. We had no cream separator of course, and when granny skimmed the cream off the milk, she made sure she got all of it. The result was that the churn was half-full, each week, of cream and milk. The churn was about four feet high and two feet in diameter. It was fitted with a very tight fitting lid, with a circular hole in its centre through which the dasher moved up and down. That dashing was really hard work. A person could only keep it up for three or four minutes at a stretch. Oh, I guess the men could hold out longer, but none of them seemed to be on hand at churning time, usually in the evenings.

Either Winnie or Evaleen or Jo would play for "the lancers" and the rest of us would dance in the kitchen, each dancing out to grab the dasher when her turn came. Thus the hour or hour and a half that it took to "get butter" passed very easily and joyously.

For years after I left the old country I remembered those 'churning' evenings, and always with a nostalgic yearning for the dear, care-free, laughter-loving days when we would all meet at holiday time and we were all young and gay. Days before Death laid his sinister and possessive hand so heavily on our family.

The first to go was Granny.

Part 5   For better, for worse

      She had been failing in appearance, but uncomplaining, for many weeks. Then she began to complain of tiredness and would lie down in the afternoons. Mother used to go up to Granny's room as soon as she came home from school to see how she was. One afternoon Granny was talking quite cheerfully and rationally, when she suddenly asked, "Is me bonnet on straight, Catherine?" Mother was startled, but Granny snapped back immediately and laughed. Then she asked, "Is Thomas home yet?" When told he was, she went off to sleep.

      Next afternoon, when Mother went up to see her, Granny had passed away in her sleep. Granddad had left her only a short time before Mother came home.

      I did not go home for the funeral. It was then the first week in November 1902, and the Christmas holidays were coming up about December 20th or 21st. I would not have wanted to look upon Granny dead.

      At Christmas we all missed her terribly, but none of us so much as did Granddad.

      The first evening I was home, I was sitting at the kitchen fire talking to him about her. He seemed so full of sadness and tired, tired of waiting, I thought. He now looked so old and bent, he who had always been so strong and straight. He spoke of how Granny and he had grown up together, and of how he had first thought of marrying her. Her family's name was Black. He had loved her very dearly. He said, "She was never a good singer, but there was always a song in her laugh, and in her heart."

Part 5   For better, for worse

Granddad had always been a good singer, - his favourite was "The Rose of Tralee". This he always sang when in a happy mood. He now sat in a deep reverie for some moments, and I felt that Granny was with us, and he too sensed her presence. He began to sing, as if to her, very softly and with such deep tenderness and pathos, the last verse of Moore's 'Last Rose of Summer'.

> "So soon may I follow
> When friendships decay
> Or from Love's shining circle
> The gems drop away.
> When true hearts lie withered
> And fond ones are flown,
> Oh! Who would inhabit
> This bleak world alone?"

As he finished it, he rose. I was sobbing, and he laid his hand affectionately on my head and said, "You will be a good girl, Aggie. You were always her favourite." And he went, bent and old upstairs to bed.

I felt as if my heart were bursting.

He passed away on Good Friday the following spring.

Dear, dear, Granddad! Granny and he had practically brought us up. He was always so honest and honourable, but withal so peccable, "The just man falls seven times a day.

Not very long after this heartbreaking loss, I began to search for some purpose in life beyond the confines of the world to which I was accustomed.

381

Part 5   For better, for worse

35391400R10219

Printed in Great Britain
by Amazon